ALSO BY SARAH ABREVAYA STEIN

The Holocaust and North Africa (coeditor)

Ninette of Sin Street (coeditor)

Extraterritorial Dreams: European Citizenship, Sephardi Jews, and the Ottoman Twentieth Century

Sephardi Lives: A Documentary History (1700–1950) (coeditor)

Saharan Jews and the Fate of French Algeria

A Jewish Voice from Ottoman Salonica: The Ladino Memoir of Sa'adi Besalel a-Levi (coeditor)

Plumes: Ostrich Feathers, Jews, and a Lost World of Global Commerce

Making Jews Modern: The Yiddish and Ladino Press in the Russian and Ottoman Empires

FAMILY PAPERS

FAMILY PAPERS

A SEPHARDIC JOURNEY THROUGH THE TWENTIETH CENTURY

SARAH ABREVAYA STEIN

FARRAR, STRAUS AND GIROUX • NEW YORK

Farrar, Straus and Giroux
120 Broadway, New York 10271

Printed in the United States of America
First edition, 2019

Illustration credits appear on pages 315–317.

Library of Congress Cataloging-in-Publication Data
Names: Stein, Sarah Abrevaya, author.
Title: Family papers : a Sephardic journey through the twentieth century / Sarah Abrevaya Stein.
Description: First edition. | New York : Farrar, Straus and Giroux, [2019]
Identifiers: LCCN 2019020324 | ISBN 9780374185428 (hardcover)
Subjects: LCSH: Levy family. | Sephardim—Greece—Thessalonikåe—Biography.
Classification: LCC DS135.G73 S74 2019 | DDC 929.208962/40495—dc23
LC record available at https://lccn.loc.gov/2019020324

Designed by Abby Kagan

1 3 5 7 9 10 8 6 4 2

To three good people I love to walk with:
Fred, Ira, and Julius

Kamina kon buenos, te hazeras uno de eyos.
Walk with good people and you will become one of them.

CONTENTS

ÉMIGRÉS

CAPTIVES

SURVIVORS

FAMILIARS

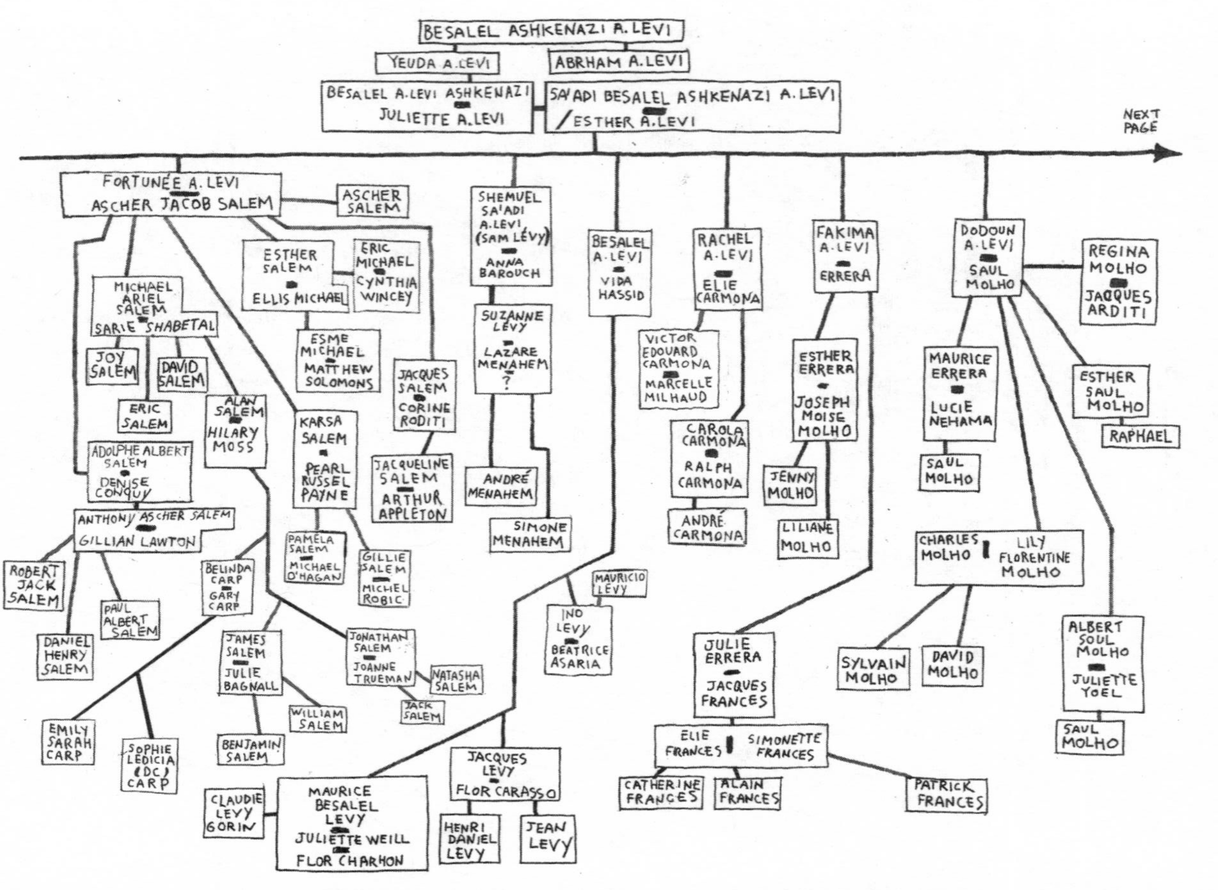
BESALEL ASHKENAZI A.LEVI
YEUDA A.LEVI
ABRHAM A.LEVI
BESALEL A.LEVI ASHKENAZI
JULIETTE A.LEVI
SA'ADI BESALEL ASHKENAZI A.LEVI
/ESTHER A.LEVI
NEXT PAGE
FORTUNÉE A.LEVI
ASCHER JACOB SALEM
ASCHER SALEM
MICHAEL ARIEL SALEM
SARIE SHABETAL
JOY SALEM
DAVID SALEM
ERIC SALEM
ALAN SALEM
HILARY MOSS
ADOLPHE ALBERT SALEM
DENISE CONQUY
ANTHONY ASCHER SALEM
GILLIAN LAWTON
ROBERT JACK SALEM
PAUL ALBERT SALEM
DANIEL HENRY SALEM
ESTHER SALEM
ELLIS MICHAEL
ERIC MICHAEL
CYNTHIA WINCEY
ESME MICHAEL
MATTHEW SOLOMONS
KARSA SALEM
PEARL RUSSEL PAYNE
PAMELA SALEM
MICHAEL O'HAGAN
GILLIE SALEM
MICHEL ROBIC
JACQUES SALEM
CORINE RODITI
JACQUELINE SALEM
ARTHUR APPLETON
BELINDA CARP
GARY CARP
EMILY SARAH CARP
SOPHIE LEDICIA (DC) CARP
JAMES SALEM
JULIE BAGNALL
WILLIAM SALEM
BENJAMIN SALEM
JONATHAN SALEM
JOANNE TRUEMAN
NATASHA SALEM
JACK SALEM
SHEMUEL SA'ADI A.LEVI (SAM LÉVY)
ANNA BAROUCH
SUZANNE LEVY
LAZARE MENAHEM
?
ANDRÉ MENAHEM
SIMONE MENAHEM
BESALEL A.LEVI
VIDA HASSID
MAURICIO LEVY
INO LEVY
BEATRICE ASARIA
JACQUES LEVY
FLOR CARASSO
HENRI DANIEL LEVY
JEAN LEVY
MAURICE BESALEL LEVY
JULIETTE WEILL
FLOR CHARHON
CLAUDIE LEVY GORIN
RACHEL A.LEVI
ELIE CARMONA
VICTOR EDOUARD CARMONA
MARCELLE MILHAUD
CAROLA CARMONA
RALPH CARMONA
ANDRÉ CARMONA
FAKIMA A.LEVI
ERRERA
ESTHER ERRERA
JOSEPH MOISE MOLHO
JENNY MOLHO
LILIANE MOLHO
JULIE ERRERA
JACQUES FRANCES
ELIE FRANCES
SIMONETTE FRANCES
CATHERINE FRANCES
ALAIN FRANCES
PATRICK FRANCES
DODOUN A.LEVI
SAUL MOLHO
REGINA MOLHO
JACQUES ARDITI
MAURICE ERRERA
LUCIE NEHAMA
SAUL MOLHO
ESTHER SAUL MOLHO
RAPHAEL
CHARLES MOLHO
LILY FLORENTINE MOLHO
SYLVAIN MOLHO
DAVID MOLHO
ALBERT SOUL MOLHO
JULIETTE YOEL
SAUL MOLHO

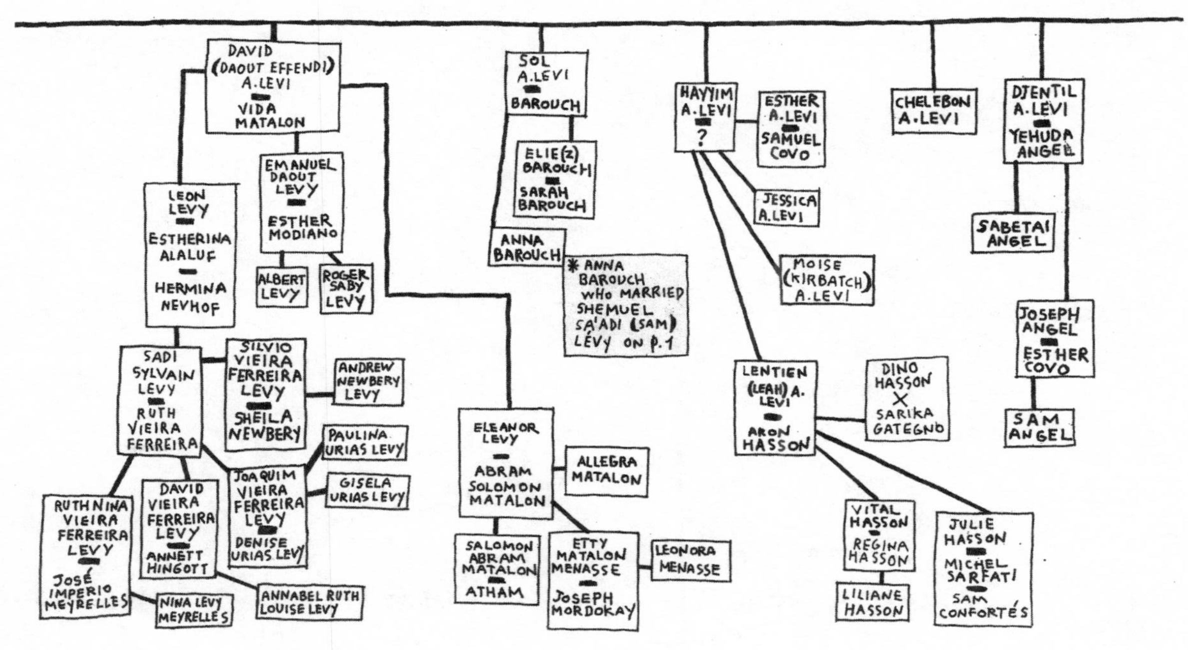
DAVID (DAOUT EFFENDI) A.LEVI
VIDA MATALON
LEON LEVY
ESTHERINA ALALUF
HERMINA NEVHOF
EMANUEL DAOUT LEVY
ESTHER MODIANO
ALBERT LEVY
ROGER SABY LEVY
SADI SYLVAIN LEVY
RUTH VIEIRA FERREIRA
SILVIO VIEIRA FERREIRA LEVY
SHEILA NEWBERY
ANDREW NEWBERY LEVY
JOAQUIM VIEIRA FERREIRA LEVY
DENISE URIAS LEVY
PAULINA URIAS LEVY
GISELA URIAS LEVY
RUTH NINA VIEIRA FERREIRA LEVY
JOSÉ IMPERIO MEYRELLES
NINA LEVY MEYRELLES
DAVID VIEIRA FERREIRA LEVY
ANNETT HINGOTT
ANNABEL RUTH LOUISE LEVY
SOL A.LEVI
BAROUCH
ELIE(Z) BAROUCH
SARAH BAROUCH
ANNA BAROUCH
* ANNA BAROUCH WHO MARRIED SHEMUEL SA'ADI (SAM) LÉVY ON p.1
ELEANOR LEVY
ABRAM SOLOMON MATALON
ALLEGRA MATALON
SALOMON ABRAM MATALON
ATHAM
ETTY MATALON MENASSE
JOSEPH MORDOKAY
LEONORA MENASSE
HAYYIM A.LEVI
?
ESTHER A.LEVI
SAMUEL COVO
JESSICA A.LEVI
MOISE (KIRBATCH) A.LEVI
LENTIEN (LEAH) A. LEVI
ARON HASSON
DINO HASSON
X
SARIKA GATEGNO
VITAL HASSON
REGINA HASSON
LILIANE HASSON
JULIE HASSON
MICHEL SARFATI
SAM CONFORTÉS
CHELEBON A.LEVI
DJENTIL A.LEVI
YEHUDA ANGEL
SABETAI ANGEL
JOSEPH ANGEL
ESTHER COVO
SAM ANGEL

WRITERS

This is the story of a single Sephardic family whose roots connect them to a place and community that no longer exist. The place was the port city of Ottoman Salonica, present-day Thessaloniki, Greece, one of the few cities in modern Europe ever to claim a Jewish majority. The community was made up mostly of Ladino- (or Judeo-Spanish) speaking Jews—Sephardic families who traced their ancestry back to Sepharad, medieval Iberia, from which they were expelled in the 1490s, but who, for the next five centuries, called the Ottoman Empire, southeastern Europe, and Salonica home.

Today, the papers of the Levy family are spread across nine countries and three continents. The single largest collection, the papers of Leon Levy, is kept by his four grandchildren in a private vault in Rio de Janeiro. It consists of nearly five thousand handwritten and typed letters, telegrams, photographs, legal and medical documents, and miscellanea—address books, expired passports, and more: by far the largest private archive I have encountered as a professional historian and near obsessive document hunter.

In a suitcase in a spare garage, in a retirement village outside Johannesburg, there is another repository of Levy family papers. Smaller than the Rio collection, the South African one is nonetheless of immeasurable historical value. It includes such cherished souvenirs as a silhouette cut in Salonica in 1919 capturing the likeness of a young woman about to emigrate from her native city, never to return.

Other family papers have turned up in private hands in England. One collection, boxed up in a home in London, has survived multiple migrations, from Greece to Great Britain to Germany to India, back to Great Britain and on to the United States. Another, housed in a scenic village outside Manchester, contains fragile glass slides taken in 1917 in Salonica's Jewish cemetery, then the largest Jewish cemetery in Europe.

Yet more documents, photographs, and objects have materialized in Brazil, Canada, France, Germany, Great Britain, Greece, Hungary, Israel, Italy, Portugal, and the United States: not only family-owned papers, but documents and photographs held by thirty archives. Travel documents; naturalization papers; birth, death, and medical records; letters exchanged by relatives, lovers, and friends; business papers; even a baptismal certificate. All told, these scattered sources have allowed me to trace an intimate arc of the twentieth century.

The Levy family papers catalogue the lives and losses of multiple generations, contain papers written in eight languages, and reflect correspondence among members of a single family spanning the globe. This is a Jewish story, an Ottoman story, a European story, a Mediterranean story, and a diasporic story, a story of how women, men, and children experienced wars, genocide, and migration, the collapse of old regimes and the rise of new nations. The Levy papers also reveal how this family loved and quarreled, struggled and succeeded, clung to one another and watched the ties that once bound them slip from their grasp.

As the first papers in the Levy family collections were amassed, around the time of the Balkan Wars (1912–1913), Salonica and its Jewish community were undergoing an irrevocable transformation. Nationalism provoked the transition of Salonica from an Ottoman city with a Jewish plurality to a Greek city with a Christian majority. Emigration drove the city's Jews, and the Levy family, across the globe.

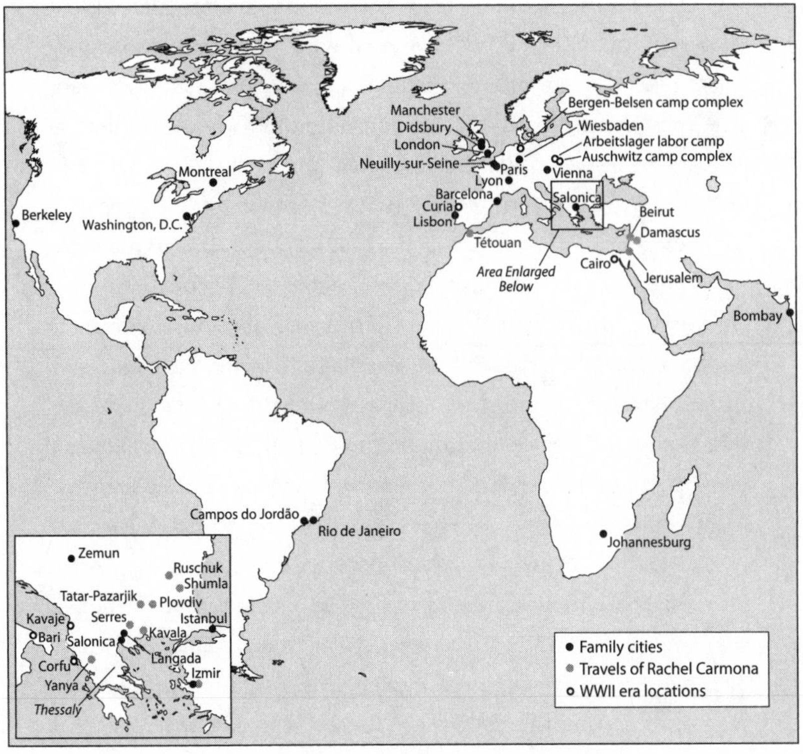

Map of the Levy family diaspora

Ladino speakers began to abandon their language in favor of various adopted tongues. Genocide eradicated 98 percent of the Jews who remained in Salonica during the Second World War, leaving survivors crippled by one of the highest rates of annihilation to affect a single community in Europe.

The Levy family lived all this. They knew Salonica when one was more likely to hear Ladino on the street than any other language. As leading publishers and editors in the city, they helped chronicle and shape modernity as it was experienced by Sephardic Jews. Wars redrew borders around them, transforming them from Ottomans to Greeks. Family members moved across boundaries and hemispheres, with some leaving in optimism and others in shame. The Holocaust eviscerated their clan, destroying entire branches of the family tree. The losses that so devastated those left behind disrupted intimacies and led to new relationships among survivors driven together by grief, seeking solace in one another and, in some cases, cooperating to file reparation claims from Germany. Slowly, agonizingly, they rebuilt.

My encounter with the Levy family has its roots in another book, one I coedited with my colleague, former teacher, and friend, Aron Rodrigue. In 2012, Aron and I published a translation of the first known Ladino memoir (Isaac Jerusalmi, *zikhrono livrakha* [z"l], of blessed memory, served as translator).[1] The memoir was composed by a Levy patriarch, Sa'adi Besalel Ashkenazi a-Levi (1820–1903), whom contemporaries called Sa'adi.

Sa'adi's memoir fills ninety-five pages of a humble notebook—the sort of ledger a small-business owner might use to keep track of expenses. Written in elegant *soletreo*, the unique cursive handwriting of Ladino, the pages are dotted with Hebrew words in calligraphic block letters. The margins show Sa'adi's meticulous additions and corrections, some in blue pencil. Sa'adi would revise and polish the document for a decade, until blindness overtook him. A lifelong publisher, Sa'adi made this notebook his last and most intimate creation.

Astonishingly, Sa'adi's notebook passed through four generations of his family, traveling from Salonica to Paris, from Paris to Rio de Janeiro, and, finally, from Rio to Jerusalem—somehow eluding destruction, even in the face of the dispersal of Sa'adi's descendants over multiple countries and the annihilation of Salonica's Jewish community. Later, after I spent years grappling with Sa'adi's words, I wondered what had become of this remarkable family from Ottoman Salonica.

The slenderest of leads enabled me to write this book. In 1977, Sadi Silvio (Sylvain) Levy, the great-grandson of Sa'adi Besalel Ashkenazi a-Levi, had donated the sole copy of Sa'adi's memoir to the National Library of Israel, then known as the Jewish National and University Library. Because Sephardic Jews tend to name children after living forebears, I reasoned that names would persist in the Levy family, even in the émigré outpost of Brazil. The hunch eventually led me to Silvio Vieira Ferreira Levy—Sa'adi's Rio-born great-great-grandson. In time, Silvio told me about the Levy collection in its vault in Rio and, with the blessing of his three siblings, shared his family's papers with me. The discovery began a decade-long historical journey.

The Levy family was known variously across the years. In nineteenth-century Ottoman Salonica, when the Levys were among the city's cultural elite, they were called a-Levi. (A contemporary Hebrew speaker might render the name Ha-Levy, but this fails to reflect the pronunciation of Hebrew among Ladino speakers of the era.) Certain family members who went to France removed the prefix and added an accent, a stroke that would testify to their Frenchness: Lévy. Those who moved through Germany considered embracing Lewy, but, in the end, did not. The Brazilian branch favored Levy, which would be more recognizable to Portuguese speakers. Women in the family, meanwhile, adopted married names, all significant to Sephardic history: Amariglio (Amarilio), Carmona, Errera, Florentin, Hasson, Matalon, Molho, Salem, Sarfatti, and more.

In this family, as in every family, much remained unspoken,

unwritten. There were facts family members could not know, secrets they would not tell. The most devastating drama of this book—the ghastly transgressions and ultimate trial and execution of a Second World War criminal who was also one of Sa'adi's great-grandchildren—makes no explicit appearance in family correspondence. Evidence of this person has also been left out of all the family trees I have encountered. In the immediate aftermath of the Holocaust, relatives hinted at the trauma in letters, alluding to conversations they had had or would have about their disgraced kin. But never did they put the offender's name (let alone details of his crimes) in print. This was a shared secret, not meant for the eyes of a historian.[2]

Of course, a historian is not charged with perpetuating or concealing her subjects' secrets. Still, the discovery of this dark chapter of Levy history has weighed heavily on me, presenting ethical dilemmas I have struggled to resolve. Few of Sa'adi's living descendants could be familiar with this tortured chapter prior to reading this book. For some, it may prove painful, for others, a distant scandal. In the end, my decision to tell this anomalous and disturbing story emerged out of a desire to write as complete and nuanced a family history as sources permitted. To do less would allow a sanitized version of the past to prevail over the messy, sometimes ugly, unshakably human one that resonates with truth.

The Levys wrote each other to give and ask for money, to share expressions of grief, to announce achievements, to conduct business, and to reveal secrets. They wrote to maintain connection over time and distance, to propose marriage, and to plan for divorce. They wrote because they had regrets and were lonely, at times simply because they were family. Papers held them together—until distance, time, and history finally tore them apart. So it is that after a diasporic Sephardic family frays, what remains is the fragile tissue that once held them together: neither blood nor belief, but paper.

DNA tests and genealogical websites have turned the search for ancestry into a booming industry, with spit and computers its essential tools. Yet in an era of expanding family trees, digital relationships, and instantaneous communication, writing or receiving letters is something few of us do—or have ever done, depending on our age. It is uncommon, in today's world, to anticipate a letter, to relish its arrival, to stain it with tears, or to pass it to children or grandchildren as an inheritence. We have infinite ways to connect. But what have we relinquished, along with family papers?

OTTOMANS

Those Levys were dangerous. All they needed was an idea to come to them like a little birdie, and they'd start chasing after it. And this idea never rested until it became a reality.

—*The Memoirs of Doctor Meir Yoel*, 1900[1]

SA'ADI

Does every generation believe it exists at a moment of transition? Looking around him, Sa'adi Besalel Ashkenazi a-Levi saw a world that scarcely resembled the one into which he was born. Young women and men dressed differently from their parents, maintained a looser relationship to religion. New train tracks connected his city, Ottoman Salonica, to Belgrade, and from there to all of Europe. His children, like so many Jewish youth, spoke languages a previous generation did not know. They were moving far from home, assuming new jobs, attempting to realize their own utopian dreams.

Sa'adi's city, Ottoman Salonica, was among the few cities in the modern world to have a Jewish plurality, if not a Jewish majority. Jews numbered between 60,000 and 100,000 of Salonica's residents in the nineteenth century, when roughly 50 percent of the city's residents were Jews.[1] The majority of Salonica's Jews were Sephardic, descendants of Jews expelled from medieval Iberia ("Sepharad" in Hebrew) in the late fifteenth century. Pushed from their homes, these expelled women, men, and children scattered northward to France and the Spanish Netherlands, and southward to Morocco. The largest number, however, moved east to the Ottoman Empire, an expanding state that would, at its height, reach across southeastern Europe, through the eastern

Mediterranean and North Africa, and eastward to the border of what is today Iran. To the Ottoman lands the Iberian Jewish exiles brought their religion, their memories, their cultural practices, and their craft, including printing, which was the a-Levi family trade. So, too, did the exiles transport their tongue—a Judeo-Spanish language they sometimes called *muestro espanyol*, which today is known as Ladino.[2] Over the course of 450 years, Jews became an integral part of the Ottoman imperial social mosaic. They were particularly influential in cities like Salonica, where they constituted a large enough group to conduct affairs in their own language.

When Sa'adi commissioned a scribe to transcribe his memoir, Salonica was the third most important port in the Ottoman Empire and a link between Europe and the Levant. The cosmopolitan city, home to Jews, Muslims, Dönme (descendants of Jews who followed the self-proclaimed messiah Shabbetay Sevi into Islam after he converted in 1666), and Greek Orthodox and other Christians, boasted more than fifty synagogues. The Sabbath was celebrated on three different days by Salonica's multisectarian residents. Still, to its early-twentieth-century Jewish residents, the city was hailed as a Jewish capital, the "Jerusalem of the Balkans."[3] So at ease were Jews in the city that they could be found praying on the quay, obstructing the path of pedestrians.[4]

A Jewish industrial-class, working-class, and middle-class workforce fueled Salonica's economy. Jews were prominent among both the stevedores who manned the port and the women and men, girls and boys who dried tobacco and shaped bricks in the city's factories. Jews owned many of the shops, cafés, and bars that lined Salonica's streets, and were teachers in the city's schools.[5] The city's most popular newspapers were also edited, printed, and written by Jews, including Sa'adi and his sons. Indeed, the a-Levi family intro-

Ottoman Salonica, c. 1860s

duced printing to Salonica, in much the same fashion as Sephardic Jews introduced printing to the Ottoman Empire.[6]

Like most of Salonica's nineteenth-century Jews, Sa'adi counted Ladino as his mother tongue. It was the language in which he spoke to his wife and children, wrote his memoir, and published some of his newspapers and the ephemera that earned him a living. Still, his family line was the product of intersecting Jewish worlds that merged in Salonica, reaching back to Iberia as well as to Amsterdam and Italy. As culturally Sephardic as the family came to be—and as influential to the shaping of modern Judeo-Spanish letters—the a-Levi line braided Sephardic (Iberian

Jewish) and Ashkenazic (European Jewish) heritage. The family's Ashkenazi lineage was for a time preserved and even flaunted by the family through select customs and through their use of the surname Ashkenazi, a name common among Jews in the Balkans and Turkey, which in many cases signaled a non-Sephardic inheritance. Sa'adi's father, Besalel a-Levi Ashkenazi, his grandfather Rabbi Yeuda a-Levi Ashkenazi, and his Amsterdam-born great-grandfather, Besalel a-Levi Ashkenazi, went by this name, as did Sa'adi himself.[7] The next generation would not emulate this practice, probably out of a desire to simplify and Westernize their family names.

Sa'adi was losing his vision in the early 1880s when he began composing his memoir. The work suggests that he was sanguine about many of the changes that were transforming Jewish Salonica. The city had only recently spilled over its medieval walls, and its sea walls had been freshly demolished in favor of a waterfront promenade. New, wealthy districts were being built on Salonica's eastern edge, and within the city, water, electricity, paved streets, and tramlines were updating the urban landscape.[8] Sa'adi didn't dwell on these developments in his memoir. Nor did he seem terribly bothered that his children's generation did not cling to the laws and mores of the past, that they embraced new political movements and fashions, or that women and men were both increasingly defiant about traditional gender roles. None of this fundamentally seemed to disturb Sa'adi—or, at least, this is not what comes through in his memoir. For Sa'adi was something of a freethinker. What he could not abide was obstructionism on the part of the city's Jewish religious elite. Though religiously observant himself, Sa'adi believed that Salonica's rabbis were fearful leaders threatened by modernity.

Sa'adi battled with Salonica's religious elite throughout his life. He triggered their ire with words, both sung and written.

By vocation Sa'adi was a printer and editor, by avocation an accomplished composer and singer. Like his grandfather Rabbi Yeuda a-Levi Ashkenazi, Sa'adi was a virtuoso of Ottoman Jewish music. His training had come at the feet of two Ottoman musical masters—one Muslim, the other Jewish—who taught him the full Ottoman and Jewish repertoires. Sa'adi also practiced and performed with the *maftirim* choirs of Salonica. Composed of Jewish, Sufi, and Muslim musicians, the *maftirim* performed mystical texts from a variety of traditions, blending their melodies and composition into a unique (and today almost lost) art form. The kind of musical blending that Sa'adi excelled at was quintessentially Ottoman, reflective of the cultural melding that was inextricable from Salonica's multiethnic, multisectarian, multilingual environment.[9] Music brought Jews and non-Jews together, allowing them to share a cultural voice. No wonder it proved an irritant to a rabbinical leadership that wished to fortify the boundaries around Judaism.

While still in his teenage years, Sa'adi was commissioned by the head of one of Salonica's greatest yeshivas to sing at the wedding of his son. For the occasion, Sa'adi composed a melody based on a secular Turkish song, to which he set the kaddish, a traditional Jewish hymn of prayer to God. The day of the nuptials, the grand synagogue was packed—filled, in Sa'adi's words, with "the entire aristocracy of Salonica." Enter the groom, enveloped in turban and robes. Sa'adi intoned the words of the kaddish, sending his newly composed secular melody echoing throughout the sacred building. His voice had "the purity of crystal, a nuanced and captivating sweetness."[10] The crowd was overwhelmed. All except one. "When [Rabbi Shaul] went home accompanied by eight to ten of his friends, he removed his cape and sat on his elevated cushion for some rest." Asked if he had enjoyed Sa'adi's performance, "the *sinyor rav* hit the roof . . . saying 'What a wicked person to sing a Turkish melody in the synagogue!'"[11] To this antimodernist fearful of losing influence and control, the blurring of musical boundaries, a celebrated tradition in the Ottoman world, seemed threatening. In Rabbi Shaul's eyes, Sa'adi was less a budding maestro than a firebrand. It was not the only time Sa'adi was threatened with excommunication (or even corporal punishment) for singing "à la turka."

Sa'adi's work as a publisher placed him in a still more combative relationship with Salonica's religious elite. He entered the publishing world at the young age of thirteen, when he inherited a ramshackle printing press from his father, Besalel a-Levi Ashkenazi. Sa'adi's father, thirty-six at the time of his death, had inherited the press from his own grandfather, the first in Sa'adi's paternal line to migrate to Salonica, from Amsterdam, in 1731. Already the family line was being preserved in print: some of the titles Sa'adi's father published, presumably with his brothers, bore the Hebrew imprint "Sons of Besalel," or "Orphans of Besalel," in recognition of the Amsterdam-born patriarch who brought the family to publishing.[12]

Sa'adi's father died when Sa'adi was still an infant. The family printing house was run by employees—but barely. Revenues were low, the staff not very competent. With family finances shaky, Sa'adi's mother entered the workforce. The a-Levi matriarch is never named by her son in his memoir, despite the outsized role she played for her family. Born in the eighteenth century, she was a seamstress and early aficionado of clothing in the "European style," though she and her husband wore traditional dress. Sa'adi's memoir offers detailed depictions of men's and women's clothing. Traditional clothing in the Salonican Jewish context, his memoir teaches, entailed, for women, a *kofya*, head covering, and a *devantal*, a long silk shirt, tight at the bodice, covered by an *antari*, a close-fitting kaftan with wide sleeves or, for men, a turban, round cap, or fez, and a belted *antari* with a long fur boa. European clothing such as Sa'adi's mother produced placed men in long trousers, a shirt with a high, stiff collar, and a frock coat. Women's clothing favored floor-length skirts, small tight waists, and high-necked blouses.

Sa'adi's mother had been taught to sew in the European style by her mother, who had in turn learned from her mother, an immigrant to Salonica from Italy. Sa'adi describes watching his mother conduct business out of the home, whisking her young daughters away from the peering eyes of male clients when necessary. Word of her skill spread rapidly through Salonica. "In an age when there were no sewing machines, all the work was done by hand," Sa'adi recalled. "All the consulates in Salonica and other high-placed personalities, as well as all the business people, wore her shirts, the outcome of her handiwork."[13] At the height of her business, Sa'adi's mother was employing three of her own daughters and three additional helpers. In four weeks' time, the seven could hand-sew eight dozen shirts.

Sa'adi may not have seen fit to record in his memoir his mother's name, or that of his maternal grandmother, who provided his mother with an informal education in the needle trade. Still, the impact of these women on the course of the family's history was deep. Sa'adi's mother's business acumen and skill as a seamstress saved Sa'adi and her other children from poverty in the early nineteenth century. Her talent then passed to her daughters, granddaughters, and great-granddaughters, one of whom would rescue her own family from financial ruin in the mid-twentieth century by using these same skills.

It is sometimes assumed that Mediterranean Jewish families were essentially patriarchal and hierarchal, with the father's word akin to law, and family honor sacred.[14] While there is some truth to this generality, the image painted by the Levys is more intimate and complex. As early as the eighteenth century, women took an active role in providing for the present and in charting a future course for this family. They continued to command authority in the centuries that followed, leaving a documentary trail that was unusually robust for women of their day.

Despite her pioneering ways, Sa'adi's mother was a creature of her times, prone to its ravages as well as its opportunities. Early mortality was the norm rather than the exception; Sa'adi's mother died before his teenage years were over. Barely educated, Sa'adi poured himself into that quintessentially Ottoman Jewish trade, printing, filling the hole in the family business his father had vacated years earlier, upon his death. Sa'adi learned to cast font and claimed to have produced personally 30,000 to 40,000 letters in Rashi script—the letters used in printed Ladino until the language was informally and inconsistently Romanized in the 1920s.[15] In time, Sa'adi acquired the press of a competitor, along with two handpresses, twenty molds with matrices, and hundreds of sheets for casting. Over the course of sixty-five years the family press would produce a staggering quantity and range of printed works in Ladino, Hebrew, and French: everything from gilded wedding invitations to rabbinical commentary, the Zohar (a compendium of Jewish mystical writing), and Salonica's most popular fin-de-siècle newspapers, the Ladino-language *La Epoka* and the French-language *Le Journal de Salonique*. Much of this work Sa'adi did with his four sons, David, Besalel, Shemuel Sa'adi, and Hayyim—*Kitapçı* Hayyim, as he was known by the Ottoman Turkish nickname that associated him with his job: Hayyim the bookseller.

There were fourteen children in all, five with the unidentified first wife of Sa'adi's who died young, and nine with his second wife, Esther. Sa'adi's memoir offers shockingly little description of his wives, lavishing far more attention on the rabbis he enraged

Studio portrait of Sa'adi Besalel Ashkenazi a-Levi and his unidentified second wife, c. 1890s

than on the women with whom he built a family. His memoir touches with an equally light hand on his children, who were adolescents, young adults, and adults at the time of his writing.

The fourteen children were born over roughly twenty-five years. The dating is imprecise because, as Sa'adi warns, like most Jews of his era, he "neglected" chronology. "That is why I failed to keep track of my children's birth dates," he confesses. Three of Sa'adi's children would not reach adulthood. Two boys succumbed to cholera at a very young age, the first passing while his father was sweating off the fever. By the time the disease reached the second son, it took only two hours to run its course. A third son died in his teenage years, after a botched surgery.

Sa'adi's children who came to maturity, like the children of Sholem Aleichem's fictional Tevye, walked down all the paths modernity offered Jews, for the centrifugal force was no less strong in turn-of-the-century Salonica than in Boiberik. If Tevye's six fictional daughters are caricatures of the possibilities that branched out before Russian Jews of the turn of the twentieth century, Sa'adi's children walked the byways favored by modern Sephardic Jews. One daughter, Rachel, worked as a teacher for the Alliance Israélite Universelle, a Franco-Jewish philanthropic organization that provided hundreds of young Mediterranean and Middle Eastern Jewish women with a secular education and an entrée into the formal workforce. One son, Shemuel Sa'adi, became an impassioned political commentator, throwing himself into his father's business, publishing, and using the family's (and, later, his own) newspapers as a mouthpiece for his eclectic opinions. Fortunée, another daughter, moved to Manchester, one of several Sephardic émigré centers abroad. Three more of Sa'adi's children would emigrate in turn. Another son, David, stayed behind, weathering the transition from Ottoman to Greek rule and serving first as an Ottoman bureaucrat and subsequently as a high-ranking official for the Jewish Community of Salonica. Not one of Sa'adi's children married a non-Jew, as did Tevye's Chava—yet the children gradually assimilated into various adopted milieus, such that their own children would grow up worlds apart even if still, for the most part, Jewish.

Loyalty to French culture; the embrace of innovative politics; emigration; an investment in Ottoman and post-Ottoman society; measured assimilation—these were the boulevards that beckoned Sephardic youth at the fin de siècle. There is, too, the undocumented path taken by Hayyim, Fakima, Doudoun, and Djentil, children of Sa'adi about whom I found very little. Like so many Sephardic lives, theirs remain obscure—though their descendants found a way into this book. Finally, two of Sa'adi's children—both in their advanced years—died in the gas chambers of Auschwitz. In this, too, they were typical of their community.

As Sa'adi and Esther's children came of age in mid-nineteenth-century Salonica, the parents made a crucial decision. Conformists offered daughters scant formal education and sent sons to receive religious training at a *meldar* or Talmud Torah, schools for Jewish learning. "A *meldar* was a room with a couch in a neighbor's courtyard," noted a Ladino memoirist of the period. "On the couch, some benches, and the floor, sixty or seventy children sat or crouched . . . pushing, pulling, pinching, or biting each other, until the teacher would see them and yell, 'Scoundrels! Bastards! Rascals!' "[16] In Sa'adi's memoir, he condemned the Talmud Torah for cultivating self-indulgent young men committed to nothing but "months of merrymaking." The school's graduates, Sa'adi complained, awoke each day late in the afternoon and passed their time hunting and "going from coffeehouse to coffeehouse and from picnic to picnic on allowances they received from their parents."[17]

Sa'adi, culturally progressive, if traditional from a religious point of view, charted his own path. The a-Levis were not wealthy, even if the family was a visible part of Salonica's non-rabbinical Jewish cultural elite. Sa'adi leveraged this status to secure a bourgeois existence for his offspring. With his friend Moise Allantini, a wealthy philanthropist and freethinker, Sa'adi helped establish the first school of the Alliance Israélite Universelle in Salonica in 1873. The brainchild of the Franco-Jewish elite, the Alliance offered Mediterranean and Middle Eastern Jewish children rigorous instruction in French, according to the educational norms of the Franco-Jewish bourgeoisie. In hundreds of classrooms and schools segregated by gender, Alliance students, both female and male, studied secular subjects, including French and Hebrew, literature and math, as well as religion and Jewish history. They were also offered moral instruction—advised not to smoke or drink, and not to play backgammon or converse in Ladino, their native tongue, which the Alliance hoped they would abandon in favor of French.[18] Sa'adi enrolled at least four of his children—two daughters, Fortunée and Rachel, and two sons, David and Shemuel Sa'adi—in Salonica's new school. The siblings were among Salonica's first Alliance graduates.

Alliance Israélite Universelle boys' school, Salonica, 1912

The imprint an Alliance education had upon the children is depicted vividly in their handwriting: or, at least, in the pen of three of the four—Shemuel Sa'adi, always in a hurry, had the most inelegant penmanship of his siblings. Their French is virtually native, the writing a touch formal. Each letter is dated in the upper right corner, with the place of writing named. Numbers appear in the French style, margins are even, punctuation is perfect, accents are precise. Were it not for the addition of Ladino phrases here and there—and, of course, the content—one could assume the correspondents had come of age in the French Republic. The a-Levi children were distinguished students, marked by drive and passion. At least three were invited, upon graduation from high school, to enroll in the Alliance's elite teacher-training college in Paris, the École Normale Israelite Orientale. The choice each made (or that was made for them) proved a tributary of sorts, carrying them on an ever-swifter current, toward different seas.

As his children came of age, Sa'adi sharpened his public persona, using the printing press he operated with his sons to denounce the rabbinical establishment of Salonica as abusive, fanatical, and exploitative of the poor. A frequent target was the rabbinical tax on kosher meat—the very same charge that the breakaway Hasidic movement of eighteenth-century Eastern Europe launched against the reigning religious establishment there. Threatened by Sa'adi's accusations, Salonica's religious elite, Chief Rabbi Asher Kovo at its head, fought with what remaining weapon it had, a writ of *herem* or excommunication. The writ was issued against both Sa'adi and his eldest son, Hayyim, in the child's case on trumped-up charges of smoking on the Sabbath in violation of Jewish law. On a climactic day in 1874, the rabbi's henchmen dragged and chased Sa'adi and Hayyim through the streets of Salonica, a mob of five hundred at their heels. The city's streets were then narrow and labyrinthine, lined with buildings in the Ottoman style. One can imagine their wooden balconies alive with onlookers, witnesses to Sa'adi's humiliation. The a-Levi home was ransacked in the melee. Father and son were spared physical harm only after the intervention of a wealthy friend who succeeded in reasoning with the mob.

Children in Salonica's Upper Town, 1907

Though the throng dispersed, the *herem* remained in place. Technically a writ of excommunication was meant to cut off the accused from the Jewish community, preventing him from joining a minyan (Jewish prayer quorum) or engaging in commercial or social transactions with other Jews. In Sa'adi's case, members of the community were warned against patronizing the family press, employees left the family firm, and Sa'adi himself stopped attending synagogue for a time. And yet, the impact of the *herem* seems only to have galvanized Sa'adi's supporters—and his own radicalism. Shortly after his excommunication, Sa'adi traveled to

Vienna to obtain new letter blocks in Rashi and Latin fonts. It was the farthest he would travel in his lifetime. Upon his return to Salonica, Sa'adi inaugurated the city's first Ladino-language newspaper, *La Epoka*. With his sons at his side, he would publish the newspaper for sixteen years, using it to give voice to his progressive sensibilities and myriad grievances. "They fired a cannonball at me," he later wrote, "I fired back in kind."

If, in practical terms, the blow wrought by the *herem* was slight, psychologically its impact was heavy. Though a critic of rabbinical excess, Sa'adi observed Jewish law, and his excommunication disturbed him deeply. In fact, it was a trauma that stayed with him all his life. Out of anger and a desire to clear his name, Sa'adi began to compose his memoir. He could not have imagined how far the document would travel, let alone that it would inspire this history.

RACHEL

Sa'adi's daughter Rachel (1862–1948) favored violet ink. Her letters are lined with the vibrant color, their rhythms charted with a steady hand. I turn to her next not because she was Sa'adi's eldest—this honor went to Hayyim, who earlier had the alleged sins of his excommunicated father visited upon him—but because her writing is the oldest of the family's to have been preserved, save Sa'adi's own.

If Sa'adi's publishing legacy passed from father to son, the family's indomitable and sometimes headstrong spirit passed equally from mother to daughter. For decades, Rachel served as a teacher for the Alliance Israélite Universelle, compelled by terms of employment to narrate her career through letters. The Alliance meticulously preserved every letter it received from its students, principals, and teachers, storing them in folders neatly classified by person and place in its Paris archive. Rachel and her husband, Elie, wrote hundreds of letters back to the Alliance over their decades of service, their missives mailed from professional posts across the Mediterranean. The letters strike a surprisingly intimate tone. Rachel left home at an early age and the Alliance became a surrogate family, with which she was obliged to correspond.

Rachel was a dutiful daughter of the Alliance, and she traveled the farthest of any of her siblings—distances unimaginable to most Ottoman women of the time. Yet her professional life was marked by struggles with her employers, and though the Alliance awarded her a medal for her service, Rachel retired dissatisfied. Personality played a role in Rachel's ups and downs, to be sure: then again, her work placed her in a series of untenable situations. Rachel taught through epidemics and political turmoil and in the face of community upheaval. Her finances and marriage were both tested because of her service to the Alliance, and despite their advanced degrees the couple lived close to poverty. Rachel boldly embraced a modernist project, but the embrace proved chilly and unyielding.

Rachel was fifteen or sixteen years old when she graduated from Salonica's Alliance school. An excellent student, she was invited by the organization to pursue teacher training in Paris, at the École Normale Israélite Orientale. Rachel's training there would have been expensive, putting a financial strain upon the family. To shoulder the burden, Sa'adi and his wife had to have believed strongly in the advantages of graduate education for their eldest daughter.

One might imagine that a late-nineteenth-century Jewish family would be loath to let a daughter travel so far. The a-Levis, however, were unusually open-minded. Like other progressive Jewish families of the era (including those in the Ashkenazi sphere), they were often more willing to expose daughters than sons to novel ideas, readings, and environments.[1] Ironically, this reflected their conviction that girls did not have the drive, ambition, or intelligence to stray. It also suggests how fully the a-Levi family had embraced the message of the Alliance, which promised education and social mobility. Paris, though geographically distant, had been offered up to Sa'adi's children as an intimate place—a cultural nursery.[2] When another Alliance student of the period learned that she had been selected to study at the École Normale Israélite Orientale in Paris, she wrote that while she would miss her childhood home, she would "jump for joy" upon seeing Paris, a "dear city" she had loved since childhood, despite never having visited it.[3] For this girl, as for Rachel, pursuing an education at the École Normale Israélite Orientale was at once bold and the natural result of choices she and her family had made years earlier.

It would take another decade before train tracks allowed a rapid, three-day journey from Salonica to Paris.[4] Rachel must have traveled by steamship when she arrived there in 1877, not yet married and prepared for two years of training. At the time, the French Third Republic was in its infancy: the city was preparing for the 1878 World's Fair, where Alexander Graham Bell's telephone, the head of the Statue of Liberty, and a human zoo of four hundred "indigenous people" were all on display. Rachel, who was in Paris to study, had modest funds, scant free time, and even less independence. There would be no World's Fair for her. The Alliance kept its protégés under strict supervision.

A photograph of Rachel at eighteen years of age, taken upon her graduation, pictures her holding what appears to be her diploma and betraying the sober, practical look of a teacher.[5] The studio portrait presents a one-dimensional story of an educated young woman. It does not tell of the strains of modernity, which both availed opportunities to Sephardic women and simultaneously imposed novel constraints upon them. Rachel's education liberated her from restrictions that had bound her mother's generation, releasing her, also, from the rabbis who had challenged her father. Nevertheless, the eighteen-year-old was now under a new, equally patriarchal authority: the Alliance, and with it, the ideals of the Western European Jewish bourgeoisie.[6] Despite the distance Sa'adi's daughter would travel, her path was

Rachel a-Levi Carmona, 1880

determined by her superiors, and she often chafed at this. Her dilemma was the need to struggle with the force that purported to free her.

Rachel's path took her to settings her father couldn't have imagined. Her first post was at a girls' school in Ortaköy, a poor Jewish neighborhood of Istanbul. Rachel's colleague Gabriel Arié, director of the neighboring Alliance boys' school, described Rachel as "very pleasant." The couple became close, yet Arié, by his own admission, was too young for marriage. He also found Rachel's ways "a bit too free." Nevertheless (or, perhaps, all the more) Arié considered the two years he spent in Ortaköy with Rachel as among the happiest of his life.[7] The very idea of premarital socializing between women and men was new to Rachel's generation. Sa'adi, by contrast, met his wife for the first time upon the marital altar, her face red and swollen from prenuptial waxing.[8]

Rachel's friendship with Arié sheds light on her independent spirit. Still, much of her life followed a script set by her family and the Alliance. Before assuming her second post, Rachel married Elie Carmona, another graduate of the École Normale Israélite Orientale, a child of Istanbul who was a few years Rachel's senior. The pair had much in common, in addition to their educational background. Both came from publishing and writing families, with the Carmonas building a small empire of newspapers in Istanbul, much as the a-Levis did in Salonica.[9] With Rachel and Elie's union, a significant publishing alliance between the families emerged. Through marriage, Rachel found a way to honor the house of the a-Levis and the Alliance at the same time.

Over the decades that followed, Rachel and Elie would travel across the Levant in the employ of the Alliance, working as a teacher and school director (in Elie's case) and as a teacher (in Rachel's), in Tétouan (in Morocco); in Beirut, Damascus, and Jerusalem (in Ottoman Syria); in Shumen, Ruschuk, Plovdiv, and Tatar-Pazarjik (in Ottoman Bulgaria); in Izmir (in Ottoman Anatolia); and in Serres, Kavála, and Yanya (Ioannina) (in Ottoman Macedonia). In their first three years of marriage, they moved at least three times.

The couple's first joint appointment placed them in the Ottoman port of Ruschuk. This was the city of Elias Canetti, future winner of the Nobel Prize in Literature, whose family was among the founders of Ruschuk's Jewish community. Canetti offers this description of the town: "Ruschuk, on the lower Danube, where I came into the world, was a marvelous city for a child, and if I say that Ruschuk is in Bulgaria, then I am giving an inadequate picture of it. For people of the most varied backgrounds lived there, on any one day you could hear seven or eight languages."[10] The cultural variety Canetti describes did not ease Rachel's arrival. Brought to Ruschuk to assume a position in the Alliance girls' school, Rachel found the school shuttered and Jewish families hesitant to enroll their daughters. Even as enrollment climbed (there were one hundred twenty girls studying in the Alliance school two years after Rachel's arrival), the majority of families proved unable to pay their fees and the majority of students were too young to study. Rachel persevered. She proposed that some of her pupils enter Bulgarian public school, so that they could learn the Bulgarian language and occupational skills. At the same time, Rachel wed her mother's ability with sewing to her own professional expertise, opening a vocational class in dressmaking for girls. The class turned a profit, but failed to find favor with parents. Alliance parents, it seems, hoped education would produce loftier options for their daughters. To her employers in Paris, Rachel complained that she was faced daily with threats and insults, and that all she was granted in return for her labor was disdain and ingratitude. Strained finances compounded the problem: both she and Elie received low and intermittent wages.[11]

By the early 1880s, Rachel had given birth to a daughter. Whether due to the stress of her employment or undernourishment, she found herself unable to produce the requisite milk to nurse. Beside herself, Rachel demanded to be relocated. "I am a mother," she wrote her employers, "and though privation has become a habit for me, I do not want my infant to suffer."[12] When the Alliance acquiesced, moving the Carmonas to Tatar-Pazarjik (a backwater compared to the thriving Danube port of Ruschuk), Rachel called it a "miserable little place." The post extended to three difficult years, the time marked by Rachel with a flow of increasingly distraught letters. Typhoid racked the town, and the whole family became sick in turn. Matters reached a crisis point when

Elie was accused of attempting to rape the daughter-in-law of the rabbi, a young woman who had become close to Rachel. Rachel declared the situation "totally insupportable."[13] The Carmonas had lost their professional credibility; their marriage, too, must have suffered. Elie and Rachel were relocated to the small Bulgarian town of Shumla. Rachel may have been relieved to distance herself from Tatar-Pazarjik. Still, she fretted that in Shumla, she was sure to perish from boredom alone.[14]

At least in southeastern Europe, Rachel's students were Judeo-Spanish speakers, and of a cultural milieu reasonably similar to her own. At her next post, in Morocco, Rachel shared no language with the bulk of her Arabic-speaking pupils, though she could communicate with some in Haketia, the particular form of Judeo-Spanish preserved in northern Morocco. Further, the family's arrival in December 1900 coincided with a famine and the outbreak of a civil war. In the spring of 1903, as violence raged in Tétouan, Morocco, Elie wrote his superiors a series of despairing letters and telegrams. Schools were deserted as families fled the city for the relative peace of the countryside. Tétouan's European population was being evacuated, panic was everywhere, violence raged just outside the Carmonas' Alliance residence. Ignoring the Alliance's rigid directive that they stay and render themselves useful to the Jewish poor of Tétouan, Elie, Rachel, and their young daughter fled to the port, only to be denied the chance to leave. "Our existence has become intolerable," wrote Elie.[15]

No sooner had tensions subsided in Tétouan than the Alliance central office fielded a letter of complaint against the Carmonas. The disgruntled writer claimed that the pair were eating non-kosher meat in their home and beating their students in school. Rachel, the letter confided, had applied pepper oil to the mouths of those who misbehaved.[16] The letter reeked of paranoia and its lurid accusations undermined its own credibility. Still, the

Alliance could ill afford a whiff of scandal, and Rachel, at least, sensed that her employers were not on her side. Within the year, the Carmonas were reassigned to Yanya (Ioannina), in Ottoman Macedonia, and, some years later, to Beirut, where Rachel facilitated a visit of the chief rabbi of the Ottoman Empire.[17]

Trials were a through line of Rachel's many decades with the Alliance. When the Carmonas arrived in Damascus with their young children in 1891, it was in the midst of a cholera epidemic like the one that had killed Rachel's half brothers some decades earlier. Decades later, they were in the Ottoman town of Kavala through the violent Bulgarian occupation that attended the Balkan Wars.[18] Rachel and Elie were trapped in conflict-ridden Tétouan when Rachel would have received the news that her father, Sa'adi, had died. Given the distance and slow pace of communications, she must have missed his burial in Salonica and the shiva that followed. Across their varied posts, Rachel and her husband lived a spare existence, particularly after Elie's father's death left him to serve as father to his seven younger siblings.[19] Rachel and Elie survived from paycheck to paycheck—and at times even this was not enough. When Elie temporarily lost his job with the Alliance, the meager monthly stipend the organization paid Rachel did not cover the couple's rent. When Elie died in 1932, he apologized to Rachel for abandoning her without resources. "At least I leave you with two children," he wrote in a final letter, "and [our son-in-law] Ralph is so good and so solicitous that he will take care of you."

At the time Rachel retired, she lamented that she had never received the full respect of her superiors in Paris. Even when the secretary of the Alliance Israélite Universelle attempted to soften his tone, his words to Rachel were sharp, as in this crudely edited letter of 1906: "~~Whether out of negligence or ineptitude~~/For one reason or another, the schools where you practiced have almost always collapsed under your direction and never progressed."[20] The secretary's choice not to retype the handwritten missive was unkind. The organization preferred to pin its failures on individual teachers rather than concede the burden it placed upon them. Though Rachel did eventually receive a medal of recognition from the Alliance, she found this recognition slight, given her lifetime of service.[21]

Yet Rachel was treasured by her family for some of the very same reasons she seemed to irk her employers. She was direct to a fault, her criticisms unvarnished. In family letters, Rachel could skillfully encapsulate a character in a line or two, with a preference for the unflattering. "Suzanne is louche," "Besalel is always suffering." Rachel's supervisors bristled at her tone: her professional letters are dotted with the marginal comments of her superiors noting occasional pique at her suggestions, complaints, and demands. But family members admired Rachel's straightforward nature. Rachel's brother Shemuel Sa'adi described his and his siblings' affection for her as exceptionally deep, conveying that he viewed her as a maternal figure. Her sister-in-law Renée spoke of her as a "true mother."[22] Rachel's nephew Leon celebrated her vibrant spirit. Rachel's daughter Carola was extremely close to her mother, faithfully nursing her through various bouts of illness. In his will, Rachel's husband, Elie, addressed her as "My much loved wife." Rachel was distinguished by her plainspokenness and candor. She was inclined to articulate what no one else could perceive, or was willing to say.

SHEMUEL SA'ADI / SAM

Rachel and Fortunée's brother Shemuel Sa'adi (1870–1959) was the Zelig of the a-Levi family, capable of adjusting to a staggering array of historical events in the course of his long life. Fittingly, he was the first a-Levi to modify the prefix of his father, adopting the surname Lévy in place of the more traditional formulation, and later going by Sam in place of his given first names. Though he altered the family name, Shemuel clearly inherited his father's hot blood. Fearless, politically passionate, frequently outraged by perceived slights, the self-proclaimed hero of all his own stories, Shemuel could ruffle feathers. But his relentlessness was also a force in the life of the family.

His education began conservatively, in a Jewish middle school where he studied the Bible and Jewish liturgy. This was followed by a six-year stint at Salonica's Alliance school, where Shemuel delved into the study of French, Italian, Greek, Turkish, and Hebrew. Shemuel was invited by the Alliance to continue his education in Paris. This was an honor for boys as well as for girls and Shemuel's path could have followed that of his sister Rachel, who spent so many decades working for the institution. Family finances were tight, however, and Sa'adi strove to keep his sons in the family business. With the help of his elder brother David,

Shemuel obtained entry as a boarder in the newly opened Ottoman imperial lycée of Salonica.

This was an usual choice for a Jew of his generation. Fluency in Ottoman Turkish (let alone in the Ottoman literary canon) was rare among Jews at this time. At the Lycée, Shemuel was one of five Jewish students out of a total of three hundred. And none of the Jewish students boarded at the lycée, as opposed to the Muslim students, who did live there.[1] Shemuel was given the Ottoman Turkish nickname Kemal, and "learned classical Turkish literature better than my Muslim peers," so much so that he was mistaken for a Muslim Turk by a delegate of the minister of education.[2] Had his temperament been more mellow, Shemuel would surely have graduated with high honors. But disagreements with classmates and teachers interrupted his studies, and Shemuel was forced to finish his education elsewhere.

Upon graduation from high school, Shemuel balanced work for the family firm with a job at the state-financed Anatolian Railway Company, a position he bitterly disliked. He would have dressed for work each day like a family friend, who wore "a starched collar, a melon hat, peg-leg trousers and a fitted jacket buttoned up to the neck, as was the fashion."[3] Certainly his clothing would have been quite unlike that of his more traditional father—or, for that matter, his brother David, whose service to the empire required a fez. At the Railroad Office, Shemuel's company sought to link Salonica to other regional centers, including Edirne, Istanbul, and Sofia—but his eyes were on Paris, a city he visited for the first time in 1893.

Shemuel's second visit coincided with one of the most important episodes of turn-of-the-century European Jewish history, the Dreyfus Affair. The cause célèbre arose after Captain Alfred Dreyfus, a young Alsatian officer of Jewish descent, was falsely accused in 1894 of passing secrets to the German Embassy in Paris. At the time of Shemuel's arrival, Dreyfus had been tried and convicted and was languishing in prison on a sweltering island in French Guiana. France roiled in his absence, dividing in two over the question of his guilt or innocence. Dreyfus supporters argued the captain had been framed, while his critics fanned the flames of anti-Semitism. Shemuel, who was studying law at the Sorbonne, lived with a friend in a cheap storeroom, subsisting on crusts of bread and *pommes frites*.

"We entered the fray head-on, especially Shemuel," remembered his roommate. "He couldn't sleep at night if he hadn't come to blows that day with some anti-Dreyfusard. There were many times when we returned to our twelve-francs-a-month storeroom with blackened eyes, bloody noses, and impressive bumps on our foreheads."[4] Shemuel left Paris with a renewed passion for French Republicanism, and an embrace of that which his Alliance teachers (and father) held dear: the redemptive value of the liberal ideal, the practical advantage of a French education, the sense that Jews should support other Jews even as they aspired to be model citizens of modern nations.

Throughout the Paris period, Shemuel continued his collaboration with his father and brothers, though his diary suggests that distance and experience left him judgmental of his brothers' intellect and the informal style of Ladino journalism.[5] But on the occasion of his father's retirement in 1898, Sam allowed himself to be pulled home (he had not been back for two years at this point) to take a more active role in the family business. Once more in Salonica, he assumed editorial direction of the family's flagging Ladino-language newspaper *La Epoka* and, a few months later, the French-language *Le Journal de Salonique*. On the masthead of *La Epoka*, he introduced himself as Sam Lévy—the name by which he would be known for the rest of his life.

The Salonica to which Sam returned was increasingly prosperous and modern. The stores were well stocked, the quay crowded with pedestrians. Carriages rolled by, the streetcar's call was loud and frequent. Outdoor tables were crowded at the many cafés where one could order a raki, nibble meze, debate politics—and riffle through a well-thumbed French- or Ladino-language newspaper for news of the world.[6]

Sabri Pasha Street, 1910

Ladino-language journalism was a relatively young institution at the turn of the century, and Sa'adi and his sons were among its pioneers. The Ladino- and French-language newspapers they edited were improvisational in style. Until the early twentieth century, editors frequently composed letters to the editor under pseudonyms. Contributions by "correspondents" from distant cities and countries were often written by the editors themselves. Exclamation points abounded. Yet the notion that ordinary readers could acquire the day's news in a language they understood was still radical. And newspapers provided more than news. Full of advertisements for the latest fashions, scientific and health exposés, serialized fiction translated from numerous world languages—newspapers were, then as now, an education.[7]

Ladino and French newspapers were, additionally, among the most important places for Ottoman Jews to debate the welter of political considerations that confronted them at the turn of the century. In the pages of *La Epoka* and *Le Journal de Salonique*, as in the pages of rival newspapers, editors and letters to the editors defended and decried a staggering number of political alternatives, particularly after the lifting of censorship that followed the Young Turk revolution of 1908. Would Jews' security and future be best served by socialism, Zionism, the bourgeois and reform-minded goals of the Alliance Israélite Universelle, or regional nationalism of one form or another? Ought they to cast their lot in with Ottomanism and affiliate with their multireligious empire?

Nowhere did these debates rage as boisterously as in Salonica, where, under Sam's watch, *Le Journal de Salonique* and *La Epoka* emerged as voices of progress. The newspapers' broad agendas embraced the idea that Ottoman Jews ought to modernize themselves and their culture and emulate Western educational norms, the French language, and a secular worldview—all the while remaining Ottomanists, faithful citizens of their multiethnic empire. Sam's temporary penchant for socialism left its fingerprints on the family newspapers, too. His affiliation with the Worker's Federation of Salonica and his labor organizing for Salonica's enormous tobacco industry translated into a flurry of articles on the needs and rights of the working class. Sam would soon abandon this position, defending employers' rights and lambasting the Federation.[8]

Brief as Sam's socialist period was, it led him to a position he would maintain all his life—his defense of Ladino, the language of Salonica's Jewish masses. In the Ottoman Balkans, as in Eastern Europe and the United States, Jewish socialists learned to appreciate the power of the Jewish mother tongue for organizing and activism.[9] Sam's respect for the Ladino language rendered him unique among Ladino editors of the day, as the Judeo-Spanish language was an object of ridicule for many other Ottoman Jewish newspapers. In the pages of *La Epoka*, by contrast, the Sephardic language was celebrated and championed as a modern language on par with any other.

Sam's most effective means of communication was the editorial. He always had a point to make, and his editorials, like his letters, are emphatic if repetitive and unruly. He once described himself as having "an impulsive and argumentative character," which strikes me as a just self-assessment.[10] I imagine him writing feverishly in a bar or café, his pages stained with traces of coffee, his fingers spotted with ink.

Publishing in the Ottoman Empire was often a family affair, and the Levys (like other publishing families) were susceptible to the business's strains. Income from paying subscribers always lagged behind what was needed to keep a newspaper afloat. And the Ottoman censor's hand was always felt, even if a bit more lightly in the world of Ladino letters than in Ottoman Turkish, French, or Greek. Nevertheless, in 1905, two years after the death of his father and shortly before the birth of his daughter, Sam temporarily relocated his young family to the small Austro-Hungarian town of Zemun (Semlin, now a suburb of Belgrade), in order to evade the censor's reach.[11] There Sam founded two

Sam Lévy, from El djiro del mundo kon sinko metalikes *(Salonica, 1905)*

new newspapers, the Ladino-language *El Luzero* and the French-language *Le Rayon*, both intended primarily for readers in Salonica.

At the time of his move to Zemun, Sam was newly married to his niece Anna Barouch, daughter of his father's sister Sol. Marriage among close relations was common at the time for Sephardic Jews. Sam, seventeen years older than his wife, had been called upon to serve as Anna's escort on various trips across Europe (some of which included extended stays in foreign capitals) when she was still a teenager. Anna's mobility is a sign that her parents were broad-minded and reasonably well-off. Anna's own mother had "traveled the world, from Istanbul to Alexandria, and from Cairo to Jerusalem." Sam and Anna's daughter Suzanne later remembered her grandmother as a magnetic raconteur who favored Stendhal's *The Red and the Black*, half singing, half telling the story of love and betrayal over the course of many nights in order to make her way to the end.[12] Anna, one can infer, was every bit her husband's equal.

Though Sam had moved to Zemun to avoid the Ottoman censor, he would find the Austrian one still more meddlesome. His new newspapers were shut down soon after they opened, and this propelled Sam, Anna, and their first and only child back home to Salonica just months after they had left. This meant they were in the city to celebrate the Young Turk revolution of 1908, with whose reformist leaders, the Committee of Union and Progress, Sam allied himself. Once it had assumed power, the Committee of Union and Progress reinstated the thwarted Ottoman constitution of 1876 and legislated new freedoms for Ottoman citizens, including a lifting of censorship. Celebrants flooded Salonica's streets after the pronouncement, with Jews, Armenians, and Greek Orthodox citizens all parading in turn. Sam's brother-in-law Ascher Salem was among them, speaking before the chamber of commerce and the multiethnic Club Commercial. *Le Journal de Salonique*, which Salem served as a commercial editor, declared his speech "superb," without offering further details.[13]

Using his newspapers as a platform, Sam expressed his patriotism for the Ottoman state. The empire's new leadership, Sam believed, would benefit Jews and other minorities. "There are no more Bulgarians, Greeks, Serbs, Romanians, Jews, Muslims," ran one of his editorials, repurposing the words of Committee of Union and Progress leader Ismail Enver Pasha: "We are all equal, and can boast of being Ottomans!"[14] Sam's fervor for the Ottoman state drove his opposition to Zionism, a movement that had little support among Ottoman Jews prior to 1908, but that gained popularity after the lifting of censorship laws. Jewish nationalism, in Sam's view, ran counter to Ottoman patriotism, while Zionists' interest in Jewish settlement in Ottoman Palestine directly threatened the empire's sovereignty. "I am an anti-Zionist," Sam declared in *La Epoka* in 1908. "I was always one under the previous regime and there is even more reason for this now."[15]

Like every patriot, Sam loved a parade. In 1911, Sultan Mehmed V visited Salonica as part of a summer tour of Ottoman Macedonia. The occasion was an opportunity for various political factions of Jewish Salonica to compete for the attentions of the ruler, as well as everyday Salonicans. When Sultan Mehmed arrived in the port, he was met by rows of local dignitaries. Chief Rabbi Jacob Meir was present, as was Sam's brother David "Daout Effendi," now an Ottoman representative and president of the Grand Cercle Israélite, an organization of prominent Jewish merchants.[16] Upon leaving the port, the sultan was led on horseback through a series of decorative arches erected specifically for the occasion.[17]

The pageantry was splendid, and who better to memorialize it than the city's most tireless editor, Sam Lévy. Over the twenty-four hours of the sultan's stay, Sam prepared on behalf of *Le Journal de Salonique* a lavish commemorative album of the sultan's visit illustrated with photographs of the celebratory arches erected by the citizens of Salonica. The morning after the sultan's tour, Sam presented the album to Sultan Mehmed V. The gesture sprang from Sam's own Ottomanist sentiments—and paid tribute to his father, who, half a century earlier, composed Hebrew and Ladino songs in honor of Sultan Abdul Medjid's visit to Salonica.[18] The sultan, for his part, awarded a pair of diamond cuff links to Sam's brother Daout Effendi, a partner in the newspaper that produced the album, and an Ottoman official. No one could have imagined that in less than three years Salonica would be lost to the Ottomans, and that in less than two decades, Jews would cease to be the dominant thread in the city's fabric.

Soon after the sultan departed Salonica, Sam, too, took leave of the city. By the end of 1911, Sam, Anna, and Suzanne were living in Belgrade because, according to one account, Sam's incendiary writing had earned him enemies at home. Prior to his departure from Salonica, Sam had folded both *La Epoka* and *Le Journal de Salonique*, which his father, Sa'adi, had created decades earlier, and which Sam had edited since 1898. A new newspaper, *El Liberal*, was created in the void, its masthead announcing that it was the result of the editorial collaboration of the "*ijos de Sa'adi Levi*" (sons of Sa'adi Levi), the Ladino phrasing echoing the Hebrew (sons of Besalel) used by Sa'adi's father's press a century and a half earlier.[19] This new newspaper would run for a decade—yet, despite its success, with the closure of the family's original papers, a chapter in the history of Jewish Salonica closed, as did a chapter in the history of the Levy family. In the Kingdom of Serbia, Sam wove his political views into an elegy called *The Decline of the Crescent*. He dedicated the volume to Sa'adi.

DAVID / DAOUT EFFENDI

A skilled linguist and a gifted mathematician, David (1863–1943) was, from a young age, charged with creating and printing calendars on his father's press. This task demanded the complex synthesis of lunar and solar, as well as Jewish, Muslim, Greek Orthodox, and Roman, time. It required one to be punctilious, numerate, and highly organized—skills that would serve David well once he left the family business to become a student of law, a high-ranking official in the Ottoman bureaucracy, and, in time, interwar head of Salonica's Jewish Community.

Like his siblings Rachel and Shemuel, David was invited to enroll in the teaching college of the Alliance Israélite Universelle in Paris upon his graduation from high school. But Sa'adi was unwilling to sacrifice his able junior partner, and compelled David to dedicate himself to the family business. Among his tasks, at fifteen years of age, was to translate into Ladino Italian, French, Greek, and Hebrew writings for publication in *La Epoka*. Working alongside his brothers Besalel and Shemuel, and in collaboration with his brother Hayyim, a bookseller who brought a-Levi products to a wider market, David helped Sa'adi shape an autonomous family business. Members of the a-Levi family controlled all aspects of production, from the creation of movable type to the writing of copy to printing and sales.

David a-Levi (Daout Effendi), 1880

David, however, had grander ambitions. In 1881, at eighteen years of age, he began to study law with two other young Jewish intellectuals. Scarcely had he begun his legal studies when his mentor, a distinguished jurist, recommended him as director of the Ottoman Passport Office. He assumed the post in 1882 under his new name, Daout Effendi, Daout being a Turkified version of his given name, David, and Effendi being an Ottoman honorific for a distinguished, well-educated man. David would be known by this august title for the rest of his life.

Daout Effendi's post with the Ottoman administration, like his brother Sam's first desk job, carried considerable symbolic significance. Working for the Anatolian Railway Company, Sam helped link Salonica to the wider region—and the world. In his professional capacity, Daout Effendi oversaw the legal transformation of the Ottoman population as Sultan Abdülhamid II reimagined the empire as a modern state. Salonica, like the empire as a whole, was rapidly changing, to the roar of trains and the rustling of legal documents.

In the nineteenth century, few residents of the Ottoman Empire—whether Jewish, Christian, or Muslim—carried legal papers of any kind. Birth certificates were rare and, when they existed, were acquired by women and men only when absolutely necessary, such as in the case of foreign travel. Most Jewish women and men were more inclined to register newborns with the Jewish Community than with the state—however, many, including Daout Effendi's father, Sa'adi, had no record of their children's births whatsoever. Those Jews who did travel abroad often carried a single legal document—a temporary travel or residency permit. It was not unusual for a man of Daout Effendi's generation to carry, fold, and unfold a sheet like this for years, or an entire lifetime.[1]

Yet over the course of the nineteenth century, the Ottoman bureaucracy, like those of the European states, was increasingly interested in identifying who belonged and who did not—who was officially Ottoman, and who was a visitor, foreign resident, migrant, or refugee. Meanwhile, individuals like Daout Effendi and his children were coming to appreciate that legal papers—and especially the right kind of legal papers—were a crucial asset. They facilitated travel and trade, dictated whether a son was eligible for military service, and, more abstractly, came to seem like a form of insurance required by the modern world. "You must know that the question of a passport is very serious.

With what passport are you traveling? What is your nationality?" Daout Effendi addressed these questions to his daughter-in-law Estherina in the frantic lead-up to the Second World War. Though the circumstances of their exchange were unique, Daout Effendi's sentiments were honed through service to the empire. He knew firsthand that life-changing opportunity could hinge on the possession of a passport. For years, he was the Ottoman official empowered to grant or deny the possession of this document to others.

As head of a passport office and personal secretary to the provincial governor, Daout Effendi was no ordinary bureaucrat. He was required to maintain contact with his superiors in Istanbul and to meet frequently with the many consular officials in Salonica. He needed to constantly test, and anticipate, the prevailing political winds. He possessed the right to judge the legal identity of women, men, and children. When Theodor Herzl wanted an audience with the Ottoman sultan to discuss the future of Ottoman Palestine, it was on Daout Effendi's door that he knocked.

Jews of more modest stature also valued Daout Effendi's wisdom and power. When a close friend of his siblings wished to attend Istanbul University at age sixteen, he knew how to circumvent the university's required age of twenty. In the young man's telling: "That's what we had Daout for." A stickler for rules, Daout Effendi at first refused the would-be student's request. But because the legal maneuver would facilitate his education, Daout Effendi relented. "So when I went to him for a travel permit, without looking at my face and acting like he didn't know me, [Daout Effendi] asked me: 'How old are you?' 'Nineteen going on twenty,' I answered as advised. 'Good.' And so Daout wrote '20 years of age' in his beautiful script on the *tezkere* [Ottoman travel papers]."[2]

In whatever language Daout Effendi wrote, he wrote elegantly. When he signed his name on official documents, in French, he added an elongated flourish beneath: a paraph (perhaps intended to thwart forgery) that could command as many as five looping curves.[3]

Fittingly, given his position, Daout Effendi tended toward greater political circumspection than his brother Sam. While Sam trumpeted the Young Turk revolution and flirted with socialism, Daout Effendi was hopeful that a robust Jewish working class, if properly integrated into the larger Jewish community, would be able to compete with a growing body of Greek Christian competitors. He was, additionally, among a small group of powerful Jewish leaders who, in response to the revolution, created a mutual aid society that offered self-help to Salonica's Jewish working poor.[4] The Young Turk revolution—and with it the rise of mass politics—had brought the brothers' divergent personalities into sharp relief. Sam, impulsive, one might even say a firebrand, while Daout Effendi was measured and in full command of himself at all times. Happily, each found a professional niche to match his nature.

In 1910, Daout Effendi assumed a new position as the Jewish Community of Salonica's director of communal real estate. An official body created by the Ottoman state in 1870 and granted a degree of legal, social, and economic authority, the Jewish Community governed all aspects of Jewish religious and secular life, managing the dispersal of charity, the care of orphans, widows, and the poor, and the control of extensive property. It collected taxes, oversaw the designation of *kashrut*, the accordance with Jewish dietary laws, and employed the chief rabbi.[5]

Daout Effendi's new position was not necessarily a step up for an Ottoman bureaucrat, but it was nonetheless imposing. In his new post, Daout Effendi oversaw a formidable economic portfolio—a measure of the power and influence of the Jewish Community of Salonica, and of the Levy family within it. It is no surprise that 1910 also brought Daout Effendi's election to the council of the Grand Cercle Israélite, a prestigious association of Salonica's Jewish upper class.[6] Though the Levys were not wealthy, Daout Effendi acquired a level of recognition that far exceeded what previous generations of the family had attained. Soon he would become the most influential official of the Jewish Community aside from the chief rabbi. Beginning in 1910, Daout Effendi's private life and the life of Salonica's Jewish Community bled into one another, so much so that many of his personal letters were written on the Community's bilingual French-and-Ladino-language letterhead.

Daout Effendi was by this point married to Vida and father to three children, Eleanor, Emmanuel, and Leon, now in their early twenties. The family must have been very proud when Daout Effendi stood, among all the dignitaries of Salonica, to welcome the Ottoman sultan Mehmed V to their city: how thrilled to hold in their hands the diamond cuff links with which the sultan honored their husband and father. In the face of so much pomp, it was unthinkable that war would soon fray the ties that bound the family and the city to the empire.

Daout Effendi had only been in his new position with the Jewish Community for two years when the First Balkan War (1912–1913) filled the streets of Salonica with Jewish, Christian, and Muslim refugees, as well as tens of thousands of Turkish, Bulgarian, and Greek soldiers. The conflict pitted the Balkan League—Greece, Bulgaria, Montenegro, and Serbia—against the Ottoman Empire, with each of the Balkan states intent on wresting territory from the Ottomans and claiming control over ethnic subjects they felt belonged within their national boundaries.

For Salonica's residents, the wars ground daily life to a halt. The port was obstructed, shops were forced to close, traffic ceased, and trains stopped running.[7] The first of the Balkan Wars resulted in the Ottomans' loss of the bulk of their European holdings, including the city of Salonica—territory the empire had held for centuries. In June 1913, the Second Balkan War, which lasted only a month, dramatically altered the fate of Salonica. The once Jewish city came under Greek control.[8]

The Balkan Wars brought changes on the grandest and also the most intimate scales. The new Greek administration was eager to banish all evidence of Ottoman society and to efface the city's Jewish and Muslim characteristics. Suddenly, Greek signs replaced those in other languages and Greek flags outnumbered other nations'. Streets were renamed to reflect the city's Hellenistic past. Sabri Pacha Street, where Daout Effendi's brother-in-law Ascher Salem's store was located, now honored Eleftherios Venizelos, the prime minister who negotiated Greece's entry into the Balkan League and secured its triumphal expansion in the Balkan Wars. Of course, Salonica's Ottoman sensibility did not disappear overnight—minarets, mosques, and multilingual street signs remained in place until the 1920s, if not later—but a process of Hellenization had begun that would never be reversed.

Daout Effendi and the Levy family were longtime Ottoman patriots who experienced the end of Ottoman rule as a calamity—at least initially. In this, they were not alone. Many young Jewish men and women in Salonica were fearful about the onset of Greek rule. Much of their anxiety sprang from the fact that, relative to the Ottoman Empire, Greece, a Christian Orthodox nation, would give preference to the Greek Christian mercantile rivals of the Jews.[9]

For centuries Salonica had been the hub of a large trading network radiating outward from the city in all directions—to Europe, to the regional countryside and the Ottoman interior, to the Arab provinces of the Ottoman Empire and the wider Middle East. Now, as Jewish businessmen were acutely aware, Salonica (renamed Thessaloniki only in 1937) was to become the second city—next to Athens—of a small country. The city remade by the Balkan Wars was, in the eyes of many Jews, doomed to financial strangulation by Orthodox Christian and Greek rule. "The prosperity of Jewish Salonicans is greatly compromised," wrote one Jewish intellectual in the course of the conflict.[10] And who would have understood the stakes better than Daout Effendi, who had the finances of the entire Jewish Community at his fingertips?

As their empire and economy frayed, the Levys, like all the city's Jews, were destined to become nationals. What kind of nationals they became was a matter of choice. They could accept the state that formed around them; they could emigrate; or they could seek the protection of a foreign power.

Daout Effendi pursued the first course. With his wife and daughter, he remained in Salonica, helping the city's Jews meet the new demands of community and state. The job wasn't easy. Under Greek rule, the official Jewish Community of Salonica continued to function like an Ottoman *millet* (a non-Muslim, self-governing religious community with a degree of autonomy), but it now existed within a modern nation-state that ostensibly elevated the rights of citizens over those of any given religious group. Inevitably, there were points of friction, as when the state introduced the Sunday-closing law of 1924, which ended the longstanding custom by which all of Salonica rested on the Jewish Sabbath.[11]

While Daout Effendi, his wife, and daughter remained in Salonica, his sons, Leon and Emmanuel, chose departure. Both young men left for France, with Leon subsequently following his brother-in-law to Brazil. In moving abroad, Daout Effendi's sons were a bellwether of change for the community as a whole. Jewish emigration from Salonica began to increase with the Balkan Wars and would continue to mount with the outbreak of the First World War, and in the aftermath of a terrible fire that swept through the city in 1917. During this relatively brief five-year period, many Jewish citizens left. In addition to Daout Effendi's sons, three of his siblings were among the émigrés: Sam, Fortunée, and Besalel, each with their own families.[12] Rachel and Elie Carmona were the rare few to undertake a brief reverse migration, returning to Salonica temporarily in 1914, after their thirty years' service to the Alliance Israélite Universelle.[13]

While some Levys remained in Salonica and others left, a third group pursued the legal protection of a foreign power. Hundreds of Jewish families in Salonica embraced this option, among them Daout Effendi's son Leon, Leon's new bride, Estherina, and Daout Effendi's nephew Ino (the youngest son of Besalel). These Levys became citizens of nations they had never lived in, without ever leaving their homes. A foreign passport cost little yet enabled travel, the evasion of military service, the shirking of taxes, and, in general, insulation from the Greek authorities. Then, as now, the right foreign passport also seemed a hedge against an uncertain future.[14] Leon, Estherina, and Ino would use their new documents to travel and emigrate, renewing their passports in consulates across Europe and as far away as Rio de Janeiro. In time, this documentation would spare Ino deportation from occupied Paris at the hands of the Nazis and the French police.

CONSULAT de PORTUGAL
à SALONIQUE.

No. 5.

SIGNALEMENT.

AGE 26 ans
TAILLE 1m 60 cm.
CHEVEUX chatains
YEUX "
VISAGE regulier
NEZ "
BOUCHE "
BARBE [illegible]
SIGNES PARTICULIERS: Néant.
SIGNATURE et PHOTOGRAPHIE DU PORTEUR:

PASSEPORT.

Nous Consul de la Nation Portugaise à Salonique, faisons savoir à tous ceux qui verront le présent passeport, que le sujet portugais:
---LEVY LEON---
agé de 26 ans, né à Salonique, de profession Comptable, fils de DAOUT, dont signalement et signature en marge part de cette ville à destination de PARIS (FRANCE) voie d'ITALIE.-

Prions en conséquence toutes les autorités [illegible] présenté de laisser passer librement le porteur et de lui donner toute aide et protection en cas de besoin pour son voyage.-

Le présent passeport est personnel et valable pour un an.-

CONSULAT de PORTUGAL à SALONIQUE
le Quatre Octobre Mil Neuf Cent dix-sept.-
Le Consul:

Vu pour l'authenticité de la signature et de la photographie ci-dessus.-

CONSULAT de PORTUGAL
à SALONIQUE.

No. 9

SIGNALEMENT.

AGE 26 ans
TAILLE (MOYENNE) 1m70
CHEVEUX chatains
YEUX "
VISAGE regulier
NEZ "
BOUCHE "
SIGNES PARTICULIERS Néant
SIGNATURE ET PHOTOGRAPHIE DU PORTEUR:

PASSEPORT.

Nous Consul de la Nation Portugaise à Salonique faisons savoir à tous ceux qui verront le présent passeport, que la citoyenne portugaise:
---LEVY ESTHERINA---
femme de LEON LEVY, agée de 26 ans, dont signalement et signature en marge part de cette ville à destination de PARIS (France) voie d'ITALIE.-

Prions en conséquence toutes les autorités civiles et militaires auxquelles ce passeport sera présenté de laisser passer librement le porteur et de lui donner toute aide et protection en cas de besoin pour son voyage.-

Le présent passeport est personnel et valable pour un an.-

CONSULAT de PORTUGAL à SALONIQUE.
le QUATRE Octobre Mil Neuf Cent Dix Sept.
Le CONSUL:

Vu pour l'authenticité de la signature et de la photographie apposées ci-dessus.-

Travel papers issued to Leon and Estherina Levy by the Portuguese consul in Salonica, 1917

Between Jewish emigration and acquisition of foreign papers, the Levy family, like Salonica as a whole, was rapidly losing a vital population. As the Salonican Jewish intellectual Joseph Nehama put it, the city was being decapitated, and the Jewish community was being starved of its collective voice.[15] In the face of this dire challenge (and many more to come), Daout Effendi worked ceaselessly to keep Salonica's Jewish Community financially stable. This endeavor, combined with personal hardships, would demand a great deal of Sa'adi's gifted son.

FORTUNÉE

In 1899, Sa'adi's second daughter, Fortunée (1877–1936), was twenty-two years old, married, a mother, and firmly middle class. A photograph shows her in front of her house in Salonica, her husband, Ascher Jacob Salem, by her side. Three children, immaculately dressed, are posed with the emblems of middle-class leisure—a hoop to roll, barbells to lift, a tall tricycle to ride. Fortunée sits in an elegant rocking chair. Behind the group, face blurred, stands a domestic, posed as if to lend credence to the family's bourgeois existence.[1]

Fortunée's story must be told in the absence of her words, for if she wrote letters or a diary, none have been preserved. Her character assumes shape through various traces: the photographs and portraits for which she posed, the homes and gardens she maintained, the manner in which she raised her children, the routes she traveled, the memories of her descendants, the grave that would, in time, mark her death.

When she married Ascher Jacob Salem, son of a successful local merchant, Fortunée was only eighteen years old, a recent graduate of Salonica's Alliance school. The Salem family grew rapidly. Fortunée had six children over eleven years, five of them (Jacques, Esther, Karsa, Michael, and Adolphe) living to adulthood. One could easily mistake Fortunée's path for a traditional

Salem family at home, 1899

one: she wed young, married a Jewish merchant from Salonica, created a family. Yet like her sister Rachel, Fortunée embraced a distinctly modern lifestyle. She and her husband moved within a new circle of elite, forward-looking Salonicans, rejecting the traditions of their parents. For example, Fortunée and Ascher gave their children non-Jewish names, enrolled them in Christian schools, and left Salonica's historic Jewish neighborhood for a posh new suburb. *Le Journal de Salonique* noted the Salems' comings and goings in its column "Arrivées et départs [Arrivals and departures]." This was a family to watch.

Fortunée's husband, Ascher, thrived as an importer-exporter. He partnered with his brothers David and Elie and traveled to Manchester, England, for weeks at a time to buy and sell goods, mostly textiles. At the time, Manchester was a great industrial city and, like Salonica, a center for textile manufacturing. For this, and because the city boasted England's second largest Sephardic community, the British port was a powerful magnet for Ottoman Jewish émigrés. Salonica afforded an entrepreneurial exporter access to partners in Vienna, Paris, or Alexandria, while Manchester unlocked trade with Britain—and the Atlantic world. So Manchester was home, by the early twentieth century, to a thriving Sephardic community, second only to London as a British center for Ottoman Jewish émigrés.

Ascher's brother Elie was the first Salem to move to northern England, establishing a branch of the family firm in Didsbury, just outside Manchester. Elie, it was said, knew "the taste of Salonicans by experience" and adeptly supplied his brothers in Salonica with "English articles . . . of the latest style, which the tailors and above all the elegant socialists tear from the shelves . . . fabrics for suits, overcoats, etc., of an elegance without compare."[2]

In addition to collaborating with his brothers, Ascher worked with both Jewish and Muslim merchants and firms in Salonica.[3] It was rare for a Jewish merchant of the time to partner with a Muslim, yet Ascher's relations with his non-Jewish business partners were close, so much so that he and Fortunée gave their second son the name Karsa. The choice broke with Sephardic naming practices, which dictated that a boy carry the name of a living relative—and a Jew. Charting their own course, Fortunée and Ascher named their son for Ascher's business partner Karsa Frères, an Ottoman Muslim family import operation with bases in Manchester, Izmir, Alexandria, and Beirut, and with which Salem & Co. had collaborated since at least the late nineteenth century. The young Karsa's particular namesake may have been Mustafa Karsa, who served as Ottoman consul general in Manchester, as well as representing the family firm in that city, and was hosted by the Salems in Salonica in 1907.[4] Fortunée and Ascher's homage holds a clue to the young couple's way of thinking about life: they honored loyalty in business—at least in this particular relationship—over fidelity to Jewish tradition. Their son Karsa would do the same in adulthood. The Salems wholeheartedly embraced secular, middle-class culture, at least as practiced in their Ottoman city.

As Ascher's business expanded, he negotiated a deal for Adolphe Nolté, a prominent photographer from Belgium. In appreciation, Nolté gave the Salems exquisite, hand-tinted portraits of Fortunée and Ascher. Today the portraits hang in the home of the couple's grandson Alan Salem in a posh village south of Manchester. The likenesses show Fortunée in an elaborately brocaded dress, her hair swept up, and pearls in her ears. Ascher sports a tuxedo jacket, his mustache waxed into a handlebar. They are elegant, refined, Salonica's quintessential bourgeoisie.

Fortunée and Ascher Salem, 1900

To clinch their lofty social status, the Salems moved to a house by the sea on the spacious outskirts of Salonica—the home, at 64 rue Reine Olga, that is shown in the 1899 family photograph. The various neighborhoods in Salonica's center were made up of narrow, meandering, partially paved streets, typically lined with open sewers. Fortunée and Ascher rejected them in favor of a verdant neighborhood known as Las Kampanyas (the Countryside), located east of the city, near the bay.

Postcard featuring view of Salonica from La Kampanyas, 1900

Newly connected to Salonica by tram, the suburb was a magnet for the city's Europeanized bourgeoisie, whether Jewish, Christian, Muslim, or Dönme. Those who settled in Las Kampanyas invested in large estates with extensive gardens that would convey their bourgeois sensibilities. This is the neighborhood where the Jewish Allatini family, with whose patriarch Sa'adi had allied to create Salonica's first Alliance school years earlier, built their grand villa, surrounded by pine trees, at the end of the tramline. It was to this palatial estate that Sultan Abdülhamid would be exiled after the Young Turk revolution of 1908.[5]

The Salems' house was in the style of an Italian villa: stone, its modest balconies lined with iron fretwork, its windows framed with heavy wooden shutters. The family inhabited a flat on the building's lower level, while a sweeping, interior marble staircase led to a second flat upstairs. The garden, with its meandering path of crushed stone, was planted with lavender, rosebushes, pine and citrus trees, with a fig and mulberry tree adjacent to the front courtyard. "The front garden was very large with several trees," Fortunée's son Adolphe remembered, "and to my young eyes it was like a forest."[6] Behind the house, a hill sloped down to the Gulf of Salonica, bordered by a low wall from which the children could fish. The garden was where the children could be found during the summer months. Family parties happened here, weather permitting, and sometimes culminated in an unusual party trick—Ascher throwing his son Michael into the water fully clothed, and the boy gleefully soaring through the air and into the gulf below. The joyous, showy act captures something of the Salems' ease in their home life in Las Kampanyas.

The same bold impulses that drew Fortunée and Ascher to Las Kampanyas drew them to enroll their children in neighborhood Catholic schools in which French was the sole language of instruction. Here, the children knelt "on the form in front of our desk [as] we recited in chorus the Lord's prayer." Ladino remained the language of the home, however—a sign that modernity in Salonica and its environs was still expressed in a distinctly Jewish tongue.[7]

In 1912, Fortunée's eldest, Jacques, moved to Manchester to create a British base of operations for the family business, becoming the first of Sa'adi a-Levi's grandchildren to emigrate overseas. In Manchester, eighteen-year-old Jacques began working for another Salonican-born Jew, a shipping merchant, as well as for his father's brother Elie, with whom he collaborated in shipping

Studio portrait of Esther and Jacques (back), Karsa, Michael, and Adolphe Salem (front), 1909

goods to his father in Salonica for resale to a Mediterranean market.[8] That Jacques would have no head for business was as yet unknown.[9] The family, eager to reap the economic opportunities a move to Britain could bring, hoped to follow him to Manchester two years later.

But the outbreak of World War I so soon after the conclusion of a violent regional conflict thwarted the Salems' plans for departure. The First World War racked Salonica, filling it with hundreds of thousands of Allied soldiers, riddling it with German bombardments, and shredding its economy for all but a few wartime profiteers, a member of the Levy family among them.[10] Fortunée's son later recalled that wartime food rations forced the normally prosperous Salem children to eat "some stodgy concoction" in place of bread. The children, picky rather than starving, made sport of haunting the perimeter of a hospital for Allied soldiers with whom they could swap cigarettes for bread.[11]

While Fortunée coped with the indignities of war at home, Jacques, the child who was meant to facilitate his family's move, faced a different sort of insult abroad. Jacques had left Salonica before it became Greek, and had entered Britain with an Ottoman passport. With the Ottoman Empire and Britain at war, Jacques—along with thousands of Ottoman-born, German-born, and Austrian-born Jewish men—became, overnight, a foreign national of an enemy nation.[12] As a Jew from Salonica, Jacques was particularly vulnerable, for British authorities were aware that Salonica's Jews had resisted the transfer of their city from Ottoman to Greek rule during the Balkan Wars. This history led Anglo officials to conclude that Salonican Jewish émigrés in Britain were Ottoman loyalists who posed a high risk to the state: a threat higher, in their view, than that of British-dwelling Sephardic émigrés from other Ottoman hubs such as Istanbul or Izmir. Jacques's political leanings only confirmed the officials' fears. The eldest Salem child was ardent in his Ottoman nationalism, and was known for his impassioned speeches in support of the cause.[13] In 1915, the British authorities took Jacques from his newly adopted Manchester home and imprisoned him in Douglas Alien Detention Camp, an internment camp on the Isle of Man.[14]

In Douglas Camp, Jacques was probably housed within a Jewish camp. From here, he would have been allowed to receive and send mail (though not easily to his family in Salonica), join a makeshift minyan, request kosher food, and possibly even leave camp periodically for work. Still, it was said that "nobody gets anything at Douglas that he does not pay for, either in money or work."[15] Fortunée's brother Sam, the fiery editorialist who always responded to an insult with a protest, wrote British officials from Paris pleading for his nephew's release. Jacques, too, lobbied on his own behalf, marshaling testimonies in favor of his honor-

Portrait of Esther, Asher, and Fortunée Salem, sent as a postcard to Jacques Salem while he was interned in an enemy aliens camp on Britain's Isle of Man, 1916

able character from the grand rabbi of Salonica Jacob Meir and chief rabbi of the Spanish and Portuguese Congregation in London Moses Gaster. But the British administration was unmoved. Jacques would remain at Douglas Camp for three and a half long years.[16]

For Fortunée the First World War surely represented a dreadful limbo. Her city had been transformed into a military camp teeming with soldiers. Her son was imprisoned far from home, her dreams of emigration thwarted. Now, even as the war raged, another tragedy rocked the family, a horrific fire that engulfed their city. This third trauma solidified the Salems' desire to emigrate—but also compelled them to leave from a position of weakness rather than strength. This story of destruction, departure, and rebuilding is the next generation's to tell.

NATIONALS

Today, my dear son . . . has returned to the barracks to continue his military service. We hope that the time will pass quickly. It's been eight months since he began and we do not know how much longer it will be. With the changes of government all the laws have changed, in time it may be twelve months, now they say eighteen, [but there is] nothing official for the moment. Whoever hopes, despairs. The thing is, this military service takes its toll on the rest of us.

—Eleanor Matalon to Leon Levy, 1936

ESTHER

One month after Greece entered the First World War on the side of the Allies, on a hot, windy August afternoon in 1917, the Salem family was enjoying a restful Sabbath in the delightful suburb of Salonica where Fortunée and Ascher, the parents of Esther (1895–1998), had settled some decades earlier. Las Kampanyas was known for its grand vista, and the Salem home offered a generous view of Salonica's red tile roofs, the bay, and Mount Olympus beyond. On this particular August day, Esther's father's enjoyment of the view was marred by the sight of flames in the distance. He called to the family to come quickly. "I went to look," wrote Esther in a letter to her brother Jacques, "and indeed a large part of the city appeared to have fallen prey to the flames. After this we couldn't stop watching the fire. We wanted to pull ourselves away but as if magnetized, we were drawn to the small corner of the terrace on the water, where we saw the whole city."[1]

Esther's brother Karsa arrived from town, frantic. Newly renamed Venizelos Street, where the family business was located, had burned to the ground. "Oh, the images that I have seen!" Karsa sobbed. "Children, women, all fleeing, and despite the horror, the city is calm; the exodus is happening in a mournful, heavy silence. A woman gave birth on the pavement! People surrounded her as she shrieked! . . . Oh, I am broken! Papa, go and

Spectators watch the port of Salonica engulfed in flames, 1917

see what must be done!" In a panic, Ascher rushed out, taking the keys to his store and leaving his wife, Fortunée, and the children at home.

As the hours passed, Esther and her family watched Red Cross and British trucks race by. Among the fleeing masses, the "parade of ghosts" that Esther saw stumble by the home was a number of family members, including her cousin Eleanor (Daout Effendi's daughter) and her husband and children.[2] Eleanor's family, and a good number of strangers, took shelter with the Salems. The garden, courtyard, and house were quickly transformed into a makeshift refuge as closets were emptied to provide clean clothes and sheets for the victims.

At last Esther's father returned, "his eyes swollen in his sockets and very red, his face pale as candle wax." Unable to save the family store, Ascher managed to rescue only a handful of account books before fleeing to the smoky streets. Despite the chaos, he had located his father- and mother-in-law, Daout Effendi and Vida, and their son Emmanuel. As the night wore on, the flames spread. Even the sea was burning, dotted with blazing sailboats. "In vain did I close my eyes in the dark," Esther wrote later, "for my imprinted retinas still saw the burning ships on the trembling sea."

Emanating from a neighborhood adjacent to the crowded port known to Salonica's Jews as Agua Nueva (New Water), the fire wrought catastrophic damage in the city's historic Jewish quarter, in the commercial district, and in the port, where most of the city's Jews lived and worked. When the fire began, the movie theaters were packed, and an Italian marching band was performing in Liberty Square. As the flames spread, the French military strategically bombed a number of buildings (including Salonica's new Talmud Torah), hoping to arrest the fire's course.[3] These efforts were futile. The fire only grew in intensity, ultimately raging for thirty hours, and covering a square kilometer thick with urban life. Thirty-two synagogues burned, along with nine rabbinical libraries, six hundred Torah scrolls, and eight Jewish schools. Though no deaths were recorded, fifty thousand Jews were left homeless, along with ten thousand Muslim residents of the city and somewhere between ten thousand and fifteen thousand Christians. The damage was estimated at a billion French francs, 75 percent of which was Jewish-owned property.[4] The city, already transformed into a wartime refugee hub, became a smoldering landscape of displacement overnight.

By morning, firefighters had managed to contain the conflagration. From the Salem home in Las Kampanyas, the city was obscured by clouds of black smoke. "Salonica has forever perished!" mourned Esther. Some weeks after the fire, as Esther closed a letter to her brother Jacques, she sent him a tender embrace, saying, finally, "I hope to go and join you, for life is becoming impossible here." This was as much despondency as Esther

Aerial view of Salonica after the fire of 1917

would allow herself. With time, she proved more resilient than her city.

It would take years for Salonica to recover. One Salonican Jewish schoolteacher, writing in 1923, bemoaned the fact that the synagogue in which he taught lacked a roof to replace the one burned in 1917, leaving him to instruct his students with snow and rain lashing their faces. "Most of all," he fretted to his superiors, "we have suffered from darkness. Many days the darkness was such that a student could not see enough to read the book he had in front of his face."[5] For the Levy family, too, the impact of the fire was profound and long-lasting. Esther's father's business had burned to the ground, and insurance could not begin to cover the losses. Her uncle Daout Effendi wrote that the fire had deprived him of "all my things and personal property," including precious papers and a collection of rugs he had been preserving for his children's inheritance.

The Salem family home had been spared by the flames, but the family's beautiful garden—site of so many joyous gatherings—was soon requisitioned by the municipality, which was desperate to house the displaced.[6] Citing a Ladino proverb drawn from musar, rabbinical ethical literature, Esther lamented: "The house of the rich empties out and still the house of the poor does not fill up; how well we understand this sad truth."[7] Esther was twenty-two years of age, unmarried, and suddenly facing depleted family coffers just as she was meant to be propelled into a new life. For her and the rest of the Salem family, as for so many others, the fire of 1917 sent them, at least for a time, on a sharp downward trajectory. Esther would, nevertheless, follow her brother Jacques to Manchester a year after the war's end, emigrating with her brothers and their parents—though not in the position of economic strength they had anticipated.

Before the Salem family left Salonica for Manchester, photographs reveal that they participated in the tradition of *ziyara* (a visit) to Salonica's Jewish cemetery. The sun is low in the sky: it is early morning or late afternoon, roughly 1919. The women wear broad-brimmed hats and are bundled in overcoats adorned with fur stoles. Esther's hat is trimmed with a large silk flower, her mother Fortunée's topped with egret feathers. Michael, thirteen years of age, wears a fine suit and tie under a wool coat, a bowler on his head, no doubt an outfit made for his bar mitzvah a few months earlier. His younger brothers sport youthful caps, wool coats, and, in Adolphe's case, the short pants befitting his age. Esther and Jacques stare directly at their photographer. They are in their twenties. Jacques couldn't have been released from captivity on the Isle of Man more than a year earlier. Understandably, their parents, Fortunée and Ascher, look somber, as they prepare to leave their homeland under difficult circumstances. Fortunée's face is drawn, her lips are pressed tightly together. She does not look at the camera.

Esther and her family visit a number of tombs. She stands at her paternal grandfather's grave.[8] The family then visits another, larger grave: the tomb of the Levy patriarch, Fortunée's father, Sa'adi a-Levi. There, the Salems gather to pray and pose.

Several photographs capture the moment. This in itself is an unusual occurrence, for cameras were considered an indulgence in those years. Today, glass plates documenting the excursion

Salem family visiting the Jewish cemetery of Salonica, 1917

are preserved in England by Esther's nephew Alan.[9] The plates are yellowed; one is stained. Still, they offer an extraordinary glimpse of a family in transition.

Salem family visiting the Sa'adi's tomb in the Jewish cemetery of Salonica, 1917

In one of the photographs, Esther and her mother stand to the left of Sa'adi's tomb, their eyes obscured by their wide-brimmed hats. To the right of the tomb stand two men, one wearing a fez, the other a large *kippah* and a traditional Salonican robe. Each holds a prayer book, and the latter rests his arm against the tomb. In all likelihood, they are *honadjis*, cemetery guides, hired to lead the Salems in prayer. It may be that the Salem men didn't feel comfortable navigating traditional mourning prayers and rituals on their own (Ascher's grandson confirms that his grandfather was not observant), or their patronage of the men was a small act of charity, a way of supporting the cemetery and its workers. To the left of the two men stands Esther's young brother, Michael, in profile, his face obscured by a tear in the negative. The damaged image also removes some of the assembled from sight, though the full group of family members appears in a second image. Stretched out behind them is the expanse of Salonica's Jewish cemetery, hundreds of thousands of tombs scattered across a hillside. Beyond the cemetery's grounds, animals graze in empty fields.

The Hebrew-language epitaph on Sa'adi's grave is only partially visible in the Salem family's photograph. It appears in full in a 1931 book on the Jewish cemetery of Salonica:

He who lies [here] in refuge
was the chief poet who composed several
poems for the visit of the sultan and his entourage [in 1859] and songs to be sung for Purim
and many Jewish hymns in praise of the Almighty,
pleasant melodies for Israel. To every gathering, for the sake of heaven,
with all of his strength and with his feet, he would run like a deer.
This man is Sa'adi a-Levi.
This tombstone was erected here
in honor of a man full of wisdom.
From him [came] counsel and insight.
He was girded with justice and faith.
Behold it is he "the great and blessed" Sa'adi a-Levi Ashkenazi, "may his soul
rest in paradise."
He was the first Jew in this city who brought to light newspapers.
In 1875 he published a newspaper in the Sephardic language
La Epoka
In 1895 he published in the French language
Journal de Salonique.

He "departed for his eternal home" on the 8th day of Tevet 5663 [1903].[10]

The epitaph is unusual for its length, biographical detail, and literary style: it was clearly designed to impress. If photographs are any indication, Sa'adi's tomb exerted a gravitational pull upon the extended Levy family, for whom visits to the grave—and, in time, bereavement over its destruction—became a ritual.

In June 1919, Esther and her family at last departed Salonica, five years after they intended. The family traveled by ship to Marseille, lugging twelve suitcases in their wake, a thirteenth having been left behind so as not to jinx the voyage.[11] One train carried the group to Paris, another two trains and a ferry took them to their new home. There, in a leafy suburb some five miles from the heart of Manchester, the Salems would cultivate one of the most robust branches of the extended Levy family tree.

SAM

Sa'adi's son Sam, newspaperman and impassioned activist, was already abroad during the series of dramatic events that transformed Salonica in the second decade of the twentieth century. With his wife, Anna, and their young daughter, Suzanne, Sam had left Salonica in 1911, just after Sultan Mehmed V's visit to the city. In the years that followed, the small family moved—somewhat frenetically—between Belgrade, Bern, Lausanne, and, finally, Paris, where they at last settled and where Sam would live (but for the years of the Second World War) the remainder of his life.

Throughout this peripatetic time, writing remained a constant, and moral outrage was Sam's favored voice. Narrow-mindedness, ignorance, and conservativism were constant goads to Sam. Even as Zionism gained ascendancy among Sephardic Jews, he continued to reject the movement, as well as nationalism in most forms. Though fiercely political, he rationalized placing journalism above politics, seeking financial support for his newspapers from both the British and the Germans during the First World War.[1] One could call this opportunism, were Sam not a man committed to the moral underpinnings of his own choices. An avid reader of French Romantic literature, he saw himself as a besieged protagonist, little understood, and haunted by fate.[2]

Sam Lévy, 1920, from Les Juifs de Salonique *(Salonica, 1933)*

Far from home, Sam remained under the spell of early-twentieth-century Salonica and the particular form of Jewish cosmopolitanism that had flourished there. From 1922 to 1930, he edited a hefty trade annual that carried his name (*Le Guide Sam*) and that offered readers a phantasmagorical regional geography in which Salonican Jews—including many of his own relatives and friends—became the pillars of modern global commerce.[3] He returned to Salonica for short visits in the decades after his emigration: for example, to deliver a series of lectures during the First World War.[4] In 1925, he returned again, this time documenting his pilgrimage to the Jewish cemetery of Salonica with a photograph. In this image, Sam stands in a dark suit beside his father's distinctive grave, his outstretched hand resting on Sa'adi's headstone.[5]

Though a dedicated follower of current events, Sam also had a deep sense of the past. His opinions about Salonica were particularly firm. In 1919, when the First World War was freshly concluded and the Allied victors were gathered in Versailles to broker terms of peace, Sam submitted an unsolicited recommendation to the assembled dignitaries. Salonica, he wrote, should be internationally recognized as a free and neutral city administered by Jews, who (he argued erroneously) constituted two-thirds of the city's population. He envisioned a city that would exist as a nation akin to other nations, replete with a voice in the newly created League of Nations. This proposal, Sam boasted, would assure tranquillity in the Balkans, thereby contributing to the promotion of peace in Europe.[6] Sam's was an audacious plan—conceivably the most audacious imagining of Salonica's future to circulate at this time.[7] He argued for a Jewish city-state that was neither Zionist nor Greek: a Sephardic government with the power to influence global politics; a Salonica that could remain a vibrant center of the Jewish world, immune to the rise of nationalism across southeast Europe. Of course, Sam's vision was pure folly. Yet Salonica was not the only place championed as a potential free and neutral European city: early-twentieth-century dreamers wanted the same for Trieste, Istanbul, and Danzig.

For Sam, Salonica was fixed in time—let us say in 1911, when a sultan's visit to the Levys' beloved city brought the family great pleasure and honor. Sam seemed to relish nostalgia for the city of his birth, for the empire into which he was born, for a time when the Sephardic community exerted considerable influence. His nostalgia was shaped abroad. Despite his intense connection to Salonica, more than half of Sam's life was lived outside his birth city.[8] Emigration and the passage of time intensified Sam's passion for an idealized Salonica of the past.

Sam's nostalgia was passed on to his only child, at least for a time. Suzanne would be the rare member of the next generation of Levys, Sa'adi's grandchildren, to perpetuate the devotion of her parents to the Alliance Israélite Universelle, serving the organization as a teacher in El Jadida (Mazagan), Morocco, from 1928 to 1932. In so doing, Suzanne was honoring an institution that her own grandfather first welcomed to Salonica and following in the footsteps of her aunt Rachel, who was also posted by the organization to Morocco—though some five hundred kilometers to the east—twenty-eight years earlier.[9]

As much as Sam looked to the next generation, he also looked backward, especially to the legacy of his father. For years, Sam worked to translate excerpts of Sa'adi's memoir. He published translated segments in Ladino in 1907 and again in the 1930s, and in French in 1933, pairing Sa'adi's original words with inventive commentary.[10] But for Sam's labor, I would not have found my way to the Levy family history.

LEON

The youngest son of Daout Effendi, Leon Levy (1891–1978), announced his engagement to Estherina Alaluf in the pages of a French-language newspaper published in Salonica, on November 13, 1916. Sadly, the happy announcement was dwarfed by news of the months-long battle then raging between Allied and Bulgarian forces at a bend in the River Crna, on the Macedonian front. But while the war was bloody, for Leon it was profitable. In late 1916, Leon was hired by the British Expeditionary Force Canteens, a unit meant to supply "for officers and men cheap shops, good rest and recreation centers, and for officers excellent hotels. From the Expeditionary Force canteens the soldier could buy cigars, cigarettes, chocolate, sweets, and all kinds of canned goods, duty free, and at prices far lower than those of the London shops. Whisky, wine, and beer could be bought duty free, under some restrictions."[1] Leon's relationship to the British Expeditionary Force Canteens entitled him to drive a truck in Salonica, which was a wartime luxury.

Within the voluminous body of papers preserved by Leon's grandchildren in Rio, the work orders of the Bank of Salonica and of the British Expeditionary Force Canteens are among the very oldest. A photograph of Leon taken at this time shows him nattily dressed, sporting a handlebar mustache, a polka-dotted tie, and a careful wave at his hairline. He exudes self-assurance. A picture of his wife, Estherina, taken at the same time, looks decidedly less self-confident. Though she is elegantly attired, her brow is furrowed, hinting at the strains that persisted throughout her life.

Armed with the Portuguese papers they had acquired in Salonica in 1917, Estherina and Leon spent the end of the First World War and the immediate postwar years on the move. They left Salonica in December 1917 for Paris, stopping for a month in Italy. From southern Europe they traveled to Lyon, where Estherina's sister Beatrice Florentin lived with her husband.[2] The visit wasn't a happy one, at least for Leon. Decades later, he had not forgotten callous treatment at the hands of the Florentins—a memory that tells as much about his inability to let go of past slights as it does about whatever rudeness his in-laws may have directed toward him. Still, Leon's memories did not prevent him from sending Beatrice money when, much later, she found herself widowed and in dire financial straits. Though he rarely relinquished a grievance, Leon was unfailingly generous to relatives in need.

Estherina and Leon reached Paris, their ultimate destination, in January 1918. Like Manchester, Paris was a powerful lure to Salonican Jewish émigrés. Though Vienna was closer, for aspirational Jews who came of age in the Alliance schools Paris was the goal, a place to gain cultural, social, and economic status. In 1900, when Ottoman Jews were only beginning to contemplate emigration, the Sephardic community of Paris was tiny. By the time of Estherina and Leon's arrival, the number of Sephardic Jews in the city had grown to six thousand, with at least four branches of the Levy family among these ranks.[3] In addition to the son of Daout Effendi, Paris was home to three of Sa'adi's children—Rachel, Besalel, and Sam—each of whom had spouses and children in the city. The children and grandchildren of three more children of Sa'adi, Doudoun, Djentil, and Hayyim, now lived in Paris as well.

Leon and Estherina were soon issued ration cards and found a two-bedroom apartment in the ninth arrondissement, a neighborhood dense with retail and Sephardic émigrés. The couple stayed in the area for two years until they resettled on rue Jean-Jacques Rousseau, in a smart apartment rented under Daout Effendi's name. Their new home was a leisurely five-minute walk to the Louvre: today the same building houses a Christian Louboutin boutique.

Alas, things did not go easily for the newlyweds in Paris. The city, like Europe as a whole, was reeling from the recent world war. Opportunities were scarce, particularly for a newly transplanted importer whose base—Salonica—was under great economic strain. Leon's business appears to have been sporadic, speculative, and possibly even a bit sketchy. Intending to transfer his skills as a military supplier to France, he imported oranges and wine—which he was accused of adulterating—from Italy, and encountered myriad problems with customs officials. Leon was also sued for using a residential apartment to conduct business. For the next two years, Leon and (even more so) Estherina traveled constantly. They visited Italy, Switzerland, Germany, and Austria, each time brandishing passports from the Portuguese consulate in Paris: renewed versions of the documents they had acquired in Salonica during the Balkan Wars.

Estherina chose the German spa town of Wiesbaden as the place she would spend her last weeks of pregnancy, and it was where she would give birth to her first child. Middle-class Jews from across Europe had been flocking to spas in Germany (and in western Bohemia, in particular) since the late nineteenth century, finding them places to rest, to pursue modern medical treatments, and to heal.[4] Leon's own family regularly retreated to the lakeside retreat of Langada (Langaza, present-day Langadas) to escape the late-summer heat of Salonica. But Langada's ancient thermal pools, a mere seven kilometers outside Salonica, were nothing compared to the spas of Wiesbaden. Wiesbaden was far from home and impressively grand; a trip there was an event—and an expensive one. Seduced by the grandeur of this Central European bourgeois oasis, Leon actually considered Germanizing the family name, adopting Lewy in place of Levy. But his brother-in-law berated him for the idea, and the family name was not altered.

Sadi Sylvain Levy, the only son of Estherina and Leon, was born in September 1920, and honored with the name of his great-grandfather Sa'adi. The birth was a most joyous occasion. In Wiesbaden, the couple received good wishes by telegram and letter in Ladino, French, and Italian, from all branches of the Levy family, as well as from the Alalufs, Estherina's relations. Back in Salonica, Leon's mother, Vida, had a mystic prepare a *kemeá* for the child. A Jewish amulet containing a strip of parchment with blessings meant to ward off the evil eye, a *kemeá* was, in the words of one contemporary member of the community, a kind of all-purpose spiritual panacea.[5]

Daout Effendi sent the charm to Switzerland on his wife's behalf. It is extraordinary to imagine Estherina and Leon receiving this gift amid the Germanic grandeur of Wiesbaden. A *kemeá* was the quintessential embodiment of Sephardic folk practices, Wiesbaden, the quintessential site of European Jewish modernity and bourgeois arrival. Nothing can reveal the brittleness of reinvention so much as a birth, or a death.

Daout Effendi celebrated the birth of his grandson Sadi Sylvain though Salonica weighed heavily on his mind. The city was in a state of suspended unrest. Despite the fact that the First

World War was over, Greece did not enter the relatively quiet interwar period of much of the rest of Europe. Instead, the Greco-Turkish War, lasting from 1919 to 1922, brought sustained violence to Asia Minor and humiliation to the Greek military. While the Levy family experienced the unrest at home, Leon felt its reverberations from afar. Even before his son was born, Leon fretted that despite his status as a subject of Portugal, he would be conscripted into the Greek army. Eager to avoid military service, Leon appealed to the Portuguese consul in Paris and also to British representatives in that city. His hope, in both instances, was that his service to the Allies during the Great War would excuse him from further duty to Greece. Whether because his efforts were rewarded or because his number was not called, Leon did not return to Salonica.

Meanwhile, Leon attempted to acquire the status of a permanent resident of Paris. His appeal to the French minister of justice listed the fact that he was a father, a six-year resident of France, and a dutiful taxpayer. His application also invoked Daout Effendi as the first French-language journalist in Salonica, and a man responsible for introducing the French language and French influence to readers across the Orient. Unfortunately for Leon, his appeal reached the minister of justice at a time of rising anti-immigrant sentiment.[6] His request was swiftly denied.

January 1924 found Leon shifting between Paris, where he continued to struggle to find economic footing, and Switzerland and Germany, where his wife, Estherina, and their young son, Sadi Sylvain, moved from sanatorium to sanatorium. Sadi Sylvain experienced a bout of scarlet fever that confined him to the Children's Cantonal Hospital of Lausanne for a terrifying eight weeks, and Estherina was herself physically frail. Leon received a series of letters from his brother-in-law Elie Alaluf in this period.[7] Writing from Rio, where he had only recently settled, Elie offered a solution to Leon's rootlessness: Leon, Estherina, and Sadi Sylvain should follow him to Brazil. The climate, Elie argued, was excellent for all kinds of maladies, the doctors first-rate, the economy burgeoning. And Rio was far less expensive than Lausanne or Paris, Elie continued, with a nascent Sephardic community.[8] Besides, Elie had arranged for a colleague in Paris to entrust his brother-in-law with a quantity of crepe de chine in a range of colors then in demand in Brazil. It was enough to make Leon an associate of Elie's import-export firm. Leon was persuaded. Under his Portuguese passport, Leon embarked for Brazil on May 29, 1925, leaving his wife and young son behind in Europe.

What must it have been like for this Ottoman-born Jew to make the fifteen-day trip to Rio and sail into its passenger port of Praça Mauá? It would have taken an hour for Leon's steamship to thread the islands that dot Guanabara Bay, pass the Pão de Açúcar (Sugar Loaf), Botafogo Bay, and Flamengo Beach, to reach, finally, Rio's urban dock. Clutching his brother-in-law's shipment of crepe de chine, Leon would have disembarked, stepping onto Brazilian soil and, quite inadvertently, into the world of fashion. Steady movement between Latin America and Europe, along with immersion in the fashion industry, would define Leon's future.

DAOUT EFFENDI

Back in Salonica, and scrolling back in time to the moment of Leon's son's birth, Leon's father, Daout Effendi, prepared a letter in his characteristically formal hand. The letter blended French and—when it came to matters of the heart—Ladino, and acknowledged the birth of his grandchild tenderly, if tersely. The bulk of Daout Effendi's letter was dedicated to other matters. Apparently, a wave of sickness had swept through the Levy home. Whether malaria, typhoid, or a gastrointestinal disorder, everyone seemed to have been affected.

Having only just emerged from a sickbed himself, Daout Effendi was already fretting about community politics. A year earlier, he reminded Leon, Salonica's chief rabbi, Jacob Meir, had left the city and his post for his native Jerusalem. Since then, the Salonican Jewish Community was abuzz with speculation about who should take his place—and what sort of future that person should represent for the city's Jews. With the community politically and ideologically divided (between Zionists, religious nationalists, socialists, supporters of the Alliance Israélite Universelle, and the rabbinical corps, among other parties), a great deal was at stake for the Levy family as well as for Salonica as a whole.[1]

By the time of his grandson's birth in 1920, Daout Effendi had been working for Salonica's Jewish Community for ten years. He had begun his service as director of communal property, in 1910, but his significance to the Community increased with time as he accrued still more authority over—and institutional knowledge of—Salonica's Jews. In 1919 Daout Effendi was promoted to the position of general director and exchequer of the Jewish Community, earning the august title Chancellor. In this capacity, he sat at the helm for some eighty employees, receiving the highest salary of any communal official other than the chief rabbi.[2] Daout Effendi presided over the Community for the next sixteen years, and continued to work on behalf of this organization thereafter. For much of this period, Daout Effendi's capable niece Julie Hasson served as his secretary. Later, it would fall to Julie to relay to Daout Effendi's only surviving child the circumstances of his father's final days.

Julie Hasson, 1937

When Daout Effendi became chancellor, Salonica was still recovering from the trauma of the first two decades of the twentieth century. Large parts of the Jewish Community's educational, charitable, religious, and social institutions were in shambles. The Balkan Wars and World War I had filled Salonica with refugees, and the fire of 1917 had once again flooded it with the dispossessed. As refugees poured into Salonica, Jews spilled out, among them many of Daout Effendi's intimates, including four siblings and two sons. When Daout Effendi's brothers Besalel and Sam emigrated to Paris, he became the family patriarch in place of his father, Sa'adi, representing his nephew before the beth din (rabbinical court), for example, when the young man sought a divorce from his first wife.[3] Now, even as Daout Effendi presided over the Jewish Community, a radical act of demographic engineering once more distorted the city's face. In 1923, the Treaty of Lausanne (one of the protracted treaties that resolved the First World War) solidified the contested boundary between Greece and the Turkish Republic. This treaty also laid the legal foundation for delineation of the religious and political boundaries between Greece and Turkey. The population exchange that ensued forcibly moved nearly 1.5 million Greek Orthodox Christians from Anatolia to Greece, and 400,000 Muslims from Greece to Turkey. Salonica absorbed enormous numbers of the displaced, bringing the city's refugee population to a staggering 92,000.[4]

The massive influx of Greek Orthodox Christians to Salonica reduced the prominence of Jews in the city. Once roughly half of the urban population, Jews now represented a mere fifth of Salonica's residents. To provide jobs to the Greek Orthodox transplants from Asia Minor, the Salonican municipality adopted emergency laws that effectively pushed Jews from certain branches of the economy. For instance, Jews were prevented from working at the port, a space once dominated by Jewish laborers. Meanwhile,

Sunday was declared a mandatory day of rest—a law that crippled the commercial operations of many Jewish merchants, who were therefore compelled either to work on the Jewish Sabbath or to forsake income twice a week rather than just once.[5] As unemployed refugees roamed Salonica's streets, Jewish emigration soared. "Each day the poor knock on the door of the Community," Daout Effendi wrote his son, "and it is I alone who must respond and comfort them."

Daout Effendi's prominence made him vulnerable to criticism. Months after the population exchanges began, Salonica's Zionist newspaper, *Pro Israel*, accused him of flagrantly disregarding the injunctions of Yom Kippur, the day of atonement and fasting. The communal leader used the occasion to luxuriate in a café, the paper alleged, and there he sat with the inspector of Jewish schools, showily drinking a beer.[6] The accusations were similar to those launched at Daout Effendi's father and brother by Salonica's rabbinical leadership decades earlier, when the city was under Ottoman rule. So much had changed yet, in each case, the charge that a Levy was flaunting Jewish law was probably trumped up, a window into the accusers' anxiety over an increasingly disparate Salonican Jewish community.

The settlement of Greek Christians from Turkish Anatolia in Salonica was part of a broader scheme hatched by Prime Minister Venizelos to Hellenize Greek Macedonia and northern Greece, borderlands dense with minorities. This effort involved erasing the traces of Salonica's Ottoman, Muslim, and Jewish past, and with this in mind, Salonica's municipality cast its eyes upon the city's Jewish cemetery. Created in the fifteenth century by Iberian Jewish exiles, this cemetery eventually held 350,000 graves spread out across eighty-six acres. This was the largest Jewish cemetery in Europe and it was situated at the very heart of the new Salonica. During the 1920s and 1930s, the municipality made repeated attempts to reduce its size or move it altogether to the outskirts of town. The plan was to make space for an expansion of Aristotle University of Thessaloniki, which abutted the cemetery. According to a highly critical report by the Salonican Jewish intellectual Joseph Nehama, the dreamed-of campus would allow, among other things, for "a field for agricultural experiments, the soil, rich in human excreta, lending itself admirably to this form of enterprise."[7] Along with Nehama, Daout Effendi's brother Sam publicly protested municipal efforts to diminish the size of the Jewish cemetery.[8]

As the assault on Salonica's ancient Jewish cemetery suggests, anti-Semitism was on the rise in Salonica, buoyed by political instability—Greece withstood over twenty regime changes between 1924 and 1935. In 1931, the groundswell of anti-Jewish feeling turned violent. Tensions between a local Zionist organization, the Maccabi, and a Greek proto-fascist one erupted into fighting and led to a riot that burned to the ground the heavily Jewish and working-class Salonica neighborhood of Campbell. This event left many Jews homeless and others hastily preparing for departure, convinced that Jews were no longer wanted in Salonica.[9]

Perhaps to mollify the shaken Jewish community, Salonica's mayor chose this moment to name a street after Sa'adi Besalel a-Levi. (The honor came soon after Sam published selected translations of Sa'adi's memoirs in Salonica's French- and Ladino-language press, which could have attracted the mayor's attention.[10]) A photograph of the ceremony shows Daout Effendi at the edge of a small crowd, standing erect and proud below the fresh Greek-language sign, but his face looks aged and strained.[11] Due to the serialized publication of a portion of Sa'adi's memoirs, newspapers had once again brought memory of the family patriarch to the fore of Salonican consciousness. Whatever the mayor's intentions, Sam's look backward, to an Ottoman heyday, resisted the nationalist redirection of Greek politics.

The naming of Sa'adi a-Levi Street, 1931. Front row, far left: Daout Effendi; back row, far left: Sam Lévy; front row: Julie Hasson(?)

Daout Effendi was newly retired from his leadership role in the Jewish Community when King George II returned from exile in London to assume the Greek throne in 1935. To mark the occasion, Daout Effendi and other Jewish notables attended an event at Salonica's Beth Shaul synagogue in honor of the king. Presided over by Chief Rabbi Sevi Koretz, it was an extravagant event. To welcome the king, the Jewish Community adorned the synagogue's courtyard with flowers that bore the word "welcome" in Hebrew and Greek.[12]

Like his colleagues, Daout Effendi wore a top hat and fine suit to the celebration, but he also sported three decorations: the Order of Osmaniye (class unknown), granted by the Ottoman regime, the Order of Saint Sauveur, granted by the Greek government, and the Order of Saint Sava, granted by the state of Serbia. "I am no doubt the only Jew decorated by the Greek government," Daout Effendi wrote in a letter to his son Leon, "and I don't say this with pleasure." In fact, other Jews had also been decorated by the Greek government but the numbers were very few.[13]

Daout Effendi Levy, decorated, c. 1935

It could not have been lost on Daout Effendi that this was the third time in two generations that a member of the Levy family had welcomed a king (of sorts) to their city. Eight decades earlier, his own father, Sa'adi, had paid tribute to the Ottoman sultan Abdülmecid. On the occasion of his visit to Salonica, Sa'adi wrote and performed panegyric songs and poems in Hebrew and Ladino in the sultan's honor.[14] Daout Effendi had himself received another sultan, Mehmed V, twenty-four years before the return of King George II. So much had changed, yet the Levy family was still engaged in the delicate business of integrating their Jewish identities into the nexus of local political power.

By 1935, Daout Effendi had spoken of retiring for years, just as he had, for years, acknowledged aging and the undeniable approach of death. In letters to his son Leon, Daout Effendi frequently reviewed the terms of his pension. He was concerned about whether it would provide enough for the remainder of his life, and if it would cover the needs of his widow after his death. Yet retirement proved elusive. Not only did Daout Effendi continue to volunteer for the Jewish Community, but also he allowed his name to be included on a list of candidates for the Greek parliament proposed in 1936 by the right-wing Freethinkers' Party and then interior minister (and future prime minister and dictator) General Ioannis Metaxas. Salonica's Ladino press called Daout Effendi "the best Jewish candidate."[15]

For months Daout Effendi had weighed the proposal, changing his mind again and again.[16] But at last he felt "obliged to accept" the call, after Metaxas "demanded" the addition of two prominent members of the Jewish Community to the party's list.[17] "I was recommended by a group of Jewish notables," Daout Effendi wearily wrote his son, "and for a month I worked like a dog." The bid was unsuccessful. Daout Effendi earned only 139 votes, not nearly enough to propel him back into government service.[18] "Happily we failed," Daout Effendi wrote his son, "and I could extricate myself from this disaster. I have nothing riding on this."

The very month that Daout Effendi informed his son Leon of his parliamentary bid, his daughter Eleanor wrote of her own son Salomon's return to military service. Salomon's deployment worried the family, and removed an essential breadwinner from the home. Daout Effendi and his conscripted grandson were each, in their way, trying to support the volatile Greek national project while simultaneously crafting a Greco-Jewish identity. The pressure on the family was apparent. Within the year, parliamentary democracy (and with it, the frightening power of the Venizelists) would be suspended as Metaxas took the helm of a right-wing dictatorship.

Daout Effendi was tired, and suffering from compromised vision, just as his father had. "After one arrives at an advanced age one desires to receive the comfort and assurance of benedictions," Daout Effendi wrote his son. "I like to hope that the All Knowing will accord us that satisfaction." These thoughts may have been conjured, at least in part, by the death of Daout Effendi's eldest sister, Fortunée, in northern England, in 1936. She was the first of Sa'adi's adult children to die. A generation was poised to pass. But even in mourning, Daout Effendi was in no position to rest.

ELEANOR

In the Levy family, it was Eleanor (1887–1943) who remained in Salonica with her aging parents, Daout Effendi and Vida, feeling abandoned by her émigré brothers and sisters-in-law and burdened by constraint. Though Eleanor was vivacious and creative, she was always the one who filled the void left by her absent siblings. "Every day, mama cries that she will die if she does not see her dear [brother] Leon," confided Eleanor's daughter in a Ladino letter written when she was nine.

By the time her brothers Leon and Emmanuel had left their childhood home, Eleanor was married and a mother of three. Her husband, Abraham Solomon Matalon—known to all as Abram—struggled to hold down a job, and to transcend his physical problems and low morale. In 1936, when Abram suffered from heart trouble, Eleanor's father attributed the ailment to his son-in-law's penchant for raki and tobacco. Both were popular in Salonica, though it is possible that to this particular father-in-law they were indications of a deeper weakness. By 1938, Abram had a new ailment—pains in his legs that made walking virtually impossible. Eleanor confessed to her brother Leon that her husband had been under a great deal of pressure. With heavy European taxation imposed on import-export operations like Abram's, her husband had been idle for a few years. Having gone through their savings, they were now forced to "sit with arms crossed." How she missed her brothers and sisters-in-law, Eleanor wrote, and how hard it was to have no one with whom to speak about that which mattered most.

With so many of her generation gone from Salonica, Eleanor was the relative who was there to welcome others home, whether, for instance, her brothers, cousins, aunts, or uncles. Yet reunions would be bittersweet for Eleanor. Those who visited would inevitably leave again, and, while they were there, she must have been compelled to seem cheerful.[1]

Eleanor's eldest, Salomon, was also reckoning with the challenge of the interwar years. The young man had finished his studies in 1932—the very year that a major earthquake rocked his native city. Salomon reminded his mother of her brother Leon, and she considered sending her son abroad. In retrospect, that may have been the best course. Unable to find work, Salomon remained at home with his unemployed father until, in 1935, he was conscripted into the Greek army. Born after Salonica was lost to the Ottomans, Salomon and his sisters were the first generation of Levys to have begun life as Greek nationals. Additionally, Salomon appears to have been the first in the family to serve under the flag. Salomon's military experiment did not last long. Months after he left home, acute appendicitis put Salomon in a military hospital where he languished for months.

Following in the tradition of her grandmother and great-grandmother, Eleanor took on work as a seamstress to make ends meet. As Sa'adi's mother (Eleanor's paternal grandmother) had offered mid-nineteenth-century Salonicans their first taste of European fashion, Eleanor now made Salonica's interwar women their first trousers. Her handiwork was so

Eleanor's cousin Sari Michael on her honeymoon visit to Salonica, 1937

fine that it was celebrated in a Ladino poem written by Bouena Sarfatty:

A Salonik se uza djup-kulot
Para ekskursion o asentar al balkon.
Es konfortable, i non se ve el pantalon.
Bevamos a la salud de Eleonora Matalon ke lo envento.

In Salonica one wears culottes
For picnics or to sit on the balcony.
They are comfortable and the pantaloons can't be seen.
Let us drink to the health of Eleanora Matalon who created them.[2]

Through her work, Eleanor was coaxing change from Salonica, one bolt of fabric at a time.

Eleanor's daughters, Etty and Allegra (or Allegritta, as she was known by family), were, in their mother's words, "fancy," and liked to dress well. When Etty turned eighteen, in 1938, Eleanor, who had not a penny for her trousseau, arranged for her daughter to apprentice to a couturier in Salonica. "She is learning and has aptitude," Eleanor wrote her brother Leon. Sewing had spared Sa'adi's mother and her children from poverty a century earlier. It had spared Eleanor and Abram from destitution when their children were young. "The needle is a weapon in life," wrote Eleanor. Now, she hoped, it would provide the funds needed for Etty to marry well.

Yet when Etty did at last marry, the following year, Eleanor was overwhelmed by the expense. Etty's fiancé was from a middle-class family like the Levys, had made a decent sum as a young man, and was well positioned to marry a woman with an ample dowry, which Etty clearly did not possess.[3] "To marry a girl is to build a temple," Eleanor confessed to Leon. Taking the hint, Leon contributed, although not the sum Eleanor desired or imagined he could afford. "If I were there I would have bought the girl something pretty," Leon replied, explaining that the turbulent times had damaged his import operation. The truth was somewhat pettier. Daout Effendi had just placed Eleanor's husband, Abram, on the deed of the family home on Salonica's rue Broufas, a decision that irked Leon. Though emigration had carried him far from home, Leon refused to think of himself as in any way diminished as his father's son. Ironically, distance seemed to strengthen the sentiment.

Tensions among the family notwithstanding, Etty's wedding was grand—grand enough, anyway, to satisfy the groom. It was a high point in an economically fraught time. The event, held in the early summer of 1939, was noted by Bouena Sarfatty:

Korbeyo de flores resevieron
Ke al otro dia las tomo el estierkero.

They received a bouquet of flowers
That the garbageman took away the next day.[4]

In the ominous year of 1939, a Salonican Jewish wedding could still be extravagant. Weeks after Etty's nuptials, Germany invaded Poland, marking the start of the Second World War in Europe.

Eleanor's last letter to her brother Leon was written in February 1940. She had used green ink, turning her paper sideways so that her words appeared within the stationery's fine red lines. Eleanor explained that although she was unaccustomed to asking for things, the family's debt had put her in a state of desperation. She promised to repay Leon every last cent. "What I ask of the good Lord is that we preserve our health, all of us, for I cannot think of the unexpected." She signed the letter: "your devoted sister, Eleanor."

ÉMIGRÉS

I bless and embrace you with all my soul. You were already grown and you didn't escape my arms and now my soul takes leave of me out of desire to see you.

—Vida Levy to Leon Levy, 1921

EMMANUEL

Some émigrés leave home with a precarious optimism, others in the hope of redemption. Emmanuel (1889–1942) fled humiliated and in debt, with hungry creditors at his heels. The years had not been kind to the youngest son of Daout Effendi. Emmanuel and his wife, Esther, had lost a child to illness in infancy.[1] In business, he seemed doomed to fail, after repeatedly making unwise investments. In 1935, he wrote his brother Leon, in Brazil, that ever since the fire of 1917, luck had been against him.

In the early 1920s, Emmanuel begged his father to buy a property in Salonica and oversee the construction of a house on his behalf. But his timing was awful. The population transfers had just flooded Salonica with thousands of displaced people. The urban, regional, and European economy was in a shambles. Emmanuel had convinced Daout Effendi that he had the capital needed to finance the building of his dream home. "I was taken for a ride," Daout Effendi later confessed. Emmanuel dramatically overspent, taking out enormous loans, with his father as co-signer. As his debt mounted, he retreated to Paris, leaving his father to face his creditors.

Once it was completed, Daout Effendi managed to rent Emmanuel's newly built mansion, but the income wasn't enough to manage the debt.[2] By now, father and son were juggling two mortgages on Emmanuel's property, as well as additional debt, and their interest rate had soared to 18 percent. In Salonica, Daout Effendi took out loan after loan, mostly from friends and family willing to forgo interest.[3] Whether these were truly loans or gifts given under the guise of a loan wasn't clear. Either way, it wasn't enough. Desperate, Daout Effendi finally sold Emmanuel's house at a loss, and was glad to be rid of it.

Eleanor—Leon and Emmanuel's sister—wrote Leon that Emmanuel's financial situation had taken a severe toll on their father. Daout Effendi barely slept, and he had turned to prayer. "Not a *sou* in his pocket" (in Eleanor's words), Daout Effendi pawned his wife's jewelry without her knowledge. In Paris, desperate to become solvent, Emmanuel engaged in various speculative investments. These gambles merely increased his debt.

For years, Daout Effendi and Emmanuel concealed the facts of their financial ruin from Leon in Brazil. No doubt they were ashamed of their failure. For those members of the family who stayed in Salonica, there may have been a desire to keep up appearances for those who left. But desperation eventually won out over pride. In 1928, Daout Effendi broke down and confessed to the catastrophe. In a seven-page letter to Leon, he insisted that his son keep the revelation a secret, not disclosing to his brother Emmanuel (or to anyone else) his knowledge of the family crisis. Daout Effendi even instructed Leon to destroy the letter that documented the Levys' misfortune. Leon refused to oblige. It is not known whether he saved this damning letter for the same reasons he saved all those others he received and wrote—because in Rio, Leon was lonely, far from those he loved, and because letters were a much-needed source of connection. Or did he recognize that his father's letter held truths he would want to confront his brother with in time?

Eventually, Daout Effendi recognized that his poverty was,

in his words, "generalizable" to the entire community. Though it was unusual for a member of the Jewish elite to fall so dramatically from grace, many of Salonica's Jewish merchants were struggling in the interwar years, while a majority of the city's Jews were dependent on charity.[4] Emmanuel's sister Eleanor felt that their father's material burdens had worn him down. The siblings' mother, Vida, confided that Daout Effendi had no one to *konyorar* (cry with), and complained that with all the misfortunes they faced, she had "had enough of life." Within a decade, Daout Effendi's debts had reached 100,000 drachmas, ten times his annual salary at its peak.

In roughly 1934, Leon began sending his parents a monthly stipend, initially in the hopes that Emmanuel would match his efforts. But Emmanuel, mired in debt of his own, could not oblige. Not surprisingly, relations between the brothers—always tenuous—frayed. Three times during Emmanuel's financial crises (in 1928, 1929, and 1930), Leon came through Paris. Each time Emmanuel failed to greet his brother at the train station, which wounded him deeply.

The brothers' letters to each other were harsh and few in number. During the one and a half decades bracketed by Leon's departure from Europe in 1927 and Emmanuel's death at the hands of the Nazis in 1942, Emmanuel sent his brother a total of six letters. During that same period, Leon wrote seven angry letters to Emmanuel. The two couldn't resist revisiting old grievances, replaying past scenes. Letters became, for the pair, the principal medium of an acute sibling rivalry that showed no signs of abating with time.

Accusations flew between Rio and Paris. One called the other "unfraternal," the other responded that his brother was "unloving." "I do not know which of us is the most violent in temperament," Emmanuel wrote Leon: "Your character has been so sour for so long, to address a single word to you requires weighing my words in order not to inflame your extreme sensitivity." When Emmanuel's baby died, Leon learned the news from their father, for Emmanuel had ceased corresponding with his brother altogether. A year later, when Emmanuel brought his eldest son, Albert, to Salonica to become a bar mitzvah in the family's home city, Daout Effendi found his son thin and exhausted. Emmanuel, for his part, remained determined to resolve his business troubles and "find his way."

Emmanuel was not the only member of the extended Levy family to struggle in the interwar years. Leon and Emmanuel's cousin Moise Kirbatch Levy, one of five children of Daout Effendi's brother Hayyim, committed suicide in Paris in 1935 rather than face his mounting debt. Ironically, the onetime editor of a satirical Ladino weekly named after him, *El Kirbatch* (the whip), Kirbatch was described by one member of the family as "the joyous Kirbatch, a veritable Musketeer." But financial strain stripped him of his lightness. Leon recalled having paid Kirbatch a visit in Paris, intending to join his cousin's family for a meal. Instead, the two ended up drinking at a bar, Kirbatch sharing with Leon a litany of woes.

In the interwar years, the strains upon Emmanuel and Leon's relationship threatened to rupture the entire Levy family. The letters the brothers exchanged nevertheless managed to create a degree of continuity. Later, after the traumas of the Second World War, Leon worked for years to reclaim his brother's modest personal effects, and to regain the deed to his Paris property on rue Jean-Jacques Rousseau, which had been confiscated during the Nazi occupation. As this process foundered, Leon wrote repeatedly—obsessively, even—that as Emmanuel's surviving sibling, he was his lawful heir. Counterintuitively, the scant, tense correspondence the brothers had maintained was a form of fraternal intimacy.

ESTHER

The simple black silhouette, cut in 1919 portraying the face of Esther (1895–1998), eldest daughter of Fortunée and Ascher Salem, captures something of her spirit. It was sent to me by Esther's daughter, Esme Solomons, from an elder-care facility on the outskirts of Johannesburg, after roughly four years of correspondence. "It has been lying around here, along with all my other hoardings," Esme wrote, "but when I found the card again I was impressed at how instantly recognisable it was. It was a very fashionable thing to have done at the time, and the family were showing off their marriageable daughter, I guess!"[1] Esther is instantly visible in the silhouette. Her prominent cheekbones, inherited from her mother, her elegant upswept hair, her radiant smile: even a silhouette captures a trace of the resilience that defined her.

The silhouette was made when Esther was in her early twenties, the very year she left Salonica for Manchester. The Salem family was still grappling with the economic fallout from the fire of 1917, which demolished Esther's father's business. Esther's mother's photograph, taken at the Jewish cemetery around the same time the silhouette was made, shows a tense woman, a woman on edge. Esther's silhouette tells a different story, as does a keepsake from 1919 preserved by Esther's brother Michael: a nostalgic watercolor of the White Tower, the iconic fifteenth-century

Ottoman monument on Salonica's waterfront.[2] These mementos reveal how the generations grappled with the rapidly changing times. All the Salems wanted to hold on to something, the older generation memories of the past and of the deceased, the younger generation a snippet of the present, a sideways glimpse of themselves in transition. Photographs of the ancient Jewish cemetery, a silhouette, a watercolor—these were among the last relics gathered by the Salems as they departed their homeland.

Despite Esther's brother Jacques's traumatic experience of the Great War—waited out in an enemy aliens camp in Britain—the Salems' was a British immigrant success story. Once in Manchester, the family was active in the Manchester Congregation of Spanish and Portuguese Jews on Queens Road (later Shaare Hayim Synagogue), the children members of Manchester's Jewish Literary Society, and Jacques, for a time, its leader. Esther and her siblings frequented the Manchester Country Club, a sporting and social center beloved by south Manchester's middle-class Jews, and they completed their education in British schools. When Esther's eldest brother, Jacques, applied to be naturalized as a British citizen in 1924, his handwritten application to the Home Office explained that "all my sympathies are with the British people among which I have lived for the past eleven or twelve years most happily also because I have no other interests than those in England viz:—My home, my family, and my business."[3] In time, nearly all of the siblings would emulate Jacques's legal embrace of Britain.

Esther met her future husband, Ellis Michael, soon after arriving in Manchester. It was not an arranged marriage, precisely, yet it had the feeling of a preordained one. Like Esther, Ellis was a Salonican Jew, and part of an immigrant family transplanted to Manchester, if two decades prior to the Salems. Esther's intended was older than she and a veteran, having served as a volunteer for the British Royal Army Medical Corps during the First World

War, at the Somme. Like Esther's brother Jacques and her father, Ascher, Ellis worked in textiles.[4] The Michaels and the Salems had a natural ease with one another, though they hadn't been acquainted in Salonica. The two families, along with a third with a profile close to theirs, formed an amiable group.[5]

In Salonica, Esther had a privileged childhood. She grew up in a wealthy suburb, enrolled in an elite Catholic school despite being Jewish, received private voice lessons, and lived in a modern mansion with every amenity. With their relocation to Manchester, the Salems lived more simply. The Salem brothers dissolved their partnership in 1924, and Esther's father's modest business was quickly eclipsed by his brother's.

After Esther and Ellis wed, the couple moved to the English seaside town of Southport for a time—until Ellis invested in four inexpensive acres with his brother, Michael Michael, hatching plans to return his young family to the pastoral outskirts of Manchester. The Michaels' property was on the River Mersey in Didsbury, a suburb five miles south of the city known disparagingly as "Yidsbury" for its heavy concentration of Jews.[6] Since land was cheap, the brothers had decided to try their hand at dairy farming. According to Esther's memory, there were no Jewish farms in the greater Manchester area at the time. But her husband and brother-in-law were optimists (or given to folly). On the new land the Michael brothers built two structures: a farmhouse where Michael Michael and his wife, Eva, would live, and a second house, New Farm, for Esther and Ellis. New Farm was completed in 1932, which was when Esther and Ellis moved in with their young children—Eric, nearly nine, and Esme, just over three.

The two families operated the farm together. With some twenty-five to thirty cows, they offered south Manchester twice-a-day milk-delivery service, sending two horse-drawn "milk floats" through the Jewish streets of the area. Their customers

Left to right: Ascher Salem, Ellis Michael, Esme Michael, Esther Salem Michael, Karsa Salem, and Adolphe Ascher Salem, at the Michaels' New Farm, Didsbury, UK, 1930s

were mostly (though not exclusively) fellow Jews, because it was such a novelty for there to be a Jewish farm in northern England, and because many of them preferred to purchase milk from a dairy farm that did not handle meat, in accordance with the laws of *kashrut*. Esme, however, gives her parents' experiment with farming mixed reviews. "Those were anxious years, and no-one, including my parents, had any money to spare," she offered by e-mail. The Great Depression furthered the strain, and neither Ellis nor his brother had any prior experience with farming. "The farm never really did very well," Esme reported. Wisely, Ellis kept a hand in imports, traveling to his Manchester office each day after tending to chores on the farm.

Though Esther had little to do with the day-to-day work of the farm, she was influential in pushing the family into yogurt production, which proved a lucrative line of business. It happened like this: in addition to producing milk, the Michaels' farm produced simple cheeses—what Esther called "Greek cheese" or "cream cheese." This process generated whey, which the novice agrarians discarded until Esther realized that they could use the by-product as a starter for yogurt, which she began to produce in the kitchen of New Farm. This decision may have come after a visit from Esther's cousin Jacques Lévy (son of Besalel and Vida), who came bearing a sample of the yogurt he was promoting for a young company then known as Danone. It had been formed by Isaac Carasso, another Salonican Jewish émigré.[7]

Esther and her family operated on a scale far more modest than that of Carasso's company, though they did bring yogurt to the palate of south Manchester, pleasing their Sephardic immigrant customers to no end. For Esther and Michael in England, Jacques in France (and, subsequently, Portugal and Spain), and, later, Jacques's brother Ino in Portugal, yogurt was a culinary link between past and present, between the Mediterranean and the Atlantic worlds. While Esther and Ellis's opening of a dairy farm could be understood in terms of survival, their yogurt-making bent the arc backward, connecting modern life to ways of the past.

In a black-and-white photograph, Esther and her brother Michael sit outside their parents' house on Central Road in Didsbury.[8] It is spring or summer, and to judge from Esther's dress, the image dates from the early 1930s. The siblings smile and appear at ease, Michael exuding charm and leaning toward his sister and the camera. The two cradle cups in their hands—and the image could be mistaken for one that captures a quintessential high tea. But what the siblings hold are espresso cups, not teacups, their drinks Turkish coffee, not tea. It seems you can take

Esther and Michael share Turkish coffee, Didsbury, c. 1935

the Sephardic out of the Mediterranean but you cannot take the Mediterranean out of the Sephardic.

Esther, Ellis, and their two children attended synagogue in Manchester—Esme recalls that her mother tried to take her and her brothers to services each Saturday, despite the fact that Esme "rebelled inwardly." But Esther's Jewishness was crucial to her identity, so much so that she volunteered for the Hevra Kaddisha, the society that fulfills the most sacred of Jewish obligations, preparing bodies for burial and comforting the mourners. Though Esther considered herself religious she was not (as she mischievously proclaimed in an interview in her ninety-eighth year) "fanatical."

In 1936, after a long struggle with tuberculosis, Esther's mother, Fortunée, died at the age of fifty-nine, having spent her last years at a sanatorium. A photograph taken at Fortunée's grave shows Esther standing with her father, two brothers, and a family

Salem family at the grave of Fortunée Salem, Manchester, 1930s

friend.[9] The four are bundled against the cold and the shadows are long. This picture is reminiscent of another graveside photograph taken four decades earlier, as the Salems were preparing to emigrate from Salonica. In the earlier image, a young Esther and her family pose next to the grave of her grandfather Sa'adi, the tombs of Salonica's vast Jewish cemetery stretched out behind them. Leading them in prayer are the *honadjis*, cemetery guides, one of whom displays a prayer book by leaning it against the tomb. In 1930s Manchester, a different sort of commemoration is required. Gone are the *honadjis*, the men's fezes, the tomb's Hebrew inscription, and the prayer books, at least from their position of prominence. The most remarkable detail lies elsewhere: in the bouquet of flowers resting on Esther's mother's grave. The leaving of flowers on the grave of the dead is a new-world ritual, neither traditionally Sephardic nor Jewish. A Jewish traditionalist would instead leave a stone: in Salonica, tradition dictated that Jews toss stones on graves, particularly during funerals. Waist high, with Doric columns at its ends, Fortunée's grave is reminiscent of the grave of her father, Sa'adi. Family history continued to matter, in diaspora and even in death.

LEON

Leon (1891–1978) valued textile samples as much as he treasured letters. Today, his textile collection is held by the Museu de História e Artes do Estado do Rio de Janeiro (known as the Museu do Ingá) in Niterói, state of Rio de Janeiro, Brazil.[1] In dozens of squat white rectangular boxes, arranged by style and stuffed to the brim, there is lace in myriad designs and colors, velour in every imaginable thickness and shade, block and floral prints, polka-dot patterns, gossamer-thin rayon, colorful tulle. Most samples bear an original tag noting exporter, item number, and color—and on many, Leon's notations record favorites and fluctuations in pricing.

For five years after Leon arrived in Rio, from 1924 to 1929, he worked with his brother-in-law Elie Alaluf, the brother of his wife, Estherina. Elie had by this time been living in Brazil for seven years. He had met his own wife, Léa, a Sephardic immigrant from Ottoman Izmir, in São Paulo, home to a vibrant Jewish community. The pair now had two young daughters.[2] At the time of Leon's immigration to Brazil, Elie was the sole owner of a shop in the Centro neighborhood, on Rio's fashionable Rua Ramalho Ortigão.[3] Leon soon joined the business as junior partner.

The shop's location placed the brothers-in-law in the middle of Rio's fashion district, in a commercially dense neighborhood that

Satin-backed velvet textile sample from Leon Levy's collection

defined the European style for white Cariocas (as residents of Rio are known) of means.[4] By the time of Leon's arrival, the Centro had been transformed by a succession of mayors who oversaw the neighborhood's massive redesign in imitation of Georges-Eugène Haussmann's Paris. The once hilly neighborhood had been leveled and hundreds of tenement homes destroyed, a grid of boulevards taking their place.[5] By the 1920s, women shoppers in this district could take their pick of the latest styles: a grand evening frock, an ermine-lined cloak, satiny gloves, or an elegant cloche. A block from the Alaluf store, shoppers could linger in Rio's first department store, the luxurious Parc Royal, after whose founder Rua Ramalho Ortigão was named.

Rio's fashion magazines of the 1920s reflect a trend away from the heavy, corseted dresses of the turn of the century, and

The main avenue of Rio de Janeiro, Centro, c. 1909–1919

a movement toward lighter fabrics, lower necklines, and higher hemlines, echoing the European vogue, while adopting it to the needs of Brazilian women, who had little reason for winter designs.[6] The House of Elie Alaluf offered shoppers the latest French imported fabric needed to tailor these looks, such as silk, crepe, and chiffon.

But shortly after Elie opened his shop in the early 1920s, the Brazilian economy fell off and sales of imported textiles began to slump. The market was already depressed at the time of the 1929 crash, when Elie and Leon dissolved their partnership by mutual agreement. When the House of Elie Alaluf folded, the operation was valued at over 250,000 milréis (roughly 340,000 dollars in today's terms), with Elie's share at 70 percent and Leon's at

30 percent. Within the context of Brazil's dramatic gap between rich and poor, even Leon's percentage placed him among the wealthiest citizens of Rio. Relative to Rio's other small-scale businesses, however, Leon was merely one step ahead of a door-to-door salesman.[7]

Leon kept the lease on the shop on Rua Ramalho Ortigão and reopened the business on January 1, 1930, under his own name. It was a terrible time to launch an import operation. Leon took charge of his new business the year that Getúlio Vargas seized control of the federal government, trumpeting the centralization of political and economic power in Brazil. In time (during the Estado Novo dictatorship of 1937–1945), Vargas's fascist, corporatist rule would claim many thousands of lives, and generally limit Brazilians' political liberty.[8] For Leon, the early Vargas years were financially disastrous. A ban on textile imports to Brazil stimulated domestic production, which was Vargas's goal, but this was the death knell to import operations like Leon's.[9] In 1934 (the very year Vargas initiated the new constitution and, with it, a process that led to total federalization and centralization), Leon complained in a letter to his father that the regime change was "a veritable tragedy" and the new injunctions a severe impediment to trade with Europe. Day by day, Leon was forced to draw down his reserves.

Family problems exacerbated Leon's troubles. His wife, Estherina, was living hundreds of kilometers away from Leon during the 1930s, spending time, for example, in mountainous Poços de Caldas, which offered medicinal hot springs. The couple's son, Sadi Sylvain, was enrolled and lodged in a Baptist boarding school in Rio de Janeiro. Leon despaired over the family's fracture. What's more, Estherina's health was poor, and her medical (and other) expenses, combined with the cost of school for Sadi Sylvain, stretched Leon financially.

Estherina and Sadi Sylvain, Poços de Caldas, 1931

It was also in this period that Leon learned of his brother Emmanuel's debt, and of his father's own descent into poverty. Year after year, Leon's letters to his father included the same laments. Business was dry, his wife unhealthy and at a remove, his son growing into a man he scarcely recognized. At fifteen years old, the boy was taller than his father, and had become (in Leon's words) "a South American." What this meant to Leon is not clear—yet he hinted at Sadi Sylvain's free ways and evidently contrasted them with the strictures of his own youth. Leon mentioned repeatedly how he yearned to visit Salonica. He was, he wrote, "crazy with desire" to see his native city and embrace his mother and father one more time. Though he had returned to Europe at least three times since his arrival in Brazil in 1924, by the 1930s, he could no longer afford the voyage.

Leon acquired a typewriter in 1933, and began using the machine for personal correspondence, though he also continued to write letters by hand. He apologized to his father and sister for the formality. "You must excuse me, my dear Papa, for writing you on the typewriter," Leon wrote Daout Effendi in 1934, "but as I wish to retain a copy of this letter, I can not do otherwise." What his desire for preservation stemmed from Leon didn't specify, but I suspect that letters had come to serve as a kind of diary, a record of the emotional tides of his life. Leon wanted to preserve this record, at least in part because it allowed him to reference his earlier words and deeds in subsequent correspondence, which he did especially in the course of quarrels with his loved ones. In this, he was uncannily like his grandfather Sa'adi, who, half a century earlier, wrote a memoir to vindicate his name after his excommunication by the rabbinical establishment of Salonica.

Letters were not the only papers that mattered, of course. Leon visited the Portuguese consulate in Rio in 1937, with the intention of renewing his Portuguese passport. He carried with him a ream of documents testifying to his history as a Portuguese subject—a status that dated back to Salonica and the 1910s, and that had enabled Leon's emigration to Brazil over a decade earlier. Rio's Portuguese consulate had, on various occasions, confirmed and renewed Leon's papers. When he petitioned the consulate this time, he understood it as a routine application. What Leon couldn't have known was that months earlier, across the Atlantic, the Portuguese foreign minister had authorized an audit of the consular practice of renewing the Portuguese citizenship of Mediterranean and Middle Eastern Jews like Leon. Though there is no evidence that the audit was driven by anti-Semitic impulses, the auditor did focus on ferreting out fraud at consulates such as Salonica, which were most often frequented by Jews.[10] To his considerable dismay, when Leon delivered his passport to the Portuguese consulate in

Rio, his request for a passport was denied. To make matters worse, his Portuguese citizenship, like that of so many other Jews, was stripped away without warning.

A new, frantic tone entered Leon's correspondence with his father. As a native Salonican, he assumed he was entitled to Greek citizenship—he even began, in Brazil, to declare himself Greek. But Leon did not know the precise date of his birth and had no legal records to demonstrate his lineage. And so he turned to his father, Daout Effendi, the former Ottoman passport official now in his eighth decade, pleading with him to find proof of his birth. Leon also needed to know if his Greek citizenship could be passed on to his son, Sadi Sylvain, and if he could pay a fee to absolve the young man of service to the state.

Miraculously, in March 1939, Daout Effendi shipped Leon's birth certificate to him. The document had been retroactively issued by the prefecture of Salonica in 1915. He also mailed his son duplicate tax receipts dating to 1924, demonstrating that Leon (or his father) had paid to relieve himself of service to the state. Finally, Daout Effendi included paperwork testifying that Leon's volunteer service to a synagogue stood for military service. For good measure, Daout Effendi even included Leon and Estherina's marriage certificate, issued by a civil official in the course of the First World War. All of this, Daout Effendi proclaimed, would satisfy a Greek consular representative in Rio—proving that Leon was originally from Salonica and that he was entitled to Greek citizenship. Few Jewish émigrés could lay claim to the richness of documentation that Daout Effendi sent his son. He could not have known that this wealth of paperwork, meant to facilitate a family reunion and legal continuity across the generations, would ultimately be used for reparation claims from Germany.

ESTHERINA

Estherina (1891–1968) was a seeker. She gravitated toward spa towns, in Europe before her emigration, and after her arrival in Brazil. She sought spiritual comfort outside Judaism, and for years embraced the Seventh-day Adventist Church. She took courses in cosmetology and imported beauty supplies to Brazil, hoping to create a "Beauty Institute" that would popularize European products and techniques for Brazilian women of means.

Estherina struggled with vision loss, which completely overtook her by her fifty-fourth year. Even once her vision was gone, she wrote long, impassioned, if unintelligible letters in her loping hand. She favored stationery from clinics and hotels, wrote on scraps of paper, over letters received, on candy wrappers, on envelopes, or on both sides of paper so thin that the bleeding of ink rendered front and back equally unreadable.

Later in life Estherina traveled to Vienna for eye care, but her encroaching blindness tells only part of the story. According to a doctor she consulted in the 1920s, Estherina was plagued by "an organic affliction on her central nervous system." Thirty years later, a psychiatric exam conducted in Rio determined that "egocentrism" caused Estherina to "lose touch with reality," resulting in "extravagant conduct." Neither diagnosis would reasonably satisfy today.

In 1927, after spending the better part of a decade seeking relief in spas around Europe, Estherina followed Leon to Brazil, in the company of their son, seven-year-old Sadi Sylvain. Their steamship, the *Alsina*, docked on November 4. Like her husband, Estherina had acquired Portuguese papers in Salonica. Nevertheless, she registered with the Brazilian authorities as a native of Greece. She would do the same a dozen years later, when she applied to become a "permanent immigrant" of Brazil.[1]

The day of Estherina and Sadi Sylvain's arrival in Rio must have been hot and humid, jarring for travelers accustomed to the northern hemisphere. Leon would have been there to meet his wife and son, perhaps with Estherina's brother and sister-in-law in tow.

An unstable decade followed. Estherina moved frequently. She was moody. Her health was poor, her eyesight deteriorating. Estherina moved to Poços de Caldas in the early 1930s and Sadi Sylvain was sent to boarding school, and then medical school. His father described Sadi Sylvain as an independent child—whether by necessity or disposition. Throughout this period, Estherina remained close to her brother Elie, her sister-in-law Léa, and their children, as well as to her mother, Flor, whom Elie had earlier brought to Brazil. Flor never learned Portuguese or acclimated to her adopted country; she spent all her time at home, much as Estherina would do later in life.[2]

By the summer of 1937, Estherina had reached her breaking point. Contradicting her doctor's advice, she embarked on a voyage to Europe for ophthalmological care. Leon scraped together the money to pay her way, but he and Sadi Sylvain remained behind. "It is true that the sacrifice will be enormous and beyond my means," he told his father, "but if you are in the dance, you must dance."

Estherina's journey across the Atlantic took more than fifteen days. It is difficult to imagine how she managed. In addition to her deteriorating eyesight, her "nerves," in the words of her husband, were "completely demolishing her state in general." The ocean liner on which she traveled, the *Neptunia*, was well equipped and well stocked. But Estherina "suffered" from sea travel—whether from seasickness, the challenge of impaired vision, anxiety, or a combination of things. A fellow traveler reported to Leon that Estherina had been treated kindly by her shipmates, particularly after misplacing the keys to her luggage.

The *Neptunia* docked in Trieste in July 1937, and Estherina traveled from there to Vienna by train. In the Austrian capital, she intended to pay a return visit to Dr. Moritz Sachs, "one of the foremost oculists" in Vienna.[3] Sachs had evaluated Estherina a decade earlier and, on the basis of correspondence with Leon, had actually urged Estherina not to return to Vienna for further care. But Estherina was stubborn, or hopeless, or both. I imagine her walking to Sachs's office on Vienna's Lichtenfelsgasse, alongside the Rathaus (City Hall) and its grand park, her eyes weak, her nerves frayed as she navigated a city of Vienna's scale. Estherina knew no one in the city of Sigmund Freud but for the names of a few Salonican Jewish émigrés passed to her by family members. Sachs's examination yielded discouraging news. Estherina's eyes had deteriorated dramatically since her last visit, in part due to subconjunctival hemorrhaging. Surgery was scheduled for ten days later.

Estherina would remain in Europe for nearly a year. During that time, her communications were erratic, her chaotic letters difficult to read, her movement spontaneous. Just as prior to emigration, Estherina was again on the move, visiting sanatoriums in Vienna, Zurich, Lausanne, and Bolzano, and paying a visit to her sister in Lyon. Not infrequently, letters sent to her were returned to their sender, as Estherina was no longer at a promised address. To the consternation of her in-laws, a visit to Salonica was scheduled and rescheduled multiple times before it was canceled altogether. In preparation for her return to her native city, Estherina's in-laws, Vida and Daout Effendi, and her husband, Leon, considered whether she could purchase carpets to be brought back to Brazil for resale. But taxes were prohibitive. It was unimaginable that Estherina could have managed the extra cargo—yet, the additional income would have meant so much to the family at the time.

During Estherina's time in Europe, the prospect of war loomed. The Nazi Nuremberg Laws, which legislated a racial definition of Jews and deprived German Jewish citizens of their rights, had been on the books for two years when she arrived in Central Europe. Estherina was in Vienna recovering from surgery when Japan invaded China, initiating the Second World War in the Pacific. She was in Lyon in March 1938, when the German army crossed the border into Austria to cheering crowds. The expansion of German race laws to Austria soon followed. Estherina's Dr. Sachs would have been pushed out of both the medical profession and his position at the University of Vienna virtually overnight.

From Rio, Leon explored alternative exit routes for his wife: would it serve Estherina to travel through Trieste, or Algiers? In Salonica, reported Daout Effendi, Jews from Germany and Austria were being denied entry into Greece. Daout Effendi was increasingly anxious and his worries were well-founded. Estherina's Greek passport had expired during the course of her travels, and she did not yet have a Brazilian one to take its place. Technically she was stateless, with war seeming imminent.

Somehow, despite her blindness, her panic, her status as a solo woman traveler and as a Jew, in May 1938 Estherina managed to obtain an exit visa from the Brazilian consulate in Geneva.

The document listed her as a Greek national.[4] On the strength of these papers, Estherina returned to her sister in Lyon with the intention of traveling from there to Marseille and, ultimately, back to Rio. But in the south of France, Estherina discovered it was impossible to obtain a transatlantic ticket. The ocean liners were jammed with passengers whose instincts told them they had more to gain than lose by abandoning Europe. A high percentage of those fleeing were, of course, Jews.

At last, Estherina managed to come by a berth and make her way from Marseille to Trieste, and from there she embarked on a ship bound for Rio in early November 1938. Her departure must have been within days of Kristallnacht, the "Night of Broken Glass," during which Nazi paramilitary men and members of the Hitler Youth destroyed synagogues and Jewish-owned homes and shops across Germany.

KARSA

Berlin, summer 1936. The city has been draped in swastikas in anticipation of the Olympics. Adolf Hitler, Führer of the Nazi Party, chancellor and self-proclaimed president of Germany, will preside over the games' opening, and the newly built Olympic stadium is filled to capacity with an international roster of athletes and a mostly German public. When the audience of thousands rise to *"Sieg Heil,"* their arms soaring upward in unison in a terrifying fascist salute, at least two people in the audience remain defiantly seated: Karsa Salem (1902–1968) and his future wife, Pearl Russel Payne.[1]

The third surviving child of Fortunée and Ascher Salem, Karsa was, aside from Leon, the member of the Levy family who traveled the farthest, propelled on a trajectory to India that was unusual in the context of the arc of Sephardic history. Karsa was seventeen years old when the Salem family migrated from Salonica to Manchester.[2] His parents wished their intellectually ambitious son would set his sights on medicine or law, but Karsa followed his own path into engineering. He studied at the University of Manchester and then in Germany, where the young man—smart, likable, charismatic, and a tremendous raconteur—made fast friends. Unfortunately, Karsa's arrival coincided with the Great Depression and the economic free fall of the Weimar

Karsa Salem's photograph of the Olympic stadium, Berlin, 1936

Republic. His salary came in the form of a suitcase of cash, its value plummeting even before he could put it to use.

Karsa found work with Allgemeine Elektricitäts-Gesellschaft AG (AEG), a company that produced electrical equipment. AEG was created in 1883 to supply electric equipment and transmission systems for industry; by the time of Karsa's arrival it was a giant, having extended its reach into multiple arenas of electrical power engineering, including lighting, railways, automobiles, and cables. In the summer of 1926, this work took Karsa to Bombay (Mumbai), where AEG was constructing a labyrinth of oil pipelines. Karsa would remain in India for over two decades, meeting and marrying Pearl, fathering two children (Pamela Fortunée and Gillian Wendy), and frequently traveling back and forth to Europe. Despite having been educated partly in English and trained as an engineer in German, French (alongside Ladino)

Karsa Salem, Delhi, 1940s

was Karsa's native tongue, and his multilingualism served him well in both his professional and his flamboyant private life. According to his daughter Pamela, during these heady years, her father even cavorted with the legendary singer Josephine Baker in Paris. Photographs of Karsa and his wife show the pair traveling the globe, whenever possible with their Cadillac.[3]

As an employee of a German firm with many friends among his German colleagues, Karsa must have followed the rise of the Nazi Party closely. In January 1933, Adolf Hitler was declared chancellor of Germany. A month later, AEG was among the German companies represented in a secret meeting with Hitler in Berlin, attended by some two dozen German industrialists and businessmen whose support the Führer was currying. AEG contributed 60,000 Reichsmarks (roughly 20,000 dollars in today's currency) to the party a month later, in February 1933.[4] Within thirty days of AEG's payment, Karsa succeeded in obtaining naturalization as a British subject.

AEG was rewarded for its loyalty to the Nazi regime, receiv-

Karsa, Pamela, and Gillie Salem at home in Bombay with Great Dane, c. 1947

ing (in a joint venture with the German radio and television company Telefunken) a contract to equip Berlin's Olympic stadium with a loudspeaker system for the 1936 games. The equipment used to directly transmit the competitions to the world—a first in Olympics history—was supplied by the same joint venture, which meant that Karsa's employer was responsible for delivering to the world images of Hitler at his most triumphant.[5] How chilling for Karsa to sit in that Olympic stadium, witnessing thousands of spectators cheer their dictator, aware that the spectacle was being enabled, from an engineering standpoint, by the company he had worked with for a decade.

Karsa returned to India after the Olympics—though just barely. His plane was grounded, and all passenger passports were seized by Nazi authorities. Karsa was among a few travelers led off the plane, and admitted back on board only after a powerful colleague bribed the officers with an emerald ring.[6] So Fortunée's son was safely home in his adopted India when war was declared. Now a naturalized British citizen, Karsa spent the war years assisting the British government—though he resumed working for a German firm after the war.

During the years of the Second World War, AEG ran a factory near German-occupied Riga that depended on female slave labor, received contracts for the production of electrical equipment in the Auschwitz camp complex, and relied upon slave labor at a sub-camp of Auschwitz III known as Arbeitslager Blechhammer (Metal Hammer Labor Camp). Within a decade of illuminating the Olympics for the world in 1936, AEG had become a cog in the Third Reich's genocidal machine. In Arbeitslager Blechhammer, conditions were so inhumane that most of its forced laborers would perish. Among the very few to survive that camp was Karsa's first cousin Jacques Lévy.

VIDA

Among the thousands of documents in the Levy family archive in Rio, one hand is all but missing: that of Vida (1866–1940), wife of Daout Effendi and mother to Leon, Emmanuel, and Eleanor. Leon preserved—and may well have received—only one letter from his mother. It is possible Vida's other letters were not preserved, or that she rarely wrote, but most likely she was illiterate, which was unusual for a woman of her class. After all, Vida never added a handwritten salutation, or even a signature, to the letters of others.

If Vida refrained from writing, she was nonetheless expressive in showing her love. Vida frequently sent well wishes in Ladino through her husband in his letters. She also instructed Daout Effendi to send her émigré sons her embraces—something their father's letters tended to lack. After the birth of her grandson Sadi Sylvain in 1920, it was Vida who had a talisman prepared for the child. In honor of the boy becoming a bar mitzvah thirteen years later, Vida readied three boxes of fruit preserves for the family in Rio. She had hoped to send a crate of oranges as well, but the entire shipment proved too heavy.

Throughout the 1930s, Vida sent her son Leon delicacies to remind him of home: *menta* (dried mint), *konfitura* (preserved or candied fruit), and *dulses* (confections). Occasionally these treasures were entrusted to friends who were traveling from Salonica to Rio, or they were shipped by sea. However they traveled, the goods' passage was carefully monitored. Letters by Daout Effendi asked about what was the quickest and safest way to send Vida's gifts. Daout Effendi would explain the purchase and preparation of the presents, their wrapping, the moment they were entrusted to a traveler. Subsequent letters appealed to Leon to tell his parents whether their offerings had arrived intact. One has the sense that these flavors of home meant at least as much to Vida as to her son.

In the early winter of 1936, when Estherina's eyesight was already failing, Vida arranged for a rabbi to oversee *selihot*, penitential prayers, in the family home on Salonica's rue Broufas. Typically, *selihot* would be recited on fasting days and in the weeks leading up to the High Holy Days, in September or October. But Vida recited *selihot* that February, indicating that she found her daughter-in-law Estherina's situation in Brazil dire. "The distance is so far," lamented Daout Effendi to Leon, "that we cannot extend a hand of comfort to allay your pain, or calm your suffering." Prayer was a constant for Vida, and as the interwar years wore on, there was ever more to fret over, to pray for. When Estherina was struggling to leave Europe in 1938, Daout Effendi wrote Leon: "Your mother has charged me with telling you that during all the days of Yom Kippur she remained in the synagogue and prayed on our behalf. *El dio ke la oyga i vos akorde salud buena i todo lo ke dezea vuestro korason* [May God hear her and grant you good health and all your heart's desires.]"[1] Similarly, when Eleanor's daughter Allegra, Vida's granddaughter, was hospitalized with gangrene, Vida prayed constantly. Vida's response to difficult times was starkly divergent from her husband's. While Daout Effendi responded with the precise questions and instructions of a bureaucrat, Vida communicated with food, prayer, and affection.

Vida Levy, 1880

There was pleasure, too. Vida spent the hottest weeks of summer in Langada, a small town northeast of Salonica famous for its Ottoman (and, before that, Byzantine) baths. She would retreat to Langada each August with her husband, Eleanor, and Eleanor's family, the relatives joining Vida for varying periods of time. Vida badly needed the restorative experience of Langada. She suffered from diabetes and neuropathy in her feet. Yet there was more to the ritual than healing, for this was a seasonal tradition. Meanwhile, Estherina and Leon traveled from Paris to Germany to take the waters in more elegant health spas. As Bouena Sarfatty's poetry reflects, it was ironic that people like Estherina and Leon traveled great distances (to "Baden Baden or Vichy") for a showier version of what they could find at home:

Tenemos kantaro; el agua es mas freska de la glasiera.
Lo merkimos a Langada.
Ke fuimos a tomar banyos kayentes de agua natural.
Kon la kalor de Salonik, te afreska muncho kuando beves un kopo. . . .
Los Selanikilis se van azer banyo a Baden Baden o a Vichi:
Ke tenemos a una ora de Salonik, agua de Langada,
Ma non ay buen charshi.
Bevamos a la salud de la agua saloridoza a lado de Salonik.

We have a bucket; the water is colder than a glacier.
We bought it at Langada.
Where we went to take the hot baths in natural water.
With the heat of Salonica, it refreshes you greatly when you drink a cup. . . .
The Salonicans go to the baths in Baden Baden or in Vichy:
While we have the waters of Langada one hour from Salonica,
But there is not a market.
Let us drink to the health of the health-giving waters near Salonica.[2]

The only letter Vida sent to her son in Rio she dictated to her daughter, Eleanor, in the late 1930s. In the letter's six and a half narrow pages, Vida repeats the Ladino phrase "*mi karo ijo*" (my dear son) six times. An ink spot conceals the precise year in which the letter was written, but the subject of the letter is eminently clear: money, and the obligation of son to father. When Daout Effendi and Emmanuel spoke of their failed business venture, it was stated in purely financial terms. To Vida the calamity was a matter of honor, pride, and loyalty. "Until now, my dear son, I haven't mentioned anything of my suffering to you," she wrote Leon, "but now it is too much. Seeing Papa, who hasn't been at all well, I've had enough of life. He's experienced one misfortune after the next and he hasn't been able to extricate himself, seeing how the crisis is grave and all the many friends he's always had are also in a bad way." For years Leon had complained about Estherina's ill health, Vida continued, never thinking to send his father a gift, or money enough to counteract his losses. Recently, Leon had protested when Daout Effendi sold off some family jewelry—his parents' remaining nest egg. His protests seemed to miss the point that Daout Effendi had no other choice, for he was a man of honor determined to see his debts resolved. "If today it's 'Mr. Daout' here, 'Mr. Daout' there, it's because everyone knows that he is honest till the end, and that in the face of every obstacle, he holds his head high. If Papa were to impugn his honor he would lose his virtue and even his job." The time had come, Vida insisted, for Leon to do what strangers had already been doing—provide Daout Effendi with the money he so desperately needed. "Now that you read this letter, my dear son, you will make 'a thousand efforts' and send him at least 60 liras, and doing this blessed deed for God will bring good health to your house and to Estherina, which we wish for with all our hearts. Saadico [Sylvain Sadi] will grow up well with the blessings his father receives." In closing, Vida blessed her son, embraced him "with all my soul," and urged him not to reveal to his father that she had written. On behalf of her mother, Eleanor signed the letter: "Your mother who misses you and wants to hear that you are well. Vida de Daout Levy."

Vida of Daout Levy: a mother who frequently sent her son love without ever putting pen to page, who communicated through prayer, the sending of salutations, and the shipment of familiar objects. This, her only known letter, is stained with tears.

It was a sudden, unpredictable event that took the Levy matriarch from the family. In March 1940, on her way home after offering condolences to a friend, Vida was struck by a speeding motorcycle as she stepped onto Aghia Triada Street. She was treated for multiple leg fractures in Salonica's best medical facility, the Baron de Hirsch Hospital. While hospitalized, however, Vida contracted an infection that spread through her legs and shoulder. Family members were by her side day and night. Apparently, she kept calling for Leon constantly until the moment of her death.

The very next week, Eleanor's daughter Etty gave birth to a premature child who soon died. Daout Effendi was doubly devastated. Of his wife, he said: "She was wonderful and devoted to her family and, in the 53 years we spent together, there was not a moment in which she did not adore me and her children like a veritable saint." Despite his financial struggles, he organized a grand funeral in Vida's honor, inviting all of Salonica's notables and community leaders. Funeral expenses were high, hospital bills higher still.

With his daughter, Eleanor, Daout Effendi opened Vida's jewelry box, to find it nearly empty. Daout Effendi himself had pawned some of Vida's treasures. On the sly, Vida had meanwhile sold off the rest one piece at a time—her diamond-and-emerald pendant, her gold bracelets, even her costume jewelry. When Leon learned that the heirlooms were gone, he pleaded with his father to send him one of the Oriental carpets that had once covered the family floors, so that he could claim inheritance from his parents. Daout Effendi confirmed that the Levy family home had contained twelve such carpets, including four of a considerable size, which "today would be worth a fortune." But half of them had already been given to Emmanuel. The remainder, earmarked for Leon, had at some point burned. In their place, Daout Effendi offered Leon the sole remaining memento of his mother's: a single gold bracelet. The resulting exchange between father and son stretched from May to October 1940. In the interim, German troops occupied France, Luxembourg, the Netherlands, and Belgium. By the time Leon wrote his father to thank him for his intention to preserve the lost carpets in his son's name, it was the eve of the Italian invasion of Greece.

CAPTIVES

Los djidios de Salonik moz olvidimos de revir
De kuando el alman paso el bridj.
Kada uno i uno se espanta de su solombra.

We the Jews of Salonica have forgotten how to laugh
Since the Germans crossed the bridge.
Each and every one of us is afraid of his own shadow.[1]

—Bouena Sarfatty

ESTHER

Of all the European branches of the extended Levy family, the branch in Manchester, the descendants of Fortunée and Ascher Salem, emerged from the Second World War the least scathed. This is not to say they were not touched by war, nor that they didn't fear the worst—but only that death did not claim as many of them.

For Fortunée and Ascher's daughter Esther and her family (as for everyone in Britain), civilian life changed quickly with the declaration of war on September 3, 1939. Weeks after Great Britain entered the conflict, Parliament introduced emergency measures for its civilian population. Esther's daughter, Esme, eleven years old at the outbreak of the war, recalled, "I can't describe the efficiency with which we were all issued with Identity Cards (mine was NTMB 145/4), pressed cardboard discs, on ribbons, with our names and ID numbers written in Indian ink, gas masks, and brown paper carrier bags with 'iron rations' (tins of bully beef, condensed and evaporated milk, biscuits, slab chocolate, dried fruit, etc.)."[1]

Immediately, Esther and her husband readied their children, Esme and Eric, for evacuation. Nearby Manchester, five miles to the north of the family farm, was a major industrial center and home to the Avro aircraft factory, rightly perceived as a target of German aerial assault. The children were sent in different directions, in pursuit of safety. Esme found herself in the small town of Stacksteads, where she was hosted by a "Salvation Army couple." For Esther, the separation from her children would be painful and frightening—both for obvious reasons and for rather less predictable ones. Esther received word that her daughter was worshipping in the small Salvation Army chapel in the town to which she had been sent, and now wished for a tambourine, so that she could take part in prayer services. Esther's sister-in-law also retreated to the countryside with her nine-month-old, only to find herself pressed into service as a housemaid by her host family.[2]

By the autumn of 1940, Esther and her husband and children were reunited at the farm in Didsbury, just as air raids targeted nearby Manchester. At this point, Esther's husband, Ellis, was serving as an air raid warden, looking for blackout violations and reporting on and coping with local bombings and detonations. When the sirens sounded, Ellis would run into the night while Esther and the children rushed to safety. Their daughter, Esme, recalls the experience vividly:

> On nights when the sirens went off, I was usually bundled down into the air raid shelter in the garden. This was an Anderson shelter, consisting of curved iron sheets fitted together, and sunk two-thirds into the earth. This structure was then covered in the soil excavated, and planted over with either grass, or whatever you wanted to put in, even flowers sometimes, but whatever it was it was camouflaged and protected above. Ours was a four bunk model, to accommodate our family. In it were stored all sorts of things, in the small space, and these included iron rations to last a few days if necessary. In ours we also had stored

> bottles of home-made elderberry wine and champagne. Occasionally we might get a shock from an exploding bottle of the champagne!

On one occasion, a bomb landed without warning quite close to the farm, terrifying everyone yet mercifully injuring no one. Manchester was not so lucky, as the city center was heavily bombarded, first in September and then during the two-day Christmas Blitz of 1940.

Like so many other immigrant families in Britain, Esther and her family, like her brother Michael and his family, threw themselves into the war effort. Esther volunteered for the Red Cross as a member of the Voluntary Aid Detachment. Her service took her to a local Methodist college, which had been converted into a hospital for convalescing servicemen. Michael served in the Auxiliary Fire Service, working during raids to extinguish fires and help the injured. Adolphe, the youngest Salem sibling, rose to the rank of staff sergeant, earning both a War Medal and a civil Defence Medal for his service.[3] Esther's daughter, Esme, was too young to volunteer. "In the mornings I would cycle to school through damaged areas," she wrote, "seeing the rubble, and there might be empty places in the classrooms."[4]

Did the grown Salem children panic when it was no longer possible to exchange letters between occupied France and Britain, or occupied Greece and Britain? Were they, like Leon in Brazil, gripped by news of the deportation of European Jews eastward, to destinations unknown? Fortunately, this branch of the Levys lost no one in the immediate family, though numerous members of the extended Levy and Salem families in Greece were among the murdered. The move to northern England had insulated Sa'adi's grandchildren and great-grandchildren, certainly relative to those who remained in Greece or moved to France. Two decades earlier, when Esther's mother, Fortunée, and her husband chose Manchester, Fortunée's sister Rachel and brothers Sam and Besalel chose Paris. At the time it was inconceivable that this choice would be the difference between life and death—if not for themselves, then for their children and grandchildren.

A marvelous collection of late-wartime photographs shows Esther during this time. The Polyfoto 48 camera captured forty-eight successive exposures on a glass negative plate: Esther probably posed for them in a Polyfoto studio in a Manchester

Polyfoto portrait of Esther Salem Michael, 1940s

department store. The portraits date to the early or mid-1940s, when that style of photography was in fashion. Esther is cheerful and coquettish, her face unlined and her hair pinned carefully in a "victory hairstyle"—a chic and functional style for women pressed into the workforce by war.[5] Overall, the Polyfoto radiates a spirit of sturdy British self-reliance. Esther probably did not yet know the extent of the devastation back in Salonica.

EMMANUEL

Emmanuel (1889–1942), the youngest son of Daout Effendi, his wife, Esther, and their son, Albert, were two of three generations of Levys living in Paris on the eve of the German occupation. Among Emmanuel's relatives there was one aunt, Rachel, and two uncles, Sam and Besalel, along with their spouses. Emmanuel's cousins were there, too: Rachel's daughter, Carola and son, Victor; Besalel's three sons, Jacques (d. 1989), Maurice, and Ino; Sam's daughter, Suzanne; and Charles Molho, son of Sa'adi's daughter Doudoun. These cousins, too, had children of their own, such that 1930s Paris was home to more descendants of Sa'adi Besalel a-Levi than Salonica.

Many in the family fled the city in anticipation of the arrival of German troops in the spring of 1940, joining roughly 25,000 fellow Jews who abandoned Paris before it was occupied. Of those who left, most escaped in the brief period between the Nazi invasion of the Third Republic in May 1940, and the occupation of northern and western France in June of the same year. Among the refugees were Sa'adi's children, grandchildren, and great-grandchildren.

Fate carried the Levys who escaped Paris in various directions. Sam and Anna Lévy made their way to the Cote d'Azur, in the "free zone" of Vichy France, where they sought refuge with their daughter, Suzanne. (The unoccupied zone was not truly "free"

Roger Viollet, "A platform at the Gare Montparnasse crowded with civilians leaving Paris ahead of the advancing German army, May 1940"

but, rather, overseen by a collaborationist French regime based in the spa town of Vichy, whose administrators would, of their own volition, promulgate anti-Semitic legislation and policy patterned on the Nazi model.) Sam's brother Besalel and his wife, Vida, also fled the occupied zone with the help of their sons, one of whom received up-to-the-minute information from an informant in the Paris police.[1] According to one family letter, the couple hid throughout the war "in a small pit [*un petit trou*] in the free zone [*zone libre*]."

A third child of Sa'adi also fled Paris in advance of the occupation. Rachel Carmona left for Provence with her son, Victor, her daughter, Carola, and Carola's husband, Ralph (Raphaël).[2] The family's flight must have been rendered all the more traumatic by the fact that two generations of Carmona women had already experienced grievous loss. Rachel was by now a widow, as her husband, Elie, had died in 1932. Even more recently, in late 1939 or early 1940, Carola and Ralph had tragically lost their only child, twenty-six-year-old André, to illness. One family member described André as the "perfect gentleman."

Besalel and Vida's grandchildren had also been shuttled away in advance of the Nazi occupation. Like so many Jewish families, this branch of the Levy family made the painful decision to send their children abroad in hopes of securing their safety. Henri and Jean Daniel, the sons of Besalel and Vida's son Jacques and his wife, Flor, were spirited off to maternal relatives in Barcelona, where Jacques and Flor and their children had lived until General Francisco Franco came to power in 1939. Jacques was a Republican, a Freemason, and an outspoken opponent of fascism, which explains his departure from Spain.[3] Were young Henri and Jean Daniel compelled to travel to Spain over the Pyrenees, by foot, as were thousands of other refugees? Were they assisted by a rescue organization? We know only that Jean Daniel Lévy was in Spain by April 1943, when he was registered as a refugee by the American Jewish Joint Distribution Committee.[4] Another of Besalel and Vida's grandchildren, Claudie, was also sent away, to the home of a maternal uncle, possibly in Italy. The choice (if the family records are accurate) is counterintuitive, for by the time of the German invasion of France, Italy had already begun to intern thousands of foreign-born Jews.[5] Nevertheless, Ino was aware that Claudie remained safe until at least 1943.

When Nazi tanks thundered into Paris, only Emmanuel and his wife and child and his cousins Maurice, Jacques, and Ino (Besalel's three sons) remained. Of the group, all except Ino were Greek citizens. In their lack of French citizenship, the Levys in Paris were not unusual. France was bursting with foreign-born Jews in 1940. Half of the country's 350,000 Jews were immigrants, and in Paris alone, Nazi authorities registered 64,000 foreign-born Jews out of a total population of 150,000 Jews in October 1940—and this after the flight of many more.[6] Alas, to be a foreign Jew in occupied France was to be vulnerable not only to Nazi racial laws, but also to the French police, who oversaw Jewish deportations under the leadership of the Vichy government.[7] Only Ino, who carried papers of neutral Portugal he acquired in Salonica during the Balkan Wars, was insulated from arrest.

The Nazi occupation of Paris interrupted communications between nations and among members of the Levy family. The mail, whether by ship or by air, was slow and unpredictable. Emmanuel's penultimate letter to his father was sent from Paris just prior to the occupation. "What has become of him?" fretted Daout Effendi in the weeks that followed. "Where is he, right now, [and is he] with his family?" Daout Effendi appealed to the Greek Red Cross for answers. His queries were met with silence.

Daout Effendi received his last letter from Emmanuel in August 1940. Emmanuel was no longer in his apartment on rue Bleue, he told his father, and he was out of work. Emmanuel may have feared the censor's hand, for the letter revealed little. Across Paris Nazi officials and the French police were seizing Jewish property and assets, storing these belongings in warehouses where slave laborers sorted the pillaged goods, repairing what was broken and preparing the best of it for shipment to Germany.[8] In time, the apartment of Emmanuel's uncle Besalel and aunt Vida was (in Ino's words) "stolen by the German bandits." Emmanuel's property, too, was seized, as was that of Emmanuel's cousin Maurice.

After property, people. The French police, working with German officials and under direction of the Vichy regime, now initiated the mass arrest of select Jews in the French capital. Their mandate was to focus on the Jewish foreign-born, proceeding with arrests based upon immigrants' and refugees' place of origin, and pursuing women and children with particular zeal. The bulk of those arrested were housed in a transit camp in Drancy, a suburb in northeast Paris. Over three years' time, from August 1941 to August 1944, some 70,000 individuals passed through Drancy. Most of the interned were Jewish women, men, and children who would subsequently be deported to Auschwitz. Roughly two-thirds were foreign-born or stateless. Among them were 8,000 children born of immigrants in France—boys and girls, like Emmanuel's son Albert, who were technically French citizens according to prewar law.[9]

Women, men, and children in the Drancy internment camp, 1941

For the first two years of the occupation of Paris, Greek Jews were not included among those specifically targeted by Vichy and German officials for arrest or deportation, though some of the Greek Jewish émigrés of Paris were caught up in the first major roundup of the city's Jews in July 1942.[10] It appears that none of the Levy family members were among them. Unfortunately, they would not remain free for long, although Emmanuel's uncle Sam fantasized that this immunity would persist throughout the war. Sam personally lobbied the German Embassy in France in January 1942 on behalf of the Sephardic Jewish community of Paris. His improbable hope was that the German authorities would consider Sephardic Jews "Ario-Latins of Mosaic faith"—a designation that would exempt them from the racist and anti-Semitic legislation of the Third Reich.[11] The tenuous appeal caught the attention of German consular representatives, who investigated but ultimately rejected Sam's proposal. In the end, it would make little difference. Sam's proposal reached the German legation just days before the highest-ranking German leadership met in a villa in the Berlin suburb of Wannsee to discuss and coordinate the implementation of the "Final Solution," the organized genocide of European Jewry.

In Paris, events quickly took a turn for the worse. The circumstantial immunity granted Greek Jews in Paris during the first two years of Nazi occupation collapsed in an instant. On the night of November 4, 1942, French police officers, on orders of the occupying authorities, conducted a midnight sweep of Paris that specifically targeted the 1,416 Greek Jews estimated by the Gestapo to live in the city.[12] Emmanuel, his wife, Esther, and his son, Albert, were arrested, as was Emmanuel's cousin Jacques. In all, 1,060 Greek Jews were gathered in that single, violent raid. Heinz Röthke, chief of the Gestapo's Jewish Office in France, delighted in the operation, not least because for once the notoriously leaky French police force had managed to keep secret their diabolical plans, which prevented more Jews from eluding the authorities. (In fact, the French police were granted only a few hours' warning about the operation, to ensure its success.) Sam later remembered it as the single most horrific night for the Sephardic community of Paris.[13]

The night of November 4 was a turning point for the Levy family in Paris, for it ripped them from their homes and from one another and flung them into conditions of debasement. Within a few hours, Emmanuel, Esther, and Albert were arrested, while Emmanuel's cousin Maurice and his wife, Flor, were taken from their apartment on rue Ordener. When the police came for Maurice's brother Jacques, they found him awake despite the late hour. Aware of the impending operation thanks to his contact in the French police, Jacques had stayed awake to keep vigil. Upon opening his door, he found two French police officers. Jacques offered the men a hefty bribe. But while one of the officials was tempted, the other held fast to his orders. It took mere minutes for Jacques's fantasies of escape to unravel. Like the others, he was pulled from his home and taken to a police station on boulevard Malesherbes, in the seventeenth arrondissement. It was five a.m., and the operation was nearing its end. Observing the shocked crowd, Jacques noted: "What was peculiar is that nearly all the victims were of Salonican origin and had among them connections of family, relatives, or friendship." Six hours later, they were placed in convoys and driven to the Drancy internment camp.

Because he held Portuguese papers acquired in Salonica during the Balkan Wars, Emmanuel's cousin Ino eluded arrest along with some 250 to 300 other Jews who held Portuguese papers and lived in France.[14] During the Second World War, despite everything, the German authorities tended to grant legal immunity to Jewish citizens of neutral states who were caught within the borders of the Third Reich—even when Portugal itself resisted repatriating its vulnerable, scattered subjects.[15] Unfortunately, some were not as lucky as Ino: other Sephardic women and men with Portuguese papers were swept up in the Paris arrests and sent to Drancy, even though their legal status ought to have granted them immunity.[16]

Later, Ino recalled the trauma of that cold November night in a letter to his cousin Leon in Rio. The letter was the first direct communication between the two men. Like all of Ino's letters, the testimony about the late autumn sweep of Paris was written in a beautiful, calligraphic hand. "You will no doubt be surprised to receive this letter, all the more from Portugal," Ino began, "because of the war, it is likely that you have heard no news from France, and I suppose these lines will be the first."

"Unfortunately," he continued:

> —and I'm sorry—they do not offer happy news, except for one bit, and this I hesitated to write. *Voilà*: until only a year ago, my parents, my brothers, your brother and his family and I all continued to live in Paris. Despite the presence of the Germans and the measures that were in effect, we were not personally disturbed. But the [4th–] 5th of November, 1942, in the night, all Greek subjects were arrested. We had the misfortune of seeing my two brothers and their wives taken, [as well as] Emmanuel and his family, along with all compatriots of the same nationality, with almost no exception. . . . [My brothers] Jacques [and] Maurice [and] their wives, Emmanuel [and] his wife and son were all deported on the 10th of November, 1942 for a destination unknown that we suppose to be Upper Silesia. All my efforts to rescue them or even to learn of news from them have been in vain. All that we have been able to learn is that the deportees were assigned different work—forced labor. I can't

> imagine the state of hygiene and nutrition that they face and we call out day and night for Providence to look after them and protect them and give them the strength to await the [arrival] of their army and their liberation, amen!

Before Emmanuel was arrested, he entrusted an assortment of belongings to his wife's aunt. The woman, Madam Benusiglio, was another Salonican Jewish émigré spared arrest by dint of a neutral country's foreign passport. Emmanuel's bundle was small, reflective of his prior losses. Some clothes, a bit of money, a woman's watch, a gold bracelet, a gold ring with a low-quality diamond, a fountain pen, a medallion inscribed with the lucky number thirteen. These were the last precious objects of a desperate family bereft of possessions.

For Emmanuel and the other Levys imprisoned in Drancy, the subsequent days and nights passed slowly. "I cannot describe the state of the camp of Drancy," Jacques later recalled. "Nothing so lamentable has ever existed." The food made everyone sick. People slept wherever they could, pell-mell. The site was filthy, despite the internees' efforts to maintain order. Some internees were in Drancy for days or weeks, receiving packages from the outside, communicating with their loved ones by correspondence and even arranging clandestine sightings through predesignated windows.[17]

The Greek Jews' sojourn in Drancy, by contrast, was relatively brief. Three days and three nights after they arrived, those arrested on the night of November 4 were divided in two groups.[18] Emmanuel and his nuclear family, along with Jacques and his wife, were included in the first group, and brought to the Bourget train station as part of a deportation of a thousand internees from Drancy. At Bourget, French police and Nazi officials loaded the women, men, and children onto cattle cars, cramming an average of seventy individuals in each. In Jacques's memory, the French police were convivial, offering words of encouragement and hope. The German overseers, by contrast, exhibited what Jacques described as "unbelievable cruelty" and were "savage, inhumane to the last." Each prisoner was given a small loaf of bread and an inedible piece of cheese; each car was stocked with two pails of water to be shared by those locked within. The doors were slammed shut, a whistle shrieked, and the convoy began to roll out of Paris.

The trip across Europe was ghastly: airless, cold, dark, panic-inducing. Even those who were well traveled and knew intimately the spiderweb of Europe's rail lines couldn't reconstruct their route. In Jacques's car, a fellow prisoner broke down and had to be subdued by the others. In other boxcars, prisoners died even as the convoy moved eastward. When the train ground to a halt, it was not at its destination, Auschwitz, but at a way station in central Germany, Kassel. The doors were opened to reveal that the station was manned by Captain Theodor Dannecker, the official in charge of organizing the deportation of French Jewry. On his orders, men under the age of fifty were told to disembark. From this group, a hundred and fifty men were selected. But Emmanuel was sent back onto the train, rejoining his family. His cousins Jacques and Maurice, however, were kept on the tracks. As Jacques recalled: "When the women realized they were going to be separated from their husbands, when the mothers realized that they would from then on be far from their sons, when the elderly and the children thought themselves forever abandoned, heart-rending scenes took shape: the lamentations, cries of deep pain, made even the toughest weep." The selected formed a line on the platform, "their hearts broken, their eyes haggard and moist, pale, their fists clenched, moving like robots."

This was the last of fifteen selections made at Kassel in just over three weeks. Jacques and Maurice were among three thousand Jewish men chosen there for forced labor. The men selected at Kassel experienced the highest rates of survival among all the Jews deported from France in 1942.[19] Both Maurice and Jacques managed to remain alive through long and devastating stints as slave laborers. Of the pair, only Jacques would survive the war. Of the one thousand Jews deported from Drancy on November 9, seven hundred fifty would be gassed immediately upon reaching Auschwitz. Among them were Emmanuel, Esther, and their nineteen-year-old son, Albert.

DAOUT EFFENDI

Four generations of Levys were living in Salonica when German forces occupied the city in April 1941. Daout Effendi was by now in his eightieth year. Living with him, under the surname Matalon, was his daughter Eleanor, Eleanor's husband, Abram, and the couple's unmarried children, Allegra and Salomon. Eleanor and Abram's daughter Etty had recently married Joseph Menasse: together, they produced the light of the family, Lenora, who was four in 1941. Extended members of the family were abundant in the city, too, under a range of surnames—Alaluf, Amariglio (Amarilio), Carmona, Errera, Hasson, Matalon, Modiano, Salem.

The last letter to travel from Salonica to Rio prior to the German occupation of Greece was dated March 7, 1941. It was written by Daout Effendi. I am sure you have written home, father assured son, though my last six letters have gone unanswered. Communications in and out of Greece were faulty, Daout Effendi lamented—who knew what letters had been lost. The family patriarch had not heard from his son Emmanuel in Paris for six months, since early November 1940. He assumed Emmanuel was in occupied France, capable of neither receiving nor sending news. Leon assured his father that all this was typical of wartime. "You mustn't forget that we are at war," he wrote, as if Daout Effendi could have forgotten. Since Italy had entered the conflict, mail service from Brazil had been broken, as the fighting had siphoned off the ships that normally carried the post. "Here in South America," Leon explained, "our communications have been almost entirely cut off from Europe."

The loss of communication with Leon was one sharp thorn in Daout Effendi's side. The quarterly stipends that Leon had been sending his father for some years, too, had been failing to reach him, despite Leon's efforts to route payment via the United States. Through 1940, Daout Effendi struggled to pay off debts to friends and colleagues, and he postponed cataract surgery to help manage his finances. In the last of Daout Effendi's letters to reach Rio, the patriarch wrote, "It is true that I have paid off my debts, except for my mortgage, on which I continue to pay interest regularly." Daout Effendi went on to confess: "But because of the actual circumstances, I have begun to suffer, and for this, I ask you again to think of me if your economic situation permits. If not, do not worry."

Within a month—possibly even before Daout Effendi's letter reached Leon's hands—Germany invaded Greece. By April, German troops were marching on Salonica. By June, all of Greece was fully occupied by the Axis powers and the country divided among Germany, Italy, and Bulgaria. As central Greek Macedonia (including its capital, Salonica) fell within the German zone, the vast majority of Greek Jewry became, by force, subjects of German rule.

Daout Effendi's grandson Salomon had already been pressed into war. The young man had been called up by the Greek army in 1940, after Mussolini's armies invaded Greece. The Greek-Italian War pushed thousands of young Jewish men into service. Some entered voluntarily, as a demonstration of patriotism. Others, like Salomon, were called to duty. The Greek infantry, which had undergone a rearmament campaign under the Metaxas dictator-

Isidore Levy (no known relation) poses with gas mask while serving in the Greek army, 1940

ship, managed to rebuff Italian forces and push into Albanian territory. The victory was short-lived. When Germany entered the fray in April 1941, Greek advances were rolled back. At some point in the struggle, Salomon suffered a leg injury, was taken as a prisoner of war, and put in a military hospital in Ravenna.

With communications between Italy and Greece at a standstill, Salomon reached out to his family in the only way he knew how: through his uncle in Rio de Janeiro. "Happily, I am being treated very very well," he confided to Leon. Salomon was anxious for Leon to notify his mother and grandfather of his circumstances. He also begged his uncle to send what money he could. Leon wired Salomon three hundred lira through a bank in Milan. It proved harder to fulfill his promise to inform Eleanor and Daout Effendi of Salomon's situation. Neither telegram nor letter reached their mark. What happened to Salomon next is not known. He may have found his way back to Salonica with other released POWs: his fellow Jewish veteran Isaac Nehama, who would later testify to his wartime experiences at the trial of Adolf Eichmann, made the journey home from Italy on foot, over three terrible weeks.[1] Or it may be that Salomon was deported to Auschwitz directly from the hospital, as was true of other recuperating Greek Jewish veterans.[2]

It would take surviving members of the extended Levy family years to piece together what happened in their native city in the ensuing months. Many stories would later be glossed over in correspondence. Others simply couldn't be relayed—there were no survivors to tell them. What was discussed in person (during postwar reunions in England, France, Spain, Portugal, Greece, or Israel, for example) is impossible to determine. However, we do know that in February 1941, Leon assured his father that he was privy to detailed reports on the war by radio, which allowed him to be current "hour by hour with the development of military operations" in Europe. Yet for nearly three years—from March 1941 to January 1944—Leon received no correspondence from the continent. By late 1941, facts gave way to rumors, and even these were few and far between. When Estherina wrote her husband from the mountain retreat of Campos do Jordão in August 1941 to ask if Leon knew what had become of her relatives in France, his response was vague. He sent Estherina a map of France on which he drew, roughly, the boundaries of occupied France and the French "free zone." He was aware that Estherina's sister Beatrice had fled Lyon for Bordeaux in anticipation of the German assault on France, only to return when that city fell into German hands. He had not heard of the rest of the family in months.

The news from home, had it reached Leon's hands, would have been bitter. After the occupation of Salonica, one of the first actions of the German authorities was to close the Jewish Community offices and begin a systematic pillaging of the Community's Jewish books, manuscripts, illuminated *Megillot* (Scrolls of Esther), archives, Torah scrolls, and synagogue ornaments. The plunder extended to libraries public and private whose holdings German representatives had catalogued even before the invasion. Within a few weeks, the Einsatzstab Reichsleiter Rosenberg had looted nearly 4,000 volumes from ten *yeshivot* (rabbinical seminaries), the 1,500-volume library of Salonica's rabbinic court, and the lending libraries of the Alliance Israélite Universelle, B'nai B'rith, and Mission laïque française, whose holdings numbered, collectively, over 6,000 volumes. In addition, 150 Torah scrolls were stolen from synagogues across the city. Some were sent to Germany: most were ripped apart and burned. After watching his own collection of historical and encyclopedia works despoiled (along with so much else), the Salonican Jewish intellectual Joseph Nehama lamented: "At the moment, the Jewish community of Salonica, which prided itself on spiritual riches accumulated over half a millennium, is without books."[3] In his testimony at the Eichmann trial, Isaac Nehama (no relation to Joseph) recalled the city's learned men weeping in the aftermath of the pillaging, keening, "These books matter, above all."[4]

At the same time, an intense famine was taking hold in Greece and Salonica was hit hard. The famine had begun earlier, during the war with Italy, and it intensified after the German occupation as the authorities claimed the nation's fresh food supply, including fish pulled from the sea.[5] With Italy diverting wheat southward and Germany diverting it northward, prices for essential food in Greece—olive oil, beans, eggs, wheat, olives—skyrocketed. The bread supply was insufficient and irregular; vegetables and fruit were rarely seen at market; meat became an unheard-of scarcity.[6] By March 1942, the Greek populace was said to be "in a very weakened condition," with no promise of aid in sight from the Axis or neighboring countries. That same month, the secretary of the Italian representative in Greece lamented, "The sole occupation of the Greek people seems to be trying to find food in order to exist."[7] Even the Swiss consul in Salonica could not get food. He confessed to his wife that over the course of a year of occupation, he had lost forty-four pounds. When confronted with a picture of her emaciated husband, his wife "could hardly recognize his likeness."[8] Salonica's inhabitants starved their way through the early 1940s.[9]

Many Jewish families left Salonica in the early months of the occupation, particularly those who held foreign passports. The Levys remained at home, suffering through the famine with their Jewish and Christian neighbors, and were in Salonica when the occupying authorities imprisoned the chief rabbi of Salonica, Sevi Koretz (a German-speaking Jew of Galician background). The occupying authorities also arrested the leadership of the Jewish Community and selected new representatives, installing Sabbetai (Saby) Saltiel at their head. When the Nazi authorities pressured Saltiel to deliver a report on the organization, leadership, and assets of the Jewish Community, to whom did the wartime president turn but the community's longtime chancellor Daout Effendi.[10]

Reading Daout Effendi's report today, one cannot help but feel that his punctiliousness—and maybe even his pride—got the better of him. Drawn entirely from memory, the report surveys the structure and function of the Jewish Community from 1870 to 1940 and estimates the value of Jewish communal property on the eve of the 1917 fire and again at the time of Daout Effendi's writing. It breaks this data down further by estimating the value of Jewish communal property neighborhood by neighborhood. To the seventy-nine-year-old Daout Effendi, the report may have offered an opportunity to showcase his knowledge and expertise. To the German occupying authorities, it would have read like a menu of potential spoliation. Certainly, the Nazis had other sources of information; they had been eyeing and assessing the wealth of Salonica's Jews for some time. Daout Effendi's resurgence is unnerving. This was a risky time to be accommodating, a point that was not lost on one so canny as Daout Effendi. As if to offset his service to the Nazi occupiers, he managed to slip a portfolio of property deeds attesting to the rights of the Salonica Jewish Community to a non-Jewish friend for safekeeping. Or at least that was the story shared after the war between his family and friends in Salonica, Paris, and Rio. It is possible that the very papers Daout Effendi hid are among those recently rediscovered in Thessaloniki in a safe-deposit box untouched since 1943 and bearing the name of the Jewish Community, or among the papers of a notary in Thessaloniki, only now recovered.[11]

As the weeks passed, Daout Effendi and his family watched the boycott of Jewish businesses, the confiscation of Jewish-owned radios, telephones, pianos, and books, the plunder of Jewish-owned shops and warehouses, and the shuttering of Jewish-owned movie houses.[12] All the men aged eighteen to forty-five in the extended Levy family registered with the German army after it was required in the summer of 1942. And they, like everyone else, became aware of a notice posted in synagogues and published in the German-controlled press on July 11, 1942, demanding men between those same ages appear in Salonica's Eleftherías (Liberty) Square the following day.

Daout Effendi and his son-in-law Abram (Eleanor's husband) were too old to heed the summons, though Eleanor and Abram's son Salomon would have been present, if indeed he had made his way back home from the POW camp in Ravenna. The nine thousand men who gathered in Liberty Square were forced to stand in

Portrait of a Jewish man held in Salonica's Liberty Square, 1942

the summer heat without hats for seven hours, performing grueling calisthenics. Many were subjected to the brutality of German SS, army, and navy officers, to the cheers of German spectators.

The men did not have long to recover from the experience. Within weeks they were again summoned to Liberty Square: this time they were organized into work battalions and sent across the region as forced laborers. The work was punishing, the food scant, and disease rampant, and large numbers of Jews succumbed to death.[13]

So much happened so quickly in the winter that followed. In late 1942, Rabbi Koretz was released from prison and installed, in place of Saltiel, as president of the Jewish Community and its liaison with the German authorities. The position required him to relay Nazi orders, earning him the subsequent enmity of the community.[14] When the Jewish Community found itself unable to raise adequate ransom to buy its men out of forced labor, the German occupying authorities seized the Community's four-hundred-year-old Jewish cemetery in place of cash and passed it to the Greek municipality, which had coveted the property for years.

The Greek municipality dismantled the site with the permission of the occupying authorities. Five hundred Greek workers razed the cemetery's eighty-six acres, erasing Europe's largest Jewish burial ground, including the graves of the Salem family that Fortunée and Ascher had visited just before their emigration to Manchester. The grave of Daout Effendi's wife, Vida, was desecrated: Sa'adi's distinctive pyramidal gravestone, too, was uprooted. Sa'adi's was one of thousands of Jewish tombs used to build new walkways across the city, some of which are still in such use today.[15] Others of the sacred stones were used to construct Aristotle University of Thessaloniki, on whose grounds fragments of bones of the Jewish dead were still found after the war.

In February 1943, the German authorities extended the Nuremberg Laws to Salonica. "One winter day we suddenly saw people in the street, each with a big yellow star on his coat in the area of the heart," Erika Kounio-Amarilio has recalled in her memoirs: "Salonika was filled with moving yellow stars which could be seen from a great distance."[16] Now Jews were forbidden to use public transportation or telephones, or to leave the city; they were also ordered to observe a curfew of five p.m., and to cease contact with non-Jews. "I remember saying, and hearing other people say: 'So, we will have to wear a star; it is not so terrible,'" Kounio-Amarilio wrote. "And then: 'So we will have to declare our assets, let this be the worst and nothing else.' 'So, we have to move to a smaller house and live with all the Jews together; it doesn't matter. It will be good to have all the families

Greek Jewish couple wearing the yellow star pose in their apartment in Salonica, 1942–1943

together.' But the orders came one after another, without giving us time to figure out what was happening."[17]

Also in February 1943, the Jewish Community was given eighteen days to relocate the city's Jews to two tightly circumscribed areas of Salonica, one in the city's east, the other in the city's western so-called Baron Hirsch neighborhood. Originally constructed to house Russian Jewish refugees, the Baron Hirsch neighborhood contained an infirmary built with money donated by the Jewish philanthropist.[18] From the perspective of the German occupiers, the fact that the area was adjacent to a railway station made it an ideal location. How ironic that the Hirsch neighborhood, repurposed as a prison, would continue to carry the philanthropist's name throughout the war. In the frenzied weeks of early winter 1943, "the city of Salonika presented a sight of mass migration of its citizens. Carts, carriages, and porters could be seen continuously, from morning till evening, moving furniture and household appliances from one end of the city to the other. A sight of mass forced eviction of thousands of families . . ."[19] At some point in this process, the Levy family house on rue Broufas, which Daout Effendi had worked so hard to keep, was emptied of its inhabitants. Four generations of Levys joined the displaced.

VITAL

I expected to discover victims in the Levy family papers, as no Jewish family in Salonica eluded the Holocaust. What I did not expect to unearth was the tormenting story of a great-grandson of Sa'adi who was a documented perpetrator, who was said to carry a whip and wear an SS uniform. He was said to have raped and sexually humiliated hundreds of women; and to have painted the backs, faces, and eyes of men in the midst of deportation, as well as the train cars on which they were herded, to mark them for annihilation. He was said to have reserved particular cruelty for Jewish veterans of the Greek-Italian War. To have killed children in front of mothers and mothers in front of children. His own wife called him a sadist. Later, in trial, he laughed at his accusers. Vital Hasson (d. 1948), known as "the Jews' nightmare," was the only Jew in Europe tried as a war criminal and killed by a state, Greece, at the behest of its Jewish community.

Vital descended from a scandalous past, but of an entirely different nature. In the late nineteenth century, Sa'adi and his son Hayyim were dragged through the streets of Ottoman Salonica by rabbinical henchmen, chased by a mob furious at their challenges to the authority of the religious elite. During the Second World War, in a horrific twist better suited to fiction than fact, Hayyim's grandson Vital, son of Lentien (Leah a-Levi) and Aron

Hasson, served the SS as head of occupied Salonica's Jewish police (or so-called Civil Guard).

A native of Salonica, Vital moved to Palestine in 1933. When and why he returned to the city of his birth is uncertain—a number of survivors suggested he was already a murderer when he did so, yet there is no evidence to support this claim.[1] Some remembered that Vital was appointed to his wartime post by Rabbi Koretz and even that the Jewish Community supplied him with an office on Gambetta Street. In other accounts, he volunteered, or was employed directly by the German occupying authorities. It is known that Vital assumed the position of head of the Jewish police of Salonica in late April or early May 1943, when Jacques Albala (the previous chief of the Jewish police) was promoted to preside over the Jewish Community in place of Koretz. As chief of the Jewish police, Vital had authority over some two hundred unarmed men, all Jews from Salonica.[2]

Among Vital's first official acts was to volunteer himself as a bounty hunter. In May 1943, he crossed from German-occupied Greece into Italian-occupied Greece in pursuit of Jews fleeing the Nazis. Some of the Jewish women, men, and children who had fled southward, into Italian-occupied Greece, did so with legitimate Spanish, Portuguese, or Italian papers issued before the war—documents of the sort that Vital's cousins Ino, Leon, and Estherina had acquired earlier. Other refugees managed to obtain quasi-legal Italian papers during the war from two Italian consuls in Salonica, Guelfo Zamboni and Giuseppe Castruccio. Vital's plan, supported by the German occupying authorities, was to search Italian-occupied Greece for escapees whom he could identify personally. Once identified, the refugees could be extradited back to the German-occupied zone, whereupon they could be punished or deported, or both.[3]

Consul Zamboni recruited a young Salonican Jew by the

name of Shlomo Uziel to fly to Athens in an Italian military plane to warn the Italian foreign minister of the imminent threat to Italian political autonomy. By this time Vital had already crossed into Italian-occupied territory, where his search likely began in the verdant hills of Thessaly. Two hundred kilometers south of Salonica, home to a small Jewish population, this mountainous region provided sanctuary to numerous Greek Jews during the war, including some women and men allied with the resistance.[4] Remarkably, Zamboni and Uziel's plan succeeded. After much diplomatic maneuvering, Vital was called back to Salonica by the German authorities.[5] His mission to the Italian-occupied zone thwarted, he initiated a reign of terror in the Baron Hirsch ghetto, abetting German plans to isolate, deport, and annihilate Salonican Jewry.

The Baron Hirsch ghetto functioned for only six months, from March to August 1943, its short life span reflecting the alacrity with which Nazi officials carried out the deportation of Greek Jewry. Within the ghetto's wooden walls, which were surrounded by barbed wire, five control towers, and three gates, more than two thousand Jewish women, men, and children were jammed into five hundred ninety-three rooms. Disease and crime were rampant.[6]

Some families forced into this ghetto were interned no more than forty-eight hours before being deported to the Nazi camps. Others remained in the cramped district for months. From March 15 to the night of August 10, 1943, Nazi overseers directed nineteen transports of Salonica's Jews, totaling 48,533 souls, to depart from the train station adjacent to the Baron Hirsch ghetto. One of these trains would head for the concentration camp of Bergen-Belsen; eighteen for Auschwitz. The journey to Auschwitz took between five and eight grueling days. Nearly all the Salonican Jews brought there were gassed upon arrival by the

Mario Mariano on his balcony in the Baron Hirsch ghetto of Salonica, reading the pro-German newspaper Nea Evropi, *1943*

Nazis.[7] As each new transport left, Nazi officials pushed Jews from Salonica and its environs into the Baron Hirsch ghetto anew.

Herbert Gerbing, a twenty-three-year-old German SS officer, was technically in charge of the Baron Hirsch ghetto. But Vital appears to have been granted great latitude to execute Nazi orders on the ground.[8] Recollections of Vital's actions, which swirl through Greek-, Hebrew-, Ladino-, and English-language survivor testimony, are nightmarish.

Vital, it was said, strutted about the ghetto, using the glistening boots of the occupiers to knock down doors and people.[9] He raced through the ghetto in a horse-drawn carriage, and made "the best people" sweep the streets.[10] He built a makeshift prison in the basement of the erstwhile Jewish mental asylum, where he tortured the wealthy to learn where they hid their money as well as Jews accused of attempted escape.[11] In fact, his reign of terror went beyond the ghetto walls, for he pursued Jews who had eluded ghettoization, visiting and revisiting their homes to ferret them out.[12] He also stole from the imprisoned, carrying around the ghetto an open bag into which the imprisoned were expected to place what jewels or money they had managed to hang on to.[13] And he identified young men to be inducted into forced labor.[14] In the words of Bouena Sarfatty, "He was like a lion let out of a cage."[15]

Vital reserved particular cruelty for girls and women. He forced them to strip naked, searched their genitals for hidden money, sheared their hair, raped them, and pimped them to others.[16] "As a young girl, I was advised not to walk around the Baron Hirsch Camp at night," Lily-Nina Benroubi recalled, "because Hasson and his friends used to pick girls for the Germans and have orgies."[17] In the course of Vital Hasson's trial, Sarika Beja (who was among those demanding material damages from the accused) interrupted her testimony to shake her finger at Vital. "He took off all my clothes, Your Honor," she said. Her testimony stops short of accusing Vital of rape. However, someone—perhaps the stenographer, or a journalist—noted in the incomplete records of the trial that Beja's "face reveal[ed] her anger at her torturer and the killer of hundreds of Jewish women and girls."[18]

By August 1943, Salonica, like Greece as a whole, had been virtually emptied of Jews by the Nazis. A few thousand Jewish women, men, and children survived in Athens, three to four thousand were in hiding with the partisans in the north, and a scant few were secretly housed with Christian families in Salonica.[19] On August 2, a special deportation carried away the families of Salonica's wartime Jewish Community leadership (including the

Jewish police) to the concentration camp at Bergen-Belsen.[20] Before his own deportation, on this very train to Bergen-Belsen, Vital's father, Aron Hasson, publicly disowned his son. Eight days later, the last transport of Jews left Salonica for Auschwitz.

Even before Salonica was emptied of its last Jews, Vital, in the words of the Italian consul, had "come to realize that his infamous acts in Salonica have come to an end and that the Germans would reward him in the manner of Judas Iscariot by putting him on the list of deportees."[21] Aware that the Italian consulate was eager to rescue the thirty-four Salonican Jews slated for the last transport to Auschwitz, Vital cut a deal.[22] In exchange for his assistance, Italian consular officials promised to help Vital enter Albania.[23] Suddenly, a deal was brokered and eight or nine "Italian" Jews interned in the Baron Hirsch ghetto were removed from the list of Jews awaiting deportation to Auschwitz. Among them was Ida Levy, Vital's lover. The very next day, hours after the last train of Salonican Jews left the city for Auschwitz, Vital packed himself and his closest associates along with a number of suitcases stuffed with looted diamonds and gold into a German car bound for Albania. With him was his wife, Regina, and their baby, Liliane, and his lover, Ida, then pregnant with Vital's son.[24]

The party made their way to Albania, where Vital was detained in Kavajë by Italian security forces who had been tipped off about his passage by colleagues in Salonica—the very consular representatives who had earlier brokered a deal with Vital.[25] The detainment was apparently comfortable and brief, though when the Allies forced the surrender of the Italian fascist leadership in Albania, Vital and his group fled once more. Their journey seems to have carried them to (or close to) Dubrovnik, where Vital chartered a boat to carry the group two hundred kilometers across the Adriatic to southern Italy.[26] The dating of this wild expedition is fuzzy. It appears that the party left the Dalmatian coast in the late summer or early autumn of 1943. The aquamarine waters shimmered as Dubrovnik's iconic red roofs, medieval walls, and shaggy cliffs slipped out of the travelers' sight.

Vital and Regina's daughter, Liliane, was baptized in the Roman Catholic Archdiocese of Bari-Bitonto by Josephino Giuseppe in January 1944. The baptismal certificate lists the child as Maria-Liliana Hassan [sic], and includes a godfather, Agnelli Gino di Guido, and a godmother, Sulli Roza di Giuseppe. How long Liliane was linked to these people—and whether her mother, Regina, was with her during this period—is not known.[27]

Meanwhile, Ida and her newborn, Enrico, were registered by the United Nations Relief and Rehabilitation Administration in a transit camp for displaced persons in Bari. The January 1945 paperwork that documents their wartime experience lists both Ida and Enrico as Greek Jews who had come to Italy from Yugoslavia.

Ida's documentation named her father, Davide, while the entry for paternity on Enrico's form was left blank.[28] In the face of all that had happened, Enrico was named according to Sephardic custom, with Enrico a Ladino diminutive of Henri, and Henri a Sephardic version of Aron, the name of Vital's still-living father. Six months after his birth, Enrico was registered in Bari as a recipient of philanthropy from the American Jewish Joint Distribution Committee.[29] Presumably, Ida remained with her baby.

While Vital's intimates were safe in Bari, he was recognized by a refugee, who reported the war criminal to the Allied authorities. Vital was again detained, yet, to the irritation of international observers, released once more. Writing from Tel Aviv, representatives of the Central Committee of the Union of Jews from Greece in Palestine complained to the War Refugee Board that "we are at a loss to explain this leniency, and steps should be taken at your end in order to have him placed under arrest until the time comes for meting out to him the severe punishment he so richly deserves."[30] For a third time, Allied representatives apprehended Vital. The intricacies of his case now known, he was delivered by British intelligence to the Greek government in exile in Cairo.

In Egypt Vital's incarceration was said to be soft, marked by his free circulation in the port city of Alexandria. His relative freedom did not go unnoticed—in Alexandria, as in Bari, Vital was identified by a Salonican Jewish refugee who reported him to the Allied authorities. For a fourth time, the British police stepped in to capture the accused war criminal. Upon the liberation of Greece in October 1944, the British returned Vital to Athens for trial.

The immediate postwar environment in Athens was chaotic, however, and Vital managed to escape the grasp of the law yet again. After so many close calls, the young man may have considered himself invincible. At this point he returned to Salonica, ostensibly to retrieve riches hidden before his hurried departure. It did not take long before Vital was identified for a final time, this time by a group of Jews who had survived deportation to Auschwitz. The group apprehended and beat Vital, and then delivered him to the Greek police. Now that he had been captured at last in his native Salonica, the Greek authorities confined him to the Pavlos Melas prison, an old army base used by the Nazis as a camp for political prisoners during the war, where, once the war was over, the Greek authorities interrogated Auschwitz survivors upon their return home. There, on the eastern edge of the city of his ancestors, Vital Hasson awaited trial.[31]

DINO

Before the war, Vital's brother, Dino (d. 1943), was said to be "less than nothing."[1] For years, he was romantically fixated on a young woman from Salonica named Sarika Gategno, whose father was an apprentice to his own father, Aron. In 1940, Sarika rebuffed Dino in favor of another man whom she ultimately did not marry. No one in the Hasson family could forgive her.

Three years later, as the Jews of Salonica were frantically preparing their relocation to the Baron Hirsch ghetto, Sarika's family was visited by Dino's sister, Julie, as well as his mother and father, to persuade them to encourage the marriage. Vital further turned up the pressure by sending his crony Albala to beat up Sarika's father, and tear apart his tailor's shop, in search of buried money. Apparently, Vital threatened to "kill everyone" if Dino and Sarika were not married soon. Sarika capitulated and she and Dino were wed. But Sarika was so overcome by depression that she wore the same dress for three months and consumed nothing but alcohol and cigarettes.

When the Gategno family was deported, Sarika refused the "privilege" of being counted among the families of Salonica's wartime Jewish Community representatives, who would soon be deported to Bergen-Belsen. Unwilling to abandon her own family, she boarded a train to Auschwitz instead. When Dino realized he could not wrest Sarika from the compartment, he persuaded a German guard to allow him to board. The pair were then deported to Auschwitz.[2]

Sarika survived some three months longer than Dino, possibly as a subject for Nazi pseudo-medical experiments, or as a slave laborer.[3] There are conflicting accounts of what happened to Dino. According to Sarika's brother, Dino was treated terribly by his fellow inmates, subjected to medical experiments, and eventually gassed in the crematorium. Dr. Ovadia Beja—who spoke in defense of Vital's wife and sister in the course of Vital's trial—recalled Dino succumbing to diarrhea; however, Beja was not interned at Auschwitz, as he escaped to Paris in the course of the deportations. Yad Vashem's Central Database of Shoah Victims' Names records Dino Hasson simply as "declared dead" on August 14, 1943.[4]

Survivors recall a different end to Dino's brief life. Alberto Safan, a native of Salonica who survived imprisonment in Auschwitz, described Dino's final hours this way: "And they left [for Auschwitz]. Later, the Jews took matters in their own hands. They lynched him in the camp because he was Hasson's brother."[5] Safan's version of events is substantiated by the chilling testimony of David Bitran, another Auschwitz survivor. "I bring you the last will of the people who died there [in Auschwitz]," he told the court during Vital Hasson's trial. "People by the name of Hasson who entered the camp did not come out alive. We wanted to do everything in our power to have them punished if we came back alive."[6]

Over coffee and cookies in a café in Salonica on a hot summer's day, I asked Rosy Saltiel—a survivor of Bergen-Belsen and a friend of Vital and Dino's sister, Julie—to help me square the divergent accounts of Dino's death. Her gentle voice sharpened. Dino was killed by his fellow prisoners, she insisted: "There were witnesses!"[7] If the collective testimony is to be believed, it would mean that two Hasson brothers were executed for wartime crimes—one extra-legally, at the hands of vengeful Jews, the other through legal means, and by the Greek state. Both deaths are clearly exceptional in Holocaust history.

ELEANOR

The Nazis deported the extended Levy family from Salonica to Auschwitz in stages. The journey took roughly six days, in freight cars jammed with more than seventy people each. Provisions, light, and air were all negligible. Prisoners wailed from sickness, pain, hunger, thirst, and fear—some died en route, forcing the living to remain pressed against the dead for hours at a time. Eleanor's father, Daout Effendi, made this terrifying journey in his eighty-first year.

"I followed your father until the last minute, that is to say, through the concentration camp [ghetto] of Salonica," wrote Julie Hasson Sarfatti (1914–1997), the sister of Vital and Dino, to her cousin Leon in a letter sent to Rio from postwar Greece. "The news that I heard from several survivors who left in the same convoy and were trapped in the same train to Poland is that your father and his brother-in-law died in the first week in the gas chamber, since, because of their age, they could not be used for forced labor." Julie pressed other survivors for the precise date of Daout Effendi's death, but none could remember with certainty. "Life in camp was a veritable hell," she wrote, and deduced that after leaving Salonica in mid-April 1943, Leon's father must have died within the first two weeks of May.[1]

Eleanor's son, Salomon, "succumbed several months later, after being used for 'experimental work,' but he died a natural death," reported Julie. This could mean that Salomon was subjected to medical experiments, as were other Salonican deportees; or that he was inducted into the Sonderkommando, as were other Greek Jewish veterans of the Greek-Italian War.[2] "Of the women [in the family] no one has told me anything," Julie continued. "It seems that the[ir] convoy had no survivors."

With his sister Doudoun Molho, Daout Effendi belonged to the oldest generation of the Levy family to perish in Auschwitz. His daughter Eleanor was murdered there, too, as were her husband, Abram, and their three children, Allegra, Salomon, and Etty. The extended families of Abram and of Etty's husband, Joseph Menasse, were also among the annihilated, as were Abram and Joseph themselves. The youngest in the family to be killed was Etty and Joseph's four-year-old daughter, Lenora Menasse, known to the family by her two pet names, Nora and Nimica.

Eleanor's father, Daout Effendi, was born in 1863, when Salonica was Ottoman, when his father, Sa'adi, could provoke the rabbinical establishment with the incendiary tools of a printing press and a violin. His great-granddaughter Lenora was born in 1939, the year the Second World War began. The two bookended four generations, yet they breathed their last breaths in the same claustrophobic space in rural Poland, inhaling a poison invented to eradicate vermin, in a chamber designed by German engineers.

In Paris, after the war, Sam Lévy estimated that his niece Eleanor was among thirty-seven members of the immediate Levy family killed by the Nazis after their deportation from France and Greece. Were one to stretch Sam's tally to the extended family, including the many branches of the family tree that reached outward from the proverbial trunk that was Sa'adi Besalel a-Levi—to the families Alaluf, Arditi, Matalon, Menasse, Modiano, Molho, Salem, and on—the number would rise exponentially. Only one among the dizzying number of relatives deported to the east survived the war: Jacques Lévy.

JACQUES

When the convoy carrying the first round of Greek Jews deported from Paris paused at the German way station of Kassel in early November 1942, fate intervened, sparing Jacques (d. 1989) and his brother Maurice—two of Besalel and Vida's three sons—from completing the remainder of the journey to Auschwitz. Chance caused the brothers' train to pause at Kassel in the first place. Had they been selected for deportation on a subsequent convoy, the selections at Kassel would have been fulfilled already, and the pair, together with their wives and children, would have gone directly to the death camp.

As it happened, Jacques and the other men who had been selected were lined up on the Kassel platform. Prisoners who did not comply with due speed were shot point-blank. Thoughts of revenge filled Jacques's mind, "hardening" and "sustaining" him (in his words) through the dreadful ordeal. Along with the others, he was put onto a truck and sent to a processing camp. Wielding whips, German officers stripped the men of whatever they held that was of value—a watch, a coin, a ring—burying the loot deep within the folds of their own pockets. The group was forced to march eastward, through the flat, verdant countryside near Leipzig and Dresden, skirting the northern border of German-annexed Czechoslovakia and into western Poland. The air grew progressively colder as the men walked, the ground icier.

The group's destination was Ottmuth, a small labor camp that was reputed to be one of the least punishing of the Nazi concentration camps in Poland. Nevertheless, the work was brutal. Prisoners spent long hours harvesting stone blocks in quarries, crushing rocks to serve as ballast along railways, building roads, draining rivers, and working to maintain the site of the Bata shoe factory, which was also manned by slave labor. The food was insufficient to support the massive expenditure of energy. Men died of exhaustion or became weak and ill. Those unfit for labor were transferred to a "convalescence camp" (Jacques himself put the words in quotation marks in a testimonial published in *Les Cahiers Séfardis*), where they were killed.[1] The euphemism deceived no one. Among the Greek/French Jewish men imprisoned in Ottmuth was one who feigned illness in order to follow his sick son to the "convalescence camp." Jacques recalled that this man's fellow inmates tried to dissuade him, for they knew that those who went to "convalesce" never returned, but the man would not be deterred, and thereby knowingly hastened his own death.

The Levy brothers Jacques and Maurice were in Ottmuth until September 1944, when the site was repurposed into a prisoner-of-war camp. But now they were separated, and that autumn marked a turn for the worse for Jacques, whose subsequent destination, the camp of Arbeitslager Blechhammer, further dehumanized him and the other surviving inmates.

Blechhammer had existed as a forced labor camp since 1942, but by the time Jacques arrived it had become a sub-camp of Auschwitz. In the spring of 1944, the camp housed 3,056 male and 150 female prisoners, most of whom were forced to labor on the grounds of the synthetic-gasoline plant of Oberschlesische Hydrierwerke AG, the same company that once employed Jacques's cousin Karsa.[2] The month before Jacques reached Blechhammer, the camp emerged as a target of American bombing. One can hardly imagine the scene that greeted him upon his arrival. Camp guards stripped Jacques of his civilian clothing, replacing it with the striped uniform of a prisoner. His arm was tattooed with a number meant to supplant his name, identity, and history. "We stopped being individuals and became NUMBERS," Jacques subsequently lamented, capital letters emphasizing the bitter sentence. "We were turned into beasts driven by handlers who recognized their chattel only by the indelible brand we wore."[3] Food in the camp was scant and inedible. The Nazi overseers hanged prisoners accused of various offenses, forcing other prisoners to watch the spectacle. When winter arrived, Jacques and his fellow prisoners froze as temperatures dipped precipitously. Roll call was scheduled before dawn, when standing in the out-of-doors would be most painful.

Forced laborers in an electrical workshop, Blechhammer, Germany

The inmate and slave labor population at Blechhammer was mixed, and included British and French prisoners of war. The POWs had access to slightly more generous rations than the Jewish prisoners and managed to slip their fellow slave laborers the occasional crust of bread or cigarette; and since some had managed to retain illegal radios, they could also communicate the occasional word of news. As the balance of war began to shift in the Allies' favor, the information was conveyed among the multilingual population through signals that grew ever more precise. So Jacques learned of the Allied landing on the beaches of Normandy in real time—or as close to real time as circumstances allowed.

Soviet troops, too, were on the march. As the Russian liberators approached from the east, the German overseers at Blechhammer organized a hasty death march of the camp's inmates in January 1945. Jacques estimated that some 5,000 women, men, and children were driven away from the camp on foot, while the remaining 500—deemed too weak to survive the march—were locked into barracks that were doused with gasoline and set afire. Before Jacques's eyes, 350 of the unfortunate prisoners were burned alive in a massive conflagration. Jacques was among some 150 women and men who watched, huddled together, "awaiting death by incandescence." The moments passed, silence fell, and the 150 realized they stood in the smoldering camp alone, survivors.

SURVIVORS

The sun was bright, but I could see shadows everywhere.

—Erika Kounio-Amarilio, *From Thessaloniki to Auschwitz and Back*

INO

In January 1944, as the Siege of Leningrad seethed, Ino Levy (b. 1895), youngest son of Besalel and Vida, composed a letter to his cousin Leon in Rio. It was posted from Curia, a small wooded town in the Portuguese interior known for its health-giving waters, and was the first familial letter to reach Leon from Europe in nearly three years. The cousins hadn't met for decades, though they had corresponded years earlier, when Ino worked as secretary to his brothers, Jacques and Maurice, for a firm that counted Leon as a client.[1] In those days, Ino was accustomed to taking a backseat to his elder siblings. Now he spoke for the family.

Ino's letter attested to the terrifying, sudden assault on the Greek Jews of Paris in November 1942. He detailed the arrest of his brothers and sisters-in-law, the flight of his parents southward, the escape of his nephews and niece. He recounted how he had evaded arrest because of his Portuguese papers—papers that were renewed versions of those that he, Leon, and Estherina had acquired in Salonica years earlier. For nearly a year after that dreadful November night, Ino wrote, he continued to live in the French capital, insulated by his status as a citizen of a neutral country.

During this dreadful period, Ino managed to leverage his Portuguese documents to obtain a new passport from Portugal's consul general in Paris. Miraculously, the passport was granted with the approval of the Portuguese consulate in Berlin.[2] On the basis of these papers, Ino joined some fifty Jewish families (a total of 137 souls) in repatriation to Portugal in November 1943.[3] With this voyage southward, Ino "returned" to a country he had never before visited or lived in. "Because of my Portuguese identity, I avoided the catastrophe," Ino relayed to Leon. "Not only the Germans left me alone, but the Portuguese government, in all its magnanimity, and in a spirit of humanity that brings great honor and that we will never forget, insisted to the authorities that it save and repatriate its subjects." What Ino did not know was that other Greek Jewish holders of Portuguese papers were accidentally swept up in the arrests and deportations in France (as, later, in Greece), and that Portugal's dictator, António de Oliveira Salazar, resisted coming to the aid of most Portuguese Jews in France until it was too late.[4] Fate had protected Ino more than the Portuguese state had.

In Portugal, police divided the Jewish refugees from France into two groups. Those who had papers issued in Portugal, which were considered by the government to be unambiguously sound legal documents, were directed to join the significant number of Jewish refugees already housed in Lisbon. A second group, of which Ino was a part, consisted of holders of "dubious" citizenship papers—namely, those issued outside Portugal. These refugees were directed to Curia, where their legal status was to be investigated. How ironic for Ino to pass time in a town famous for its healing waters as his family suffered.

Though Ino found Curia small and charming, he and his fellow refugees had been granted few resources, and were petitioning to be transferred to Lisbon. Their desire for relocation was understandable: the Portuguese capital housed large numbers of Jewish refugees, had a pre-existing Jewish community, and was a

European hub of wartime Jewish philanthropy and activism second only to Geneva. Ino's appeals to the Portuguese authorities, however, remained unanswered. In his letter to Leon, Ino suggested that this was because he lacked the contacts that Leon's own family commanded. This was an inadvertently insensitive comment given that Leon's father, sister, and extended relatives had already been deported from Greece, their historic connections useless in a time of war, occupation, and genocide.

Fortunately, there was a bright spot in Ino's life. Before his departure from Paris, he had met a young woman, a Jewish refugee by the name of Beatrice/Beatrix Asaria. Beatrice, twenty-five years Ino's junior, was Viennese-born, of Sephardic parents from Istanbul and Ruschuk.[5] The couple became acquainted in Paris, developed (in Ino's words) "feelings for one another," moved to Portugal at the same time, and planned to marry after the war's end.[6] Before they were wed, however, Ino was determined to right his finances. In a letter to Leon in Rio, Ino asked if his cousin was interested in collaborating on an import-export operation. Ino had made connections with a local production house, he explained. He was able to supply Portuguese wine, champagne, brandy, olive oil, chestnuts, and walnuts. With Leon's knowledge of Brazil, Ino postulated, the two would both benefit from such a collaborative business venture. Ino dredged from his memory the names and addresses of several import houses in New York, St. Louis, and Chicago with which his family had done business before the war. He urged Leon to make contact. Leon demurred, arguing that the products available to Ino were plentiful in Brazil and, in any case, that Ino's knowledge was outdated—he had long ago moved out of the wine and food trade.

Ino had no contact at all with his deported family at this time, and only the most intermittent contact with his parents in the

Ino and Beatrice Levy, 1940s

south of France. He was aware that his uncle Sam and aunt Anna had joined his parents in Vichy France in the spring of 1944; and he was also aware that in the autumn of that same year his father, Besalel, had required emergency surgery for an undefined stomach ailment. Meanwhile, Ino had no contact with the rest of the Levys.

Yet Ino was the first to supply Leon with concrete news of the extended Levy family. He also helped Leon in his attempts to trace the whereabouts of the family through the Red Cross offices in Portugal, though the endeavor failed. Even before the war ended, however, Ino had some sense of what had become of his family. He believed his brothers and their families had been deported to a "work camp" in "Upper Silesia" in 1944—that is, Auschwitz. He knew that the vast majority of Salonican Jews had been deported. In October 1944, Ino's parents, Besalel and Vida, managed to send Ino a postcard written in code.[7] It revealed the joyful news that both of Ino's brothers, Maurice and Jacques, had been found in a forced labor camp, alive.

In the summer of 1945, newsreels alerted viewers across the world to the horrors of the extermination camps. The first footage, taken during the Soviet liberation of the camps at Majdanek and Sobibor, was devastating. Ino saw the footage in Portugal, and it caused his normally steady prose to boil with rage: "You can imagine all the hate that I have in my heart for this bandit people for whom the sole claim to glory is the atrocity that the whole world has been able to see in the films shot in the concentration camps and if it were up to me I would slit their throats without any pity, all these nasty worms from the smallest to the biggest, to rid the earth of these bloody monsters whose ideal is to dominate all other peoples through the massacre and the torture of weak, defenseless people. Let God punish for all eternity all of Germany for the crimes that country has not ceased to

Ino and Beatrice Levy, c. 1950s

commit since it existed. One should not find a single voice in the universe that will demand pity for those who always close their heart and their conscience."

Meanwhile, the Levy family faced a range of logistical challenges. Ino's parents and brother Jacques had returned to Paris by the summer of 1945. Besalel and Vida were sick, depressed, and fearful of leaving their apartment. The family knew nothing of Ino's other brother, Maurice. Jacques had not heard from (or of) Maurice since they were separated the previous September, and sought to remain optimistic. After months without news, however, the devastated family was obliged to presume him dead.[8]

Mauricio Levy, c. 1950

Ino and Beatrice decided to remain in Portugal. There, Ino would prosper as an investor, and he and Beatrice bore their only child, whom they named Mauricio, after Ino's lost brother. A generation removed from Salonica, in diaspora from the extended family, Mauricio would inherit the most indelible trait of the Levy family, an aptitude for languages.[9] His cousins remember him also as a passionate train buff, who studied and rode the rails all across Europe.[10] It was as if Ino's son were retracing his family's jagged history by train, covering transcontinental crossings they had made decades earlier as travelers, émigrés, refugees, prisoners, survivors, and displaced persons.

JACQUES

Again and again, Ino's brother Jacques cheated death. He fled Spain for France on the eve of the Spanish Civil War, witnessed the Nazi occupation of France, experienced the mass arrest of the Greek Jews of Paris and the horrors of the Drancy internment camp, and was boarded by Nazi officers onto an airless train car crammed with desperate women, men, and children bound for Auschwitz. When their train stopped at a way station, Jacques and his brother Maurice were separated in an instant from their family. Jacques lost his wife, Flor, when she continued on to Auschwitz without him, and was separated from his brother Maurice in the course of their enslavement. He endured forced labor and starvation, and the degradation of having one's identity replaced with a number. With 150 other prisoners, Jacques watched as the Blechhammer labor camp was set on fire by Nazi overseers aware that Allied liberators were on their heels.

Jacques and his fellow inmates were liberated without liberators, for Allied troops had yet to reach Blechhammer. The survivors spent two weeks hiding in the nearby environs, subsisting on food abandoned by their former captors. When the Soviet military arrived, the survivors were given food, medical care, and the documentation they needed to walk eastward, toward the protection of a displaced persons camp. Jacques set out together with two other men. Temperatures plummeted to sixteen degrees below zero Fahrenheit and the men were so weak they could barely walk five kilometers a day.

As they traversed the countryside, Jacques and his companions encountered streets that were empty but for the flow of Soviet soldiers heading in the opposite direction. Along the way, the men entered a seemingly abandoned house in search of food, only to confront three Soviet officers. Jacques was fearful and tried to leave, until one of the Russians—a general—treated the men with kindness. When Jacques, his two comrades, and this Soviet officer found themselves alone, the general asked if the three were Jewish. Upon receiving a yes, the officer revealed that he, too, was a Jew—a writer of stories in the Russian folk tradition who became a soldier after the violent murder of his wife and children during the Siege of Leningrad. "Sublime Jewish solidarity," Jacques declared in his subsequent testimony: "you are not a pointless word!"

With the help of Soviet repatriation officers, Jacques secured passage on the steamer *Monowai* in the spring of 1945. Commissioned for service during the war, the *Monowai* was busy ferrying freed Allied prisoners of war eastward (if they were Soviet citizens) and westward (if they were British or French), along with Jewish survivors of the camps. Jacques boarded the ship in Odessa together with a convoy of French former prisoners of war. The accommodations and food were overwhelming for the recently released inmates.

En route, the boat paused in Istanbul. Standing on deck, Jacques could see the contours of the palace, mosques, and minarets of Sultanahmet, the old city. His uncle Daout Effendi had represented that capital as an official: his grandfather Sa'adi had composed lyrical poems in honor of its sultanic leadership. Jacques stood only six hundred kilometers from the family's mother city, Salonica—a city in ruins, its Jewish population effaced. The *Monowai* docked in Marseille on May 10, 1945. Jacques was the sole member of the Levy family deported to the east by the Nazis to return home.

Jacques reunited with his sons in the French countryside (the boys had survived the war in Franco's Spain).[1] Paris was his next stop. There, Jacques rejoined his parents, Besalel and Vida, moving in with them, into their former apartment, which they had managed to reclaim. The three were shell-shocked, each in his or her own way. Ino noted that his brother Jacques was convalescing slowly but was in despair over the loss of his wife. At some point in his incarceration on the eastern front, Jacques had lost vision in one eye. He needed, in his brother's view, "seriously to heal himself."

Paris, filled with memories of all Jacques had lost, was not a place for healing. Within a year, Jacques returned to Barcelona, his former home, where his boys, Jean Daniel and Henri, now lived. There, Jacques worked for the firm of his father-in-law, Isaac Carasso, with whom he had begun to work prior to his departure from Spain. Carasso, who had reached Spain before the war, was working to introduce to western European consumers a food native to Salonica if new to the European palate: yogurt, under the commercial name Danone. During the war, Carasso had moved to New York City to expand the firm (Dannon, in the United States), and now Jacques assumed control of the Barcelona operations.[2]

Jacques and Ino's father, Besalel, died in 1946, becoming the first of the Levy family to be cremated, in a break with Jewish tradition and certainly with Levy family tradition.[3] Jacques and

Jacques and Ino Levy reunite in Barcelona, c. 1960

Ino were terribly worried about their mother, Vida. After her husband's death, she remained in Paris, infirm and alone, still with limited French despite having resided in France for decades. Now Vida and her children were spread over three countries—France, Spain, and Portugal—a Salonican Jewish diaspora all their own.

VITAL

For months, the surviving Jews of Salonica awaited the trial of Vital Hasson. "Every single Jew in Salonika expects that this trial will be some vengeance for the tens of thousands deported," recorded a relief worker stationed in the city.[1] Twelve others were tried alongside Vital, including Jacques Albala (who also served as head of Salonica's Nazi-appointed Jewish police), several henchmen of Vital's, and Vital's father, Aron, sister, Julie, and wife, Regina, who were also accused of collaboration and of aiding and abetting Vital's crimes.[2] The trial was a civil one, brought by the Jewish Community of Salonica and conducted in a Greek court. In this, it had no precedent in all of postwar Europe. Of the hundreds of trials held to assess the guilt of those who assisted the Third Reich in their criminal acts, in no other country than Greece was a trial carried out in a public court at the behest of a Jewish community. Indeed, there is no record of any other Jewish collaborator executed by the state for his wartime crimes.[3]

It was, for Greece, a time of trials.[4] The experience of war had been catastrophic for the country, and the immediate postwar months were rife with division and recrimination. The frenzy to judge Nazi collaborators was stoked by the violent assault against communists initiated by the Greek government (with British and American aid) in the buildup to the Greek Civil War (1943–1949).[5]

A Greek constitutional act passed in January 1945 outlined sanctions to be imposed on collaborators, whereupon a Collaborators' Court was established in Salonica.

Salonica's prisons were quickly overwhelmed despite the repurposing of numerous buildings into makeshift jails, including the city's Byzantine citadel (Yedi Kule, a site of internment since the nineteenth century), and an old tobacco warehouse, once Jewish-owned. Vital was among the accused collaborators crowded into the Pavlos Melas prison, a three-story army base used by the Germans as a place of detention and torture. According to a British survey of Salonica's prison, the men imprisoned in Pavlos Melas in the immediate postwar period slept on a cement floor and were given nothing aside from a thin blanket and daily rations amounting to a tin of fish shared three ways.[6]

On July 2, 1946, a crowd descended upon Salonica's courthouse. Dozens of Jewish spectators were present, along with more than thirty plaintiffs, twenty witnesses, ten lawyers, a presiding judge, two people's judges, and the accused. The environment was unruly. When, early in the trial, Vital's lawyers argued that their client was not so foolish as to have used violence, the audience erupted into noisy shouts, drowning out the judge. The courtroom was cleared of the protesters but they crowded into hallways and stairwells, refusing to leave the courthouse. And they remained there through the break in trial and lunch and the midday siesta. It was early summer, and the courthouse was stifling. But the assembled wished to bear witness to the trial: to express their opinions about who had been asked to testify and who had not, and about what had been said and what had not; and to censure the accused, who repeatedly spoke out of turn, against the judge's orders.

Inside the courtroom, the witnesses delivered their testimony—at times flatly, at times with deep emotion. Some spoke of their experiences at length, without interruption. Others were heavily questioned. Still others wished to speak but were so traumatized by the testimony of others that they lost heart.[7] The transcript is chilling.

And Vital? During the trial, he smiled, laughed, and repeatedly rose from his seat to challenge witness testimony. Vital's interjections infuriated the judge, who at one point admonished the accused: "You are not to speak without my permission. This is not a camp here." Much of the time, Vital simply listened. He listened as witnesses described him as a monster, worse than the Nazis themselves. He listened as his wife, sister, and father denounced him. He listened to the silence of no one rising to his defense.[8] He listened when the judge ruled his father, wife, and sister innocent of the accusations lodged against them. And he listened when the judge ruled that his own actions had facilitated the plans of the German occupation, that he was responsible for the rape of Jewish women, the theft of money and valuables from Jews slated for deportation, the arrest and assault of Greeks who were hiding Jews, and the search, arrest, and deportation of sixteen individuals named by the Jewish Community as well as many more unnamed Jews and non-Jews. Vital listened as the judge sentenced him to death.[9]

After the trial, Vital was returned to the Pavlos Melas prison for roughly a year, until he was transferred to the island of Corfu, where he would receive the ultimate penalty.[10] Many observers feared that on Corfu Vital would escape the law again. In the spring of 1947, the Salonican Jewish newspaper *Evraiki Estia* reported with outrage (and perhaps a bit of paranoia) that Vital was moving around the island freely. He was serving as an assistant to the prison's chauffeur, the report alleged, and was at risk of fleeing to Italy, where his lover, Ida, lived.[11]

Against the protests of the Central Board of Jewish Communities in Greece, Vital had filed a request for clemency in the wake of his trial. This request was denied by the Greek minister of justice.[12] The execution was set for March 4, 1948. It was scheduled to coincide with the execution of six communists who protested that they did not want to be shot together with "the traitor Hasson." Vital in turn refused to be buried near the communists, for fear of contamination, and he lashed out at the other prisoners prior to his execution.[13]

Yet Vital was apparently calm when the day of his execution arrived. According to Jewish law, he recited the *shema* (a declaration of faith) and, with the help of a *hazan* (cantor), the *viduy*, a deathbed confession seeking God's forgiveness for wrongdoing. Vital insisted to the *hazan* that he had been slandered, and tried unfairly. His only sin, he objected, was his occasional mistreatment of troublemakers at the Baron Hirsch ghetto and his adulterous affair, which had resulted in a child born out of wedlock. Vital requested burial in a Jewish cemetery, and pleaded on behalf of his daughter, Liliane, whom he claimed was being mistreated in Salonica. He reminded the Jewish Community that his sister, Julie, the Community's former secretary, was familiar with its property and finances. Perhaps he imagined the information would protect Julie from harassment.

Among Vital's last actions was to pass a handful of messages to the *hazan*: these were promptly confiscated by the head of the prison. When he stepped before the firing squad, Vital faced a fellow Greek Jew, Shlomo Behar. A native of Demotica (Didymoteicho) and a survivor of Auschwitz, Behar had volunteered to join the firing squad in order to avenge the deaths of Vital's many victims, and to be able to testify back in Salonica that justice had been served.[14]

This, at least, is how Vital's last day was described in the Jewish press of Salonica. Was it accurate reporting or a wishful rendering of the man's final hours? The Levy family papers do not offer a counterpoint. Nowhere are Vital's crimes or his execution mentioned directly in the thousands of letters and documents that make up the Levy family archive. The closest we get is in a heartbreaking letter written by Vital's sister, Julie, just after news of her brother's final hours circulated in the Salonican press. In this letter, Julie laments that she had been abandoned by her family in France, England, and Brazil. "They say that you have the life you make for yourself," Julie wrote: "But what can a person do if they are drowning in the ocean and no one extends a hand? I don't ask anything of anyone because I already know what they are going to say. Now, more than ever, I feel completely abandoned to my sorry fate." Vital was dead but his immediate family would be forever haunted by his actions.

JULIE

Her home was immaculate. She soaked cotton balls in jasmine oil and positioned them in bowls that would disperse the scent through her apartment. She loved beautiful crepe-de-chine nightgowns and wore gloves so that her hands would remain soft and white and her nails pristine. She modeled herself upon Grace Kelly.[1] She served peaches cut in half, stripped of their fuzzy peel, filled with brandy and whipped cream, and topped with a cherry.[2] She posed for photographs like a starlet leaning casually against a wall, wearing a string of pearls, nails lacquered, eyebrows arched, and boudoir slippers tufted with marabou feathers.[3] This was before the war, and again later, much later, when the trauma of the war began to fade, even if it never wholly disappeared. In the war's immediate aftermath, Julie was demonized because of the crimes of her brother Vital, and because she was deported not to Auschwitz, with the majority of Salonica's Jews, but to Bergen-Belsen as a family member of a Salonican wartime official.

When Julie returned to Salonica from Bergen-Belsen at the end of the war, she and her father were among two thousand Jews from their city who had survived. What Julie and Aron encountered was a city in ruins. Salonica was unrecognizable. Entire neighborhoods had been purged of their residents. Sunken ships littered the harbor. The roads were impassable. Nearly all

Julie (née Hasson) Sarfatti Confortés, 1950s

of Salonica's synagogues had been gutted and ransacked. Here is how Cecil Roth, the distinguished Anglo-Jewish historian, described his visit to the city in the summer of 1946:

> Everywhere one could see traces of loot. I found a child in the street sitting on a synagogue chair carved with a Hebrew inscription; I was given a fragment of a *Sefer Torah* which had been cut up as soles for a pair of shoes; I saw carts in the cemetery removing Hebrew tombstones, on the instructions of the Director of Antiquities for the province, for the repair of one of the local ancient churches.[4]

The emotional terrain, too, was in tatters. Christians who had moved into Jewish property during the war generally resented those who had returned, or were unmoved by their plight. And rampant recriminations divided the survivor community. Those who had managed to hide during the war doubted and even blamed those who had survived the camps. Jews who had served in the resistance were judged by others to be communists, while those who survived in the mountains were suspicious of those who returned from the camps. Auschwitz survivors who struggled back to Salonica from Poland on foot found themselves spurned, and even physically threatened, by Jews who had come out of hiding. Some camp survivors slept on park benches for weeks.[5]

When fifty-three members of the Bergen-Belsen transport, mostly the families of Salonica's wartime officials, returned to Sidirokastro (a town some hundred kilometers from Salonica) in September 1945, the reaction within the survivor community was explosive. The leadership of the postwar Jewish Community convened an emergency meeting to discuss what to do with the group of perceived traitors. The assembled concluded that sixteen on the list must stand trial for their crimes, while each of the fifty-three, children included, should appear in court to explain what had earned them the "special favor" of being counted among the Bergen-Belsen transport. Other survivors were urged to submit depositions outlining the crimes of those interned in Bergen-Belsen.[6]

Julie's name, along with those of her brothers, Vital and Dino, her father, Aron, and her sister-in-law Regina, was on this list. She was accused both of having been a part of the Bergen-Belsen transport, and of using her position as a secretary to the Jewish Community of Salonica (for which she had worked since the spring of 1932) to assist her brother in his crimes.[7] For these transgressions, of which she would be found not guilty by the same court that condemned Vital, other Jewish survivors forcibly shaved Julie's head in the wake of the war, a punishment typically reserved for prostitutes who gave their bodies to the occupiers. When the brother of Sarika Gategno (the woman forcibly married to Julie's brother Dino) spotted Julie on the streets of Salonica after his own return from Auschwitz, he "wanted to beat her." But Julie protested, insisting that she was not to blame for Sarika's forced engagement. At that point, Gategno let her be.[8]

As Bergen-Belsen survivors, Julie and her father, Aron, were denied rations offered other survivors by the Jewish Community.[9] They subsisted on olives and bread. "I have encountered the lowest levels of human degradation," she recounted. In the requisitioned apartment Julie and Aron eventually shared with two Greek students, the young woman lived close to starvation, slept on a table, and suffered terrible pains in her jaw. Watching the wave of weddings that swept through Salonica's survivor community in late 1945 and early 1946, Julie mused that the newlyweds "don't feel like us and sadness passes over them like water over rocks in the bend of a river. It doesn't penetrate them. We absorb it all."

Aron was among the oldest Jewish survivors to return from the camps, and to many, this fact alone seemed evidence of complicity. It was a point that arose repeatedly in Vital's trial, wielded by some witnesses as proof of Vital's guilt and the "comfortable" conditions that "privileged" Jews had confronted in Bergen-Belsen, relative to the conditions that awaited their peers in Auschwitz. Indeed, a photograph of Aron from 1946 reveals a man of sixty-five who looks surprisingly youthful. In the context of the survivor community of postwar Salonica, to be sixty-five was to be ancient, a relic of a lost world.

Julie was thirty-four and a widow. Her husband, Michel Sarfatti, was also an employee of the Jewish Community before the war, and was included in the Bergen-Belsen transport with Julie and Aron.[10] Michel survived the camp along with most of

Aron Hasson, 1946

the Bergen-Belsen deportees from Salonica. But he succumbed to disease after liberation.

When the Nazis sought to empty Bergen-Belsen of its prisoners prior to the camp's liberation by Allied forces, they loaded most of them onto trains headed for Theresienstadt. However, the train that carried Julie and Michel and other members of the Salonican transport missed its mark. For two weeks, it meandered through Central Europe under Nazi oversight, even after Bergen-Belsen had been liberated. Finally, Julie and Michel's train stopped at the eastern German town of Tröbitz, where it was liberated by Russian troops.[11] But Michel would not survive to make the journey home.

A family friend who traveled from Paris to Salonica in the

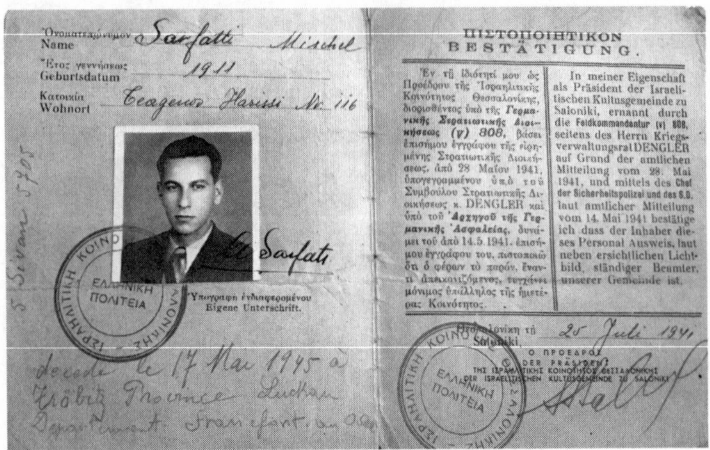

Ὀνοματεπώνυμον / Name: Sarfatti Mischel

Ἔτος γεννήσεως / Geburtsdatum: 1911

Κατοικία / Wohnort: Tsagenou Harissi No. 116

5 Sivan 5705

ΕΛΛΗΝΙΚΗ ΠΟΛΙΤΕΙΑ

Ὑπογραφὴ ἐνδιαφερομένου / Eigene Unterschrift.: M. Sarfati

décédé le 17 Mai 1945 à Tröbitz Province Luckau Department Francfort an Oder

ΠΙΣΤΟΠΟΙΗΤΙΚΟΝ
BESTÄTIGUNG.

Ἐν τῇ ἰδιότητί μου ὡς Προέδρου τῆς Ἰσραηλιτικῆς Κοινότητος Θεσσαλονίκης, διορισθέντος ὑπὸ τῆς **Γερμανικῆς Στρατιωτικῆς Διοικήσεως (V) 808**, βάσει ἐπισήμου ἐγγράφου τῆς εἰρημένης Στρατιωτικῆς Διοικήσεως, ἀπὸ 28 Μαΐου 1941, ὑπογεγραμμένου ὑπὸ τοῦ Συμβούλου Στρατιωτικῆς Διοικήσεως κ. DENGLER καὶ ὑπὸ τοῦ **Ἀρχηγοῦ τῆς Γερμανικῆς Ἀσφαλείας**, δυνάμει τοῦ ἀπὸ 14.5.1941 ἐπισήμου ἐγγράφου του, πιστοποιῶ ὅτι ὁ φέρων τὸ παρόν, ἔναντι ἀπεικονιζόμενος, τυγχάνει μόνιμος ὑπάλληλος τῆς ἡμετέρας Κοινότητος.

In meiner Eigenschaft als Präsident der Israelitischen Kultusgemeinde zu Saloniki, ernannt durch die **Feldkommandantur (V) 808**, seitens des Herrn Kriegsverwaltungsrat DENGLER auf Grund der amtlichen Mitteilung vom 28. Mai 1941, und mittels des **Chef der Sicherheitspolizei und des S.D.** laut amtlicher Mitteilung vom 14. Mai 1941 bestätige ich dass der Inhaber dieses Personal Ausweis, laut neben ersichtlichen Lichtbild, ständiger Beamter, unserer Gemeinde ist.

Θεσσαλονίκη τῇ / Saloniki, 25 Juli 1941

Ο ΠΡΟΕΔΡΟΣ / DER PRÄSIDENT
ΤΗΣ ΙΣΡΑΗΛΙΤΙΚΗΣ ΚΟΙΝΟΤΗΤΟΣ ΘΕΣΣΑΛΟΝΙΚΗΣ / DER ISRAELITISCHEN KULTUSGEMEINDE ZU SALONIKI

Selection from 1945 passport of Michel Sarfatti

spring of 1946—weeks before Vital's trial was to begin—reported to Julie's great-uncle Sam that the young woman was "brave, courageous, of superior intelligence and comprehension, but she cries a lot and it is necessary for her to leave Salonica." It was Sam who informed Leon of the survival of this younger cousin, who had been only three years old when Leon left his native city. It was Sam, too, who prodded Leon to support his young cousin financially. Leon sent Julie a modest initial check for ten pounds British sterling in January 1946, which sparked a correspondence that would continue, fitfully, for some thirty years.

"My dear cousin," Julie began her first letter to him:

> After the departure of the German barbarians from our poor city, I am unfortunately the only relative who remains in Salonica from the fraternal side. Permit me to introduce myself. My name is Julie, widow of Michel Sarfatti, née Hasson. My mother was named Leah Levy, daughter of Haim Sady [Hayyim Sa'adi] Levy, beloved brother of your deceased father

> Daout. You are thus the first cousin of my mother, and as a result we are second cousins. To clarify for you, my mother was the younger sister of Moise Levy (Kirbatch). My name is of the Sarfatti family because I married before the war, in 1941.

In this first missive to Leon (as in her first letter to her uncle Sam), Julie expressed anguish at Daout Effendi's death. Her great-uncle was like a "spiritual father" to her, she wrote. He was responsible for her being hired by the Jewish Community, the two worked together closely for eleven years, and they shared—despite the difference in their ages—the same "practical spirit."

Later, Julie would marvel that Leon shared Daout Effendi's "clean and precise" style. Her words were tender, though sometimes with a bite. Grief stricken as Leon was over the death of his father and brother and the state of his marriage, his letters offered little sympathy for Julie. True, he sent her money, clothing, and food. But while he often dwelled upon his own grief, Leon never asked Julie about her wartime experience.

In her second letter to her cousin, Julie reported that she had approached a Greek lawyer as Leon had asked her to, to help him learn more about the status of the Levy family home. The lawyer demanded a hefty fee. "With this sum," Julie wrote Leon, "my father and I could eat for 15 days"—and yet she acknowledged that the lawyer had expertise and the necessary contacts, and that it would surely be prudent to engage him.

Like other Salonican survivors who rushed to marry after the war, the very newlyweds she scorned, Julie was desperate for financial support, stability, and a measure of comfort. Nevertheless, she was cautious. Her cousins in Manchester, the Salems, offered to try to bring her to England, until the paperwork faltered and Julie realized she did not feel an emotional connection to this branch of the family. Her great-uncle Sam, in Paris, also urged the young woman to leave Salonica, and again Julie declined. In Palestine, Julie had no known relatives, and British immigration officials required a visa she thought unobtainable. There were letters in which she begged Leon to take her in—she could be his secretary, she required little in the way of attention, space, or niceties—while, at other moments, she said she must stay in Salonica. She had neither the concentration nor the energy, to face a move. She was obliged to tend to her aging father. "You must think me a great enigma," she wrote to Leon.

Miraculously, someone did come to Julie's and her father's aid. At a time when the leadership of the postwar Salonican Jewish community, mostly survivors of Auschwitz, spurned them as Bergen-Belsen survivors, Ovadia Beja was hugely helpful. Beja was, in Julie's words, "an old friend, and very dear." It seems as if he was asked to keep an eye on Julie by her great-uncle Sam, in Paris, who studied with Beja in Lausanne in his youth and also considered him a close friend. A native of Salonica, Beja had a French wife, was a doctor, and commanded respect. According to Rosy Saltiel (a friend of Julie's I met over coffee in Thessaloniki), Beja provided Julie with her first, necessary visa to reenter Salonican society. Julie's letters suggest that Beja helped her gain access to much-needed dental care, assisted her and her father in finding lodgings, brought them provisions, and facilitated Julie's introduction to a lawyer on Leon's behalf. At Sam's urging, when Leon shipped Julie letters, clothing, and other supplies, he sent them care of Beja. Julie insisted that her name not be placed on the outside of any package. Why this was so, Leon never inquired. In her correspondence with Leon, Julie never spoke of her brothers, or of Vital's trial, or of her vilification by other survivors.

Leon's correspondence, which Julie claimed (in early letters to him, anyway) as a lifeline, came in fits and starts, with years-long pauses. In time, Leon explained he could not maintain a correspondence of the intensity she craved—that even with his sister, Eleanor, he had exchanged only three or four letters in the decades that he was abroad. Still, Julie experienced the silence as punishing.

The emotional energy of her letters ebbed and flowed in those early years, with the tide of events in Salonica. Not surprisingly, Julie was at her lowest during Vital's trial—and later, when her brother's appeals for clemency were denied and his execution approached, she was in despair. "How egotistical the world is!," she wrote Leon at this time, thinking little about how it would feel for him, in Rio, to piece together so complex a puzzle, to shoulder such intensity. "People are so petty," Julie wrote, "they think only of themselves."

Economically, times were very hard, too. Julie found odd jobs—as a nanny, doing secretarial work—and still finances remained tight for years. Aron, Julie's father, was too old to find work, particularly after an accident left him temporarily unable to use one arm. In their poverty, Julie and Aron were not exceptional. The postwar economy of Salonica was in a shambles, the city bereft of its once vibrant mercantile community.

At last, Julie made a strategic decision. By the end of the 1940s—roughly simultaneous with the end of the Greek Civil War—the apartment Julie and her father had been sharing with two Greek students was partly repossessed by its owner, whom Julie found a very hostile woman. When a co-worker with whom she was intimate, Sam Confortés, invited Julie and her father into his large, centrally located apartment on the waterfront, she quickly accepted.[12] Confortés (I will call him by his last name, as Julie herself sometimes did, to avoid confusion with Sam Lévy of Paris) was seventeen years Julie's senior—as close to her father's age as to her own. Julie referred to him as "the ideal companion." Confortés was a cosmopolitan businessman and a speaker of multiple languages. To Julie, he seemed an apparition from a lost world. "This man is for me not a friend, a lover, or a husband," Julie wrote Leon; "he represents something . . . he represents all that is lost and doesn't exist anymore."

Among the qualities Confortés revived in Julie was her sense of Jewishness. Earlier, Julie had written Leon that she had no particular attachment to religious practice, and that she had only prayed in earnest for the first time in her life upon hearing of the mass gassing of the Jews of Salonica. Confortés seemed to shift her thinking. "Here in our home there is the true atmosphere of Judaism," she observed. "Each Friday night papa and Confortés go to Temple together and papa recites the [mourner's] kaddish with solemnity. My dear Leon, it is necessary to have lost this to appreciate it. Before the war I thought that I was not pious and all these ceremonies, the kaddish [hymn of praise to God], the [Passover] seder were for me a kind of pantomime that I respected by inclination, but I had no religious learning. But captivity revealed to me that I am Jewish and all the beauty that there is exists in the simplicity of our ceremonies . . ."

Confortés's attachment to religion was more potent to Julie in the 1940s than it was a decade later, when her preference was once again for a secular life. In the late 1950s, when Julie's cousin Karsa visited Salonica with his family, Karsa's young daughters were struck by the contrast between Confortés's piety and Julie's atheism, and by Confortés's deep kindness. One of these girls, a poet in adulthood, would write "A Survivor from Salonika (memories my uncle gave me)," in honor of Confortés. The poem includes these lines: "Afterwards, intact and unfathomably full of love/he married a gentle soul, quiet survivor of another hell."[13] These words contained some truth, but they were not entirely accurate about Julie, who was a tormented soul, yet outgoing with the right company.

When Julie's protective cousin Leon balked at her arrangement with Sam Confortés (and, especially, at the fact that the couple were living together though not yet married), Julie rushed to reassure him. Their arrangement did not pose the threat of scandal it once would have, she argued. Julie was economically independent, and Salonica no longer characterized by a tight Jewish community that maintained the power of social censure. On the other hand, Salonica could no longer boast a rich Jewish milieu as it had in the past. "You have been abroad for so long," Julie chided Leon, "you cannot know what solitude means." The vast majority of Salonican Jews had been annihilated: of the modest number of survivors who had returned to Salonica after the war, many had subsequently left. Nontraditional as her early relationship with Confortés was, it (and the couple's eventual marriage) allowed Julie to live the life she desired, akin to the one she once knew.

Still, the taint of the past was never quite behind those Salonicans who survived Bergen-Belsen. As late as 1957, Julie's friend Rosy would be questioned as a suitable match for her fiancé, Nico, since she had survived the war in Bergen-Belsen and he had survived in hiding.[14]

SAM

A single telegram brought Sam back into his nephew Leon's life after fifteen years without communication. Dated July 18, 1945, it contained six suspenseful words: "Collected details concerning [our] lost[.] letter follows." Sam composed the promised letter a day later and it reached Leon after a delay. The contents were crushing. Of the thirty-seven members of the Levy family deported from France and Greece by the German authorities, Sam wrote, only one (Jacques Lévy) was known to have survived the war. Sam's sister Doudoun and brother Daout Effendi were among the oldest generation deported and likely killed.

Sam's letter detailed to Leon the émigré's most intimate losses. Leon's brother Emmanuel, together with his son, Albert, were infirm upon their deportation from France, and the hardship of captivity weakened them further, steadily, until both were sent to a camp of "convalescence" (Sam himself put the word in quotation marks), where they died. Of the rest, Sam hoped for a miracle while expecting the worst. Salonica's Jews had been hit very hard. "They say that among the liberated (more than 300,000) who were found in Russia, there would be some Jews," Sam wrote. "Perhaps some of our own will be among them! Time will tell. Let God will that the blow is not too cruel." Of his own return to Paris and of his experience of the war, Sam wrote nothing. Remarkably, his letter to Leon was written on the same lined notebook paper that his father, Sa'adi, used to write his memoir nearly a century earlier. It was signed, affectionately, "Sammana."

For the next decade, Sam and Leon engaged in an intensive epistolary dialogue. Through letters, they clung to one another, each finding in the other something of what he had lost. Leon's father, siblings, and extended family had been murdered by the Nazis. Sam had seen so many fall to the same regime. Soon after the war's end, two more of his siblings (Besalel and Rachel, neither of whom had been in the camps) died, leaving Sam the last of his generation.

These traumatic times inspired intimacy, though relationships could prove fragile. At some point during the war, Sam and Anna had a falling-out with their daughter, Suzanne. By Sam's telling, Suzanne had waged a "tricky revolution" against her parents after she married a wealthy man. (Rachel Carmona echoed her brother's account, saying that Suzanne spurned her parents after she came into money.) By the end of 1945, neither Sam nor Anna had communicated with their daughter "in many years." In time, the grandparents would not be invited to the wedding of their granddaughter, Simone, despite an expansive guest list. "It is the greatest sadness in our life," Sam confessed, "and we submit to it with superhuman resignation."

Sam's ruptured relationship with his daughter made his reunion with his nephew especially emotional. "You have written to me as an affectionate son," Sam wrote Leon. "I wish also to be like a tender father . . ." Indeed, the two did come to love each other like father and son, and—like some parents and children—they exchanged barbs as well as words of affection. The two men had much in common. Both had left home at a young age. Both were quick to anger. Both sustained their correspondence in the face of private emotional failure—and no doubt in some measure because of these failures.

Meanwhile, Sam and Anna were managing with little. Their clothing was threadbare, their apartment, in Neuilly-sur-Seine, northwest of Paris, was cramped. A doting spouse, Sam fretted about how Anna (seventeen years his junior) would fare financially when he died. Writing from Rio, Leon insisted on reimbursing his uncle for the money Sam had loaned his brother Daout Effendi before the war. This was possibly a nephew's way of offering relief without bruising his uncle's pride. To Anna, Leon offered fabric for new clothing, which she accepted gratefully. When Leon made the same offer to his aunt Rachel, she asked him to send any cloth but black. "Mourning is in the heart," Rachel explained, "not in the color of your clothes."

Immediately upon his return to Paris, Sam threw himself into volunteering for the Union des Israélites Séfardis de France and the Association Culturelle Sépharadite de Paris, organizations focused on the financial needs and cultural contributions of Sephardic Jews in France. Quickly, however, Sam realized that the complexity of the postwar period required the particular skill set of the Levy family, journalism. With the initial support of the American Jewish Joint Distribution Committee, Sam founded a new journal, *Les Cahiers Séfardis*, that would appear thirteen times between 1946 and 1949 (once in 1946 and quarterly for each of the following three years). The periodical was dedicated to exploring the richness of Sephardic culture, to documenting the extent of wartime loss, and to assessing the postwar needs of Sephardic Jews across Europe. Day and night Sam pursued this endeavor, with Anna working alongside him. Never one for understatement, Sam described it as a "titan's labor."

Elements of *Les Cahiers Séfardis* (and another, smaller journal

Sam published at this time, *Les Foyers Séfardis*) were reminiscent of the Levy family's earliest French- and Ladino-language newspapers, published when Salonica was still Ottoman and newspapers were a new medium. As with the Levy family's earlier publications, *Les Cahiers Séfardis* was an in-house affair—Sam and Anna actually produced the journal in their small apartment. The contents were mostly written by Sam, under his own name or a variety of pseudonyms. "Correspondents" tended to be family members or friends, and each of the thirteen issues contained a number of hagiographic articles dedicated to close relatives: Sa'adi, Daout Effendi, Rachel, Jacques. In one issue, Leon contributed a piece on the Sephardic Jews of Brazil, and a cousin in Pasadena wrote of the Sephardic community of Los Angeles.[1] Even Leon's son Sadi Sylvain was the basis of a feature on the occasion of his certification as a surgeon in Brazil. Adding to the intimate nature of the journal was its dedication to Sa'adi (whom Sam called "one of the pioneers of the renaissance of Sephardic culture in the Mediterranean Orient") and to the thirty-seven members of Sam's immediate family who were lost to the Nazi genocide and whose names were listed in the dedication. The murdered included Sam's siblings, cousins, nieces, nephews, great-nieces, and great-nephews.

Familial homage though it was, *Les Cahiers Séfardis* conveyed a wealth of information about Sephardic experiences during the Shoah and about the Jewish death toll in the Balkans, topics most other eyewitnesses and journalists of the day were giving scant attention. Among the most devastating and impressive of Sam's achievements was to publish lists of the Sephardic and North African women, men, and children deported from the Drancy transit camp, including the deportees' addresses, places of origin, and dates of deportation. This information would not see print again until 1978, when the French historian Serge Klarsfeld included it in his monumental *Mémorial de la déportation des Juifs de France.* Klarsfeld notes in that volume that his team labored mightily to transcribe the information, as the original pages on which they based their publication were printed on flimsy, nearly transparent paper.[2] Sam almost certainly based his research on the same original documents decades earlier, his eyesight fading and his labor solitary.

Les Cahiers Séfardis was among the few publications in which Sephardic survivor testimony (including Jacques Lévy's account) was printed in the immediate aftermath of the war. Alongside the testimonies and lists of the dead, insights could be found into the Jewish death toll in Greece, in general, and in Salonica, in particular. These figures were generated by Joseph Nehama, the historian and native of Salonica who returned to the city after being released from Bergen-Belsen.[3] Nehama contributed original articles to *Les Cahiers Séfardis*, but he also conveyed additional information to Sam through their mutual friend Ovadia Beja. Julie, too, wrote an essay about the deportations from Salonica, insisting it not be published under her name. The resulting collective accounting (of the death toll in Salonica and of the number of survivors who returned to the city after the war) is startlingly accurate, given how soon after the conflict they were working, and their modest resources.

This work weighed heavily on Sam. By the time the fourth installment of *Les Cahiers Séfardis* appeared, he was exhausted. Not only was he in charge of the administrative aspects of the journal, but he also did the rigorous and emotionally wrenching fact-finding, and much of the editing. He and Anna had no assistants. It was an enormous help when the Joint Distribution Committee loaned Sam an Underwood typewriter.[4] When an issue of *Les Cahiers Séfardis* was printed, the cumulative papers weighed 125 kilos, requiring Sam to take twelve or fifteen bus rides to distribute the material. Leon advised his uncle to slow down, to which Sam responded: "My dear friend, in rest my head works with intensity, so that I am as fatigued as if I walked in the woods. The work relaxes me and I think only of this subject."

Like the Levy family's earlier generation of newspapers, *Les Cahiers Séfardis* was culturally and historically significant if financially unprofitable.[5] Though Sam and Anna distributed the journal to nearly 900 families, only 225 were paying subscribers. And after the Joint Distribution Committee terminated its subsidy in late winter 1947, the financial situation became far worse.[6] Needless to say, all Sam's efforts were unpaid although, as he emphasized to Leon, worthwhile because of his boundless devotion to "Sephardism," a philo-Sephardic cause that was more or less of his own creation.[7] In Sam's words, his work granted him profound satisfaction not known by most, leading him to pursue his "apostolate" with joy, a comment destined to drive his nephew Leon crazy for its Christian overtones and grandiosity.

Sam and Leon fought over the way *Les Cahiers Séfardis* should be handled. Sam wanted Leon to promote the journal actively, and to fund-raise on its behalf. Leon was also critical of Sam's notion of Sephardism, which he found out of touch with the postwar world. In Leon's view, after the Holocaust, Jews had an obligation to support their fellow Jews and not simply their tribe. Leon was also annoyed that Sam seemed more invested in supporting survivors in France than those in Greece, Serbia, or Bulgaria, all Sephardic centers of southeastern Europe devastated by the war. Sam insisted that his cause had allies across the globe, and that it was Leon alone who questioned its value. Recriminations flew, with Leon accusing Sam of hypocrisy and Sam accusing Leon of not listening. "I told you earlier that we did not speak the same language," Sam wrote Leon. "We do not see the same way at all, neither people nor life through the same glasses. Men are like this. We all have faults and qualities. One contradicts himself, the other is stubborn. One does not remember what he writes, the other repeats himself from morning to night." The pair would quarrel, make up, and fight all over again—all by letter, and with the built-in delay imposed by overseas mail.

The question of Zionism and, in time, of the creation of the state of Israel, muddied the waters further. Early in his life, when the idea of Jews claiming or negotiating their way to a Jewish state was a nascent idea, implausible to many, Sam had denounced Zionism in the pages of Salonica's press. He had received criticism for this position, to be sure, but it was not an altogether controversial stance in the context of early-twentieth-century Ottoman Jewish society. Some forty years later, Leon (who declared himself "no Zionist" at the time, though he would become one) was afraid Sam would translate his support for Sephardism into a critique of Zionism or the new Jewish state that would alienate his readers.

To Sam, the problem with Zionists was that they tended to be ignorant of Sephardic culture and history, and oblivious to the importance of Sephardic activism such as he was engaged in with his journal. Sam felt his work bolstered Judaism and all Jewish people, and resented its dismissal by the Zionist establishment. Nor could he comprehend the Zionist movement's growing attachment to Palestine. In late 1948 (six months after the founding of the state of Israel), Sam wrote the American Jewish Joint Distribution Committee to ask why that organization hadn't cast its eyes to Turkey's northeast as a destination for Europe's displaced persons, since in that region (Sam explained) the "climate and possibilities are identical to those of Palestine."[8]

Sam's sentiments were elastic, even if his language could be bombastic. On meeting with a delegation of Argentinian Zionists bound for the new state of Israel, he criticized their naïveté, yet marveled at their conviction. "I think that if I were twenty I would become an Israeli propagandist," he wrote Leon. Sam yearned to have trees planted in Jerusalem's Mount Herzl cemetery in memory of Leon's brother, Emmanuel, and his wife and son, near the tomb of the Zionist leader Theodore Herzl. Herzl, he reflected, "did a kindness to our family" when he honored Sam's brother Daout Effendi with a professional visit. Should Anna's health improve, Sam dreamed that they would attend the planting ceremony. Unfortunately, the plan was never realized, for Israeli governmental officials informed Sam that the "technical requirements" of his request could not be met.

On the occasion of Leon's son Sadi Sylvain being certified a surgeon, Sam offered the young man congratulations and the following reflection on the legacy of the Levy family. "My dear child," he wrote:

> We have writers of philosophy, poets, composers of lines in the Levy family. You are the first doctor in the family. We hope that you will succeed and return a bit of glory to the name of the descendants of the first editor [Sa'adi's grandfather] Besalel Sa'adi [a-] Levi, who came to live in Salonica in 1720. The Levys have contributed to the development of progress among the Sephardim. You will do the same, and serve as a surgeon with honor.

In 1951, Sadi Sylvain paid his great-aunt Anna and great-uncle Sam a visit. He was staying with the couple for Yom Kippur when Sadi Sylvain was granted the honor of leading the congregation in the blessing before the weekly Torah reading. When the visitor was called to the *teva* [the Ladino term for the elevated platform where the Torah is read], the cantor welcomed him as the great-grandson of Sa'adi Besalel a-Levi, the grandson of Daout

Effendi, and the nephew of Emmanuel. The community inclined toward the *teva* with anticipation, Sam later recounted, and his own eyes filled with tears of joy.

A measure of stability had returned to Sam's life by the 1950s. He and Anna were recently reunited with their daughter, who had divorced her first husband and remarried. Now close with their grandchildren, the couple celebrated the birth of a great-grandchild. *Les Cahiers* had folded, but Sam was busy writing another book—a history of the Jews of Spain designed for juvenile readers.

LEON

For two and a half agonizing years, from the summer of 1941 to January 1944, Leon received not a single family letter from Europe. His import business, dependent on goods from the continent, was at a standstill. His son, Sadi Sylvain, was consumed by his medical studies. Leon exchanged only occasional letters with his wife, Estherina, for the couple were not on good terms. She lived hundreds of kilometers away, in various mountain towns in the state of São Paulo. By the mid-1940s, husband and wife had not seen each other for several years, though they did continue to correspond.

Leon considered himself "well informed" about the goings-on in Europe from British and American news. He knew, as early as March 1944, that the Nazis had deported the Jews of Salonica. Through the summer of 1944, he braced for bad news about the family, aware that "deportation" was a dark euphemism: "You know what this word means," Leon wrote his cousin Ino, not daring to put the translation to paper. It would take time to understand the vast scale of destruction.

As 1944 turned into 1945 and the Germans' defeats mounted, Leon wrote the Jewish Community of Salonica for information again and again. He seemed mystified by the lack of response. Not only did Leon crave information about his loved ones, but also he wished to make contact with someone who could accept support from the União dos Israelitas Sefardim do Brasil, a philanthropic organization he had founded in Rio to disperse aid to Sephardic Jews in war-torn Europe. Was Salonica's Jewish Community so disorganized, Leon mused, that its representatives couldn't reply to an offer of aid? Were they so wealthy as to be indifferent to charitable donations from Brazil? The questions revealed just how much Leon did not yet know.

In July 1945, two months after Germany surrendered to Soviet forces, Leon received that terrible letter from his uncle outlining the extent of the family's losses. Shortly after digesting his uncle's devastating news, Leon recited the mourner's kaddish (the Jewish prayer of mourning) for his father for the first time. This was within days of the United States dropping the atomic bomb on Hiroshima. By now, the war was rushing headlong to its bitter conclusion.

Leon found himself preoccupied with the fate of his father. In his eighty-first year, Daout Effendi would have been among the oldest generation victimized by the Nazis; Leon assumed his father would have had the strength neither to survive nor to "martyr himself." Leon imagined that he would travel to Europe to assess the losses, and to seek out Daout Effendi's remains. His improbable hope was to return his father's body to Salonica for burial alongside his mother, Vida, Daout Effendi's wife of more than five decades. Perhaps he could contact the Jewish community near where Daout Effendi died, to seek help with his disinterment, wondered Leon. Could not the date and place of Daout Effendi's death be pinpointed?

To these questions, Leon's cousin Julie offered concrete responses. Daout Effendi had certainly been deported with his daughter, Eleanor, and her family, Julie reported in early 1946.

What was more, the cemetery of Salonica had been razed, its stones used by the Nazis to build a swimming pool. (The tombstones were also used by Greek Christians in the construction of churches, walkways, homes, and the Aristotle University of Thessaloniki, though Julie did not write this in her letter.) There was no longer any Jewish cemetery in the city to which Daout Effendi's body could be returned, no longer a stone for Vida standing in wait for its match. "I will never be able to go cry and pray at the tomb of my mother," Leon replied."[1]

False, incomplete, and imprecise information strained the mourner. In the spring of 1946, Leon received a letter from an old friend in Salonica who assured him that Daout Effendi had died in Salonica and from natural causes, before the deportations began.[2] Perhaps the confidante knew the information was false, yet felt it would offer succor, or perhaps the misinformation was simply sown by the circumstances of war. Leon was understandably buoyed by the news, and sought confirmation from another source in Salonica. The contact urged him to accept Julie's initial, sobering account. "It is necessary to be courageous and brave in face of the bad news," came the reply.

In the months after the war had ended, corresponding was trying even for Leon, the inveterate letter writer. Missives from Leon's principal correspondents could take ten days or ten weeks to arrive. His own letters traveled circuitous and lengthy routes—for example, from Rio to Paris via New York. Leon lacked contact information for family members in France who had returned home in the wake of the war. In some cases, he didn't even know family members' original addresses, having previously contacted them through his brother Emmanuel or his business partner and cousin Maurice. In other instances, the survivors had been forced to take up new residences after the war. Ino moved several times in the course of corresponding with Leon, causing a number of Leon's letters to miss their mark.

Leon's letters from the 1940s were confused, panicked, and full of despair. He spoke of his heart being shattered, of wishing he had been among the victims. "Inconsolable" was a word he used frequently. Leon channeled a portion of his grief into philanthropy. Working with the União dos Israelitas Sefardim do Brasil and the Red Cross, he collected and shipped dozens of crates of food, clothing, and other supplies to Salonica. Through his uncle Sam (and a bank account in Sam's name that Leon had established in Paris after the war), Leon doled out yet more money to his desperate relatives in Europe: his cousin Julie, his uncle Sam, his aunt Rachel, his sister-in-law Beatrice Florentin.

Rachel described her experience of the war years to Leon in the sparest terms: "Our successive flights through towns and villages took months and we lost all our things. It was necessary to move every few days from the monsters that kicked us from our homes. . . ." By the time she wrote her nephew these words, Rachel and her children, Victor and Carola, had returned to Paris. In Paris, hunger and deprivation were the war's inheritance, and Rachel and her children experienced both. When Leon heard of their plight, he sent his beloved aunt 3,000 francs: money, Rachel confessed, that "came just in time."

In Rio, Leon poured himself into the herculean (but ultimately successful) effort of establishing a discrete Sephardic cemetery that would exist in close proximity to the city's larger Ashkenazi one. This was fruitful work—to this day, Rio's Sephardic cemetery bears a plaque recognizing Leon's contribution.[3] What Leon could not do for those members of his family lost in the Shoah, he would ensure his descendants could do for him.

Leon, understandably, greeted the 1940s with anger. He was already predisposed toward strong and shifting moods, and the agony of the times exaggerated these tendencies. He grew impatient with his relatives abroad, at times because they wrote and asked for too little, at other times because they wrote and asked for too much. His relationship with Beatrice Alaluf Florentin, Estherina's sister and Leon's sister-in-law, was particularly strained. Beatrice's husband, Elie Florentin, was, in Sam's words, "trapped in the open street of Lyons in August, 1944 and executed because he was Jewish, his body abandoned like a dog in a charnel house."[4] After the war, Beatrice had nothing. "My only nutrition is from milk," she wrote, adding that if her relatives could get her sugar it would add calories to her diet and help her digest the liquid. Leon sent Beatrice funds as a favor to his brother-in-law (and onetime business partner) Elie Alaluf, Beatrice and Estherina's brother. Nevertheless, Leon also sent the widow withering prose, reminding her of the cruelty he felt the Florentins had shown him when he and Estherina visited Lyon as newlyweds decades earlier.

Leon was furious when he learned that his brother Emmanuel's brother-in-law, Sam Modiano, held a small collection of Emmanuel's things entrusted to an aunt during the war—a watch, some money, a few pieces of jewelry. Leon's family in Paris felt Emmanuel's brother-in-law ought to be allowed to keep the items, as he was close with Emmanuel before the war and in dire straits in its wake. To Leon, this was an outrage. Emmanuel was Leon's only brother, Leon told his uncle Sam, who was mediating the dispute between Leon and the Modiano family, and Leon was also the sole living survivor of their nuclear family. Only Leon was entitled to his brother's belongings, in Leon's view.

The family of Emmanuel's wife, Esther Modiano, was also eager to honor her memory, however, and may have judged

Leon's proprietary attitude as insensitive. After all, prior to her marriage to Emmanuel, Esther held Italian citizenship, which may well have spared her from deportation. But in accordance with Italian (and most other national laws of the day), Esther was stripped of her native citizenship upon her marriage to a foreigner, whereupon she was granted his Greek citizenship in its stead.[5] It was these Greek papers that were Esther's undoing, as she was deported from Paris with the other Greek Jews in that city on the night of November 4, 1942. As for Esther's brother, he, like Leon, had lost most of his family and was desperate for a remembrance of his sister and for the barest of means with which to begin to rebuild his life. Eventually, the family agreed on a neutral solution—to donate Emmanuel and Esther's remaining possessions to a philanthropy that would honor the memory of the couple and their son, Albert. The solution took years to work out, with each side suspicious of the other's proposals.

Leon was further crushed to learn from his cousin Julie that prior to the war his father had transferred ownership of the family house on Salonica's rue Broufas to his son-in-law, Abram, without consulting Leon. Since Abram was murdered in Auschwitz along with his wife, Eleanor, and their daughters, sons-in-law, and grandchild, Leon asked his cousin in Greece to begin inquiries into the feasibility of reclaiming the family house from the strangers who took possession of it during the war. Clearly, Leon's desire for his childhood home was emotional as well as financial. His business in Rio was rebounding and expanding. The process of reclaiming property in Greece, on the other hand, demanded a significant expenditure of energy—and some cost.[6] Still, ownership of the family home would offer Leon a way of offsetting any concern he might have had about being at a remove from his family. For the émigré in Rio, the two revelations—one concerning the challenge to Emmanuel's meager inheritance, the other concerning the legal loss of the childhood home—were painful. Perhaps Leon's furious letter writing, his attempts to write his way into intimacy with his family from afar, were to cover his fear of being less integral to the family than he wished? This may help to explain his passionate pursuit of restitution and reparation in the 1950s and 1960s.

FAMILIARS

I can't find my way around anymore.

—Leon Levy, 1959

LILIANE

Liliane (b. 1942) was just one year old when she was whisked out of Salonica by her father, Vital Hasson. They were headed for the Albanian border with her mother, Regina, and her father's pregnant lover, Ida. Within a year the child's parents were each separately imprisoned in Salonica, awaiting trial as accused war criminals. Vital, as we know, would be found guilty at trial, the other innocent.

And Liliane? After the end of the war, the child spent her first dozen years in Salonica, in fractured contact with her mother, her aunt Julie, and her grandfather Aron. During these years, Liliane lived unhappily in a Catholic boarding school in the city, without knowing why she had been separated from her family. When Liliane and I first met, in 2016, she remained unable to explain the unusual circumstances of her early life.

Liliane remembered her years in the Catholic school as difficult. She was routinely picked on by her peers and the Sisters, bullied for reasons unknown to her. Anti-Semitism was acute in Greece after the war, and this could explain the tension. It is also possible that the young girl was being targeted as the daughter of Vital, as it was not unknown for survivors in Salonica to act out upon the children of accused collaborators.[1] Unhappy, Liliane remained with the Sisters in Salonica until her thirteenth birthday

Liliane and Regina Hasson, c. 1952

and she felt she had been "brainwashed" to associate Jews with the killing of Christ. Jews were, however, an intimate part of her life. She spent most weekends with her mother, grandfather, and aunt, though not all at the same time.

There always seemed to be a gulf between Liliane's mother, Regina, and her sister-in-law, Julie, and father-in-law, Aron. Liliane was never sure why. A photograph from 1946 shows Aron and Julie standing close to each other, while Regina stands at a remove, hands folded tightly in on themselves, wedding ring still in place.

Julie, who always appeared proper, even grand, in photographs, spoke to Liliane (and the Sisters, with whom she served as an intermediary) in refined French. Regina, on the other hand, was closed off, and very hardworking—a woman with little time

Regina Hasson, Aron Hasson, and Julie (née Hasson) Sarfatti, 1946

to shop or primp. She spoke to her daughter in Greek, and never of the past. As for her grandfather Aron, Liliane adored him. On weekends and holidays, the pair would explore Salonica together, eating the street food that her aunt scorned.

As Liliane's thirteenth birthday approached, the family put plans in motion to move her to another Catholic school, in France, either because Liliane had aged out of the first or because the environment had became too much to bear. A photograph taken just prior to her move captures Liliane posing in front of Salonica's White Tower with Julie and Aron. Julie is looking smart as always, a handbag draped self-consciously over a gloved hand. Liliane hovers at the edge of the group, her height artificially boosted by the curb on which she stands. Like any thirteen-year-old, she, too, is hovering: between childhood and adulthood, dependence and autonomy.

Liliane's journey to Paris took two days by train. Her family found an escort of sorts, a Greek student heading abroad for studies. The trip was long and strange and Liliane young. It forms another figurative chapter in a book full of chapters marked by uncertainty and self-reliance. When she told me of the journey, Liliane admitted to its intimidating qualities but did not complain about having to travel so far from family. She has always been lucky, she emphasized, and learned early to take care of herself.

The institution to which Liliane moved in her thirteenth year was a simple two-story structure, abutting the train tracks that connect Paris and Brest, with an arched front door and interior courtyard. Established in 1901, the Maisons d'enfants [Childrens' homes]—of which Liliane's school was a part—were state-sponsored "medico-social" establishments that attended to troubled children, including foreign minors who found themselves in France without family. Today, it continues to be used by a Catholic organization dedicated to education and overseen by Sisters committed to an apostolic life.

Whether she knew it or not, Liliane had relatives in France. Sam (brother of Liliane's great-grandfather Hayyim) was there with his wife, Anna; Charles Molho (son of Hayyim's sister Doudoun) with his wife, Lily; as well as Sam Angel (grandson of Hayyim's sister Djentil). Though the connections were distant, these were people who might have chosen to act as family—still-more-distant relations in the Levy family chose to treasure their bond. Yet not one member of Liliane's larger family was aware of her existence until her eighteenth year.

Fortunately, Julie, Regina, and Aron remained close to Liliane, and Julie's husband, Confortés, covered the cost of her room and board. Julie's communications with her niece were regular until, in January 1959, Julie informed her cousin Leon that she had not heard from Liliane in over a month, and that she and her husband were disturbed by that. Julie and Leon had exchanged intimate letters for thirteen years before Liliane's name ever came up. The letter reached Leon at the start of his first trip back to Europe since the war, on a cold winter's day in Paris. "I have long hesitated to ask for your help in a matter," Julie confessed. "I have a niece in a boarding school in [France]. She hasn't written me in more than a month and I want to find out why. Would you be willing to make inquiries?" The name she gave was Liliane Hasson; the address was that of the Maison d'enfants. Leon agreed to visit Liliane, and both Julie and her father were touched by the gesture.

But Leon and Liliane would not meet until early March. After making the necessary inquiries, Leon approached Liliane as she sat in a window of the Maison d'enfants one long afternoon. Mademoiselle Hasson? Leon asked. Liliane said yes, and the stranger announced that he was her relative from Rio. "You can imagine the pleasure she felt in knowing it was she I was looking for," Leon reported to Julie. Liliane and Leon obtained permission to leave the children's home and meandered through the neighborhood together. "She is very nice and agreeable and intelligent," Leon recounted to Julie, "and hasn't forgotten that she is Jewish despite being in a Catholic school."

Contact between Liliane and Leon was suspended in the weeks that followed, as Leon's uncle Sam became ill and died, and Leon found himself caught up with the extended family in Paris. Sam's death was an occasion for a reunion among cousins. Leon spent time with Charles Molho, his first cousin, and Charles's wife, Lily, relatives with whom he hadn't been in close contact before. The couple expressed a great interest in Liliane and spoke of the teenager's complex history.

With Liliane's eighteenth birthday approaching, the Sisters informed Julie, who told Leon, that the young woman's time at the Maison d'enfants must soon end. Leon speculated that this determination may have been provoked by the fact that Liliane chose not to live a religious life. Liliane had a matter of months to secure a suitable new living situation, as the Maison d'enfants was to close for the summer in early July. After that date the young woman would no longer be affiliated with the institution, nor permitted to lodge with the mother of one of the Sisters with whom she had been boarding of late. If no alternative in France was identified, the Sisters announced, they would send Liliane back to Salonica.

Though it is not clear what Julie and Confortés imagined would befall Liliane if she returned to Salonica, their anxieties were considerable. Even a layover in Salonica, Julie stressed, could prove damaging to Liliane. Did Julie fear the return would place her niece at risk of social ostracism, emotional vulnerability, or physical danger? Or were her concerns more inwardly focused: Did she not wish to reopen her own wounds? In any event, news of Liliane's impending displacement sent waves of concern through the extended family.

Once again, the extended family was faced with the plight of a young woman no one felt capable of taking in. Regina was dismissed by the extended family as an unfit steward (rather rudely, it must be said). Julie was by now quite ill. Leon considered his own life too chaotic to take on the responsibility. And Charles and Lily were too advanced in years to think about housing their young relative. In Israel, the nephew and niece of Sam Confortés suggested that Liliane would benefit from the structure, spirit, and hard work of kibbutz life. With Liliane's approval, inquiries were initiated with the Jewish Agency (*ha-Sokhnut ha-Yehudit*), an organization created in 1929 to encourage Jews to move to

Palestine and, after the creation of the state in 1948, to the State of Israel.

The bureaucracy in Israel moved slowly, however, and weeks passed without any sense that the right kibbutz had been found for Liliane. Documentation was part of the problem since Liliane's baptism had been kept secret from the Jewish Agency, and it could not be demonstrated that she had Jewish parents.

Six days before Liliane's summer break began, plans had yet to be made. By mail, Charles and Leon bickered over the best course of action. Leon had by this time traveled from Israel to Salonica, his first return to his native city since before the war. There he made contact with Regina, who now made her first cameo appearance in family correspondence.

At the last moment, a breakthrough was brought about by Charles. The Jewish Agency would accelerate plans for Liliane's emigration to Israel and place her on a kibbutz. In the meantime, she would live with Sam Angel, the grandson of Sa'adi's daughter Djentil, and a relative on her mother's side. As Liliane readied herself to leave school, Leon told her to abandon all indications of her Catholicism. An urgent set of postscripts to his cousin in Paris stressed the point first in French, in a penciled scrawl, and then in Ladino, in blue ink. The intention was to give emphasis, though the result was to make the sentences infuriatingly difficult to read. "The Jews must not have any part of what the priest gave her. If she has a baptism document, she should give it to you and keep . . . nothing that would betray her to the Jews." Liliane did not heed her relative's advice, and still today keeps the baptism certificate issued to her in southern Italy when she was a young refugee.

Less than two weeks after Liliane left the Maison d'enfants for the last time, she boarded a train for Marseille. From there she set sail for Haifa, where she disembarked in a new land, among strangers who spoke an unfamiliar tongue.[2] Liliane was due to be greeted in Haifa by Confortés's niece or nephew, but neither appeared. Liliane was still seventeen. For her first night in Israel, she was housed with a representative of the Jewish Agency until she set off for the kibbutz, alone.[3] The family soon discovered that she was learning Hebrew and taking courses to be certified as a nurse. Leon returned to the Maison d'enfants to retrieve items the young woman had left behind—clothing, mostly—and to take care of her bill.

There are at least two ways to understand Liliane's move to Israel—one shaped by Leon's letters, the other by Liliane's own memories. Leon's papers suggest that Liliane was in crisis and haunted by the past. "If she is to be lost," reflected Leon, "she might as well be lost in Israel." But Liliane saw the move to Israel as self-propelled, prompted by her own desire to learn about Judaism and undo the "brainwashing" she had received at the hands of the Sisters. In Liliane's version of events, her life was once again being shaped by good fortune. The kibbutz proved a congenial home and there, immediately upon her arrival, she met her first husband.

In 1962 Liliane and her husband welcomed their first child. Her mother and grandfather came to meet the baby in the fall, in time to celebrate the Jewish New Year. But while Aron returned to Greece, Regina remained in Israel. She helped Liliane raise her children, was intimately involved in their lives, and, later, would follow her daughter once again when the family moved to Canada. Always, Regina lived with Liliane and her family. When I first visited Liliane's home, a yahrzeit candle stood burning in front of her mother's photograph, the frame resting on a star of Greek lace. Regina had died but a year earlier. If you had spoken with her directly, Liliane mused, she may have told you more.[4]

JULIE

In the postwar period, the grandchildren of Sa'adi a-Levi were scattered throughout the world. There was Ino in Portugal, Jacques in Spain, Charles in France, the Michaels and Salems in Britain, Karsa in India, Leon in Brazil, and Julie in Greece. One by one, the cousins visited Salonica, each reconnecting with the only surviving relative of their generation to remain in their native city: Julie. These reunions brought together family who became acquainted after the Second World War, through the letters they exchanged.

The first postwar homecoming was Leon's, which eventually happened in 1959, after multiple postponements due to financial and personal hardship. Leon traveled on a Greek passport by way of Paris. He had been a year shy of forty the last time he was in Salonica, when his parents and siblings were alive and the city's Jewish core vibrant and intact. At the time of his 1959 return, he was a man of nearly seventy years. Salonica was much smaller when Leon left in the 1910s; a city of 158,000 people. By the time of Leon's postwar visit, the number of residents had exploded to half a million, and the city itself had been grossly altered—by fire, war, and genocide, by waves of refugees, by aggressive urban redesign. Yet for Leon, Salonica was haunted by the past. "I feel profound emotion on returning to my home town after an absence of more than 43 years," Leon reflected. "Everywhere I look our birth city is transformed." To a distant cousin who had not yet returned to postwar Salonica, Leon confessed, "I can't find my way around anymore."

Family reunions left Julie feeling emotionally fragile. When Leon went back to Brazil after spending several months in Salonica in 1959, Julie confessed that she wept "like a young girl." A day later, she composed a letter to her cousin, her eyes still swollen. "It will take me a long time to get used to your absence," she wrote Leon, "because you have left a hole in our lives. Your dear presence represents for me all of the past that never disappeared and your affection reminds me of the loved ones that I loved so much, especially your dear Papa whose memory I will carry with me until my last breath." For days, Julie continued to set her table for four, as if Leon were still there to linger over food, drink, and conversation with her, her husband, Confortés, and her father, Aron.

Despite its transformation, Salonica provided Leon and the other returning cousins with a good deal of pleasure, in large part because Julie, Confortés, and Aron (until his death in 1964) were there to greet them. When Fortunée Salem's son Karsa arrived in 1962 with his wife, Pearl, and their two daughters, their visit fortuitously coincided with Leon's second return home. Karsa's family had traveled from Bombay, where Karsa had become a successful civil engineer and businessman. After their reunion in Greece, Karsa wrote to his cousin: "Our meeting in Thessaloniki was the happiest feature of our holiday and Pearl and the children were as delighted as I was to share a few hours with you, Sam, and Julie."

Karsa was one of the few Levys of his generation to refer to his native city by its Greek name rather than its Ottoman or Ladino name. Salonica / Salonico (in Ladino), Saloniki (in Hebrew), and Salonique (in French) were designations that most Jews from the city refused to relinquish, even after the city's conquest by Greece, its Hellenization, its demographic transformation into a majority-Christian city, their own emigration, and the city's formal renaming as Thessaloniki in 1937 (it had unofficially been known as such since 1912).[1] Karsa's choice, Thessaloniki, reflected not only how very far he had traveled, but that he lived outside the main Salonican Jewish diaspora. Karsa, perhaps not coincidentally, was also the only one of the cousins to raise his children as Christians.

Karsa's daughter Pamela considered the reunion with Julie and Confortés as a highlight of her family's travels. She and her sister knew little of their father's past, she told me when we spoke in 2017, and as adults they could only imagine how emotionally intense that trip home must have been. The girls were especially eager to hear Julie's story, but their mother silenced their questions.[2]

Some in the family proved unable or unwilling to visit Salonica in the postwar years, particularly the older generation of Levys. Sam never went back after the Holocaust, whether out of poor health, financial constraints, or the traumas he had known. His homecomings were vicarious, in print rather than in the flesh. After Sam's death, his widow, Anna, too, longed to return to Salonica, and Julie pleaded with her to make a two-month stay in 1966. Anna was deeply touched by Julie's gesture, writing that she dreamed of visiting her "native country." Unfortunately, rheumatism prevented her from leaving home. In his advanced years, Fortunée's husband, Ascher, was encouraged by his son to accompany him to Salonica—but Ascher's strength did not allow for the journey.[3]

Salonica was not the only site for family reunions. Manchester was another family hub, as the Salems were regularly visited by cousins from abroad. The sun and sea of southern France also drew the cousins together, while others reunited in Jerusalem, Tel Aviv, Lisbon, Barcelona, and Paris. Among these destinations, Salonica stood out. Though the city was birthplace to all the cousins, in the postwar period it was inhabited by few family members, and many ghosts. The city was a measure of how much the family had lost, and how very far its branches had spread.

Left to right: Jacques, Beatrice, Ino Levy, and possibly one of Jacques's sons reunite in Barcelona, 1960s

What of Salonica did Julie show the cousins—what was important to see and record? Some answers emerge in photographs taken during Jacques's 1960s return. The photographs, originally Julie's, are now in the possession of her niece Liliane, who spread them across her dining room table for me to survey in 2016.[4] In

Jacques Lévy, Julie (née Hasson) Sarfatti Confortés, and Sam Confortés on Sa'adi a-Levi Street, c. 1960s

one photograph, Jacques, Julie, and Confortés pose in front of Salonica's iconic White Tower, just down the promenade from the Confortéses' apartment. In another, the three stand close together in front of a crumbling building, its grand shutters closed against the day's light. It appears to be the Levy home on rue Broufas.

A third photograph of Jacques's homecoming features the reunited cousins standing stiffly beneath a sign marking Sa'adi a-Levi Street, the name by which the street continues to be known to the present day. At the moment the image is frozen in time, a curious young Greek (presumably Christian) woman peers out at the group through an apartment window above their heads. Did she grasp the gravity of the moment? Or was she assessing whether the party assembled outside her window had its eye on reclamation—their visit less a reunion than an act of strategy? Ignorant of (or indifferent to) the extent of Greek Jewish loss in

Julie (née Hasson) Sarfatti Confortés and Sam Confortés in front of their Salonica apartment, with the White Tower behind, c. 1960s

the Holocaust, the majority of Christian Greeks viewed Jews' return to Salonica as a threat and an intrusion, while considering their quest for restitution an expression of greed. These sentiments were extremely self-serving, as many Christians in postwar Salonica lived in property that had been stolen from or forcibly abandoned by Jews during the Holocaust.[5]

For all the trauma it had absorbed, Salonica felt familiar to those Levy cousins who returned. Stripped of its Jews, the city's light and scent were nonetheless familiar, its waterfront promenade intact, its café culture lively, its foods largely unchanged. Despite the turbulence of the twentieth century, Salonica retained a Jewish hue.

By the late 1960s, Julie and Confortés led a comfortable life, especially in the context of postwar Greece. In addition to Confortés's income as a "manufacturers' representative & commission agent" (and, later, as a "timber agent"), Julie worked as a high-level secretary for an oil company. The pair lived in an apartment that looked out upon the Gulf of Salonica, a short walking distance from the White Tower. Yet Julie was not well physically. She experienced terrible headaches that left her immobile. Julie and Confortés consulted specialists in Athens, Paris, London, and beyond, but the diagnoses varied and were ultimately inconclusive. One physician thought that Julie's pain was the long-term result of typhus acquired in the Nazi camps. In 1963, she was diagnosed with a brain tumor, which afflicted her for years.

Despite her ailments, Julie came to serve as a maternal figure for the extended Levy family, years younger than most of her cousins though she was. Since Julie had no children of her own, she doted on the cousins who returned. The fact that she and Confortés (and Aron, until his death) remained in Greece was balm for the extended family, tying them to their past and to one another.

In 1997, Julie was buried in Salonica's new Jewish cemetery, in the suburb of Stavroupolis. Julie's niece Liliane composed an unusual epitaph for her aunt. In a break with tradition, it centers not on the deceased, but on her relationship to those who lived. "To my dear aunt, who loved me," reads the engraving in Hebrew and French, "and who acted, toward all the family, like a mother." Rachel Carmona had played a similarly maternal role for the Levy family in the first half of the twentieth century. There were other Levy mothers, of course, but arguably Julie was the last motherly figure capable of holding together the sprawling family.

LEON

Leon was the most prodigious letter writer of his generation, and also the person who tried hardest to keep the extended Levy family whole. He managed to visit all the cousins except Karsa in the postwar decades. He traveled relentlessly. From home and from the road, Leon wrote a dizzying number of letters to his relatives, at times chastising them when their own correspondence did not keep pace. His letters tethered the cousins to one another, binding them together with news, gossip, and confession.

More than one relative claimed that Leon was the one they held most dear. Yet he was difficult, even on the page. Leon berated his relatives for neglecting him, for taking him for granted, and for falling short of his expectations. Once, Leon chided Charles for sending postcards, a medium he found superficial and unworthy of him. Leon could let entire months pass without word from him: nonetheless when he wrote, he thirsted for an immediate reply. He was stubborn, and drove an issue—whatever it may have been—very hard. These were qualities Leon displayed before the war, and they intensified as he aged, especially in the postwar decades.

The immediate postwar years also found Leon in pursuit of restitution and reclamation claims. But the quest was more emotional than financial. Leon's business had rebounded in the mid-

1940s, and had blossomed in the 1950s.[1] Nonetheless, he felt the family inheritance should be restored to him. He expected this to happen in the course of a quick trip to Europe in 1959. In the end, the work took six months and involved visits to myriad bureaucratic offices in two countries.

In the course of the 1959 visit, Leon managed to reclaim the apartment of his brother, Emmanuel, in Paris on rue Bleue in the ninth arrondissement. However, the reclamation of the family's Salonican property at rue Broufas 3 and the resolution of a legal dispute regarding the family's ownership of land in the vicinity of Yeni Djami (an Ottoman monument, erstwhile mosque, refugee shelter, and, since 1986, site of the Archaeological Museum of Thessaloniki) proved more arduous, requiring years to resolve.[2]

Leon and Estherina had been legally separated for decades, though Brazilian law did not permit divorce in deference to the Catholicism of its ruling majority. The marriage was legally annulled according to Jewish law in 1967, in time for Leon's marriage to Hermina (née Eizikowitz) Neuhof, a Hungarian Jewish Holocaust survivor who had migrated to Rio by way of Israel. Leon's marriage to Hermina dispelled so much of the loneliness that had characterized his life.

As the 1960s and 1970s unfolded, and particularly after the death of his uncle Sam, Leon emerged as the family historian. Aside from Karsa, Leon was the cousin who had traveled the farthest from home. He carried with him few physical mementos of Salonica, but those he kept he treasured. Especially one. The most prized of Leon's heirlooms was the studio portrait of his grandfather Sa'adi and his first or second wife, taken on the occasion of the publication of the premier issue of *Le Journal de Salonique* in the late nineteenth century. The pair are dressed in the traditional garb of Ottoman Salonican Jewry: Sa'adi wears a fez and stands in an *antari* (an ankle-length, wide-sleeved robe) belted with a *tarabulu* (a

Leon and Hermina (née Eizikowitz) Levy, Jerusalem, 1971

long fabric sash), and covered by a fur-trimmed overcoat, a *kyurdi*. His wife sits on a high-backed chair, sporting her own *antari*, *kofya* (headdress), *sayo* (outer garment), and *kapitana* (fur-lined jacket).[3] Leon made sure this extraordinary portrait made the rounds of the Levy family. It was first sent in the immediate aftermath of the Second World War from Rio to Paris, where Leon's uncle Sam received it with great emotion. Leon subsequently gave copies of the same photograph to cousins in England, Spain, Portugal, and Greece. Julie's copy made a second journey after her death, from Greece to Liliane's home in Canada, where it hangs today.

Thanks to the generosity of the Levy family, Leon's photograph found its way to me, too. When Aron Rodrigue and I were working to publish Sa'adi's memoir, Leon's grandchildren generously retrieved and scanned their grandfather's original for us. The photograph of Sa'adi had traveled from Salonica to Paris to Rio de Janeiro, and then on to Paris, Manchester, Barcelona, Lisbon, Salonica, and California, ending up in the homes of Levy descendants across the globe, and, ultimately, onto the cover of a book bearing the patriarch's name.

In the 1960s, Leon began his own Spanish-Portuguese translation of his grandfather's handwritten memoir, though he never made it past the opening passage. Leon was the third generation to attempt to preserve Sa'adi's impressions of his rapidly changing world. (In addition to Sa'adi himself, his sons had previously published selections of the memoir in Ladino and French.) When Leon took on the challenge of translating his grandfather's writing, his adopted country of Brazil was entering its own period of dizzying transformation. A nationalist leader had risen to power, inflation was rampant, and the country's military elite was laying the foundations for a coup that would usher in decades of repressive rule. By the time Leon shared his translation with cousins who had survived the war, they replied with enthusiasm for his achievement, and with concern for his security.[4]

The first deaths in Leon's generation (at least by those who survived the Holocaust) occurred in the late 1960s. Estherina was the first. She died in 1968, after spending some two decades living between the country and the hospitals and sanatoriums that continued to exert their pull. Adolphe Salem, the youngest child of Fortunée and Ascher, was the last cousin to die, in 2011, just before my work on the Levy family papers began in earnest. The others had died in turn, with Leon passing in 1978, at eighty-seven years of age.

The cousins, all grandchildren of Sa'adi Besalel Ashkenazi a-Levi, had lived under Ottoman, Greek, German, French, Spanish, Portuguese, British, Indian, and Brazilian rule; they had witnessed the 1917 fire in Salonica, the Balkan Wars, the First and Second World Wars; and they had emigrated in multiple directions, some more than once. When Sa'adi died in 1903, his grandchildren were mostly old enough to carry memories of this old-world figure into the late twentieth century. Their own children grew up in a global diaspora, with no one speaking Ladino, the family's historic mother tongue.

Back row: Ruth Vieira Ferreira Levy, Silvio Vieira Ferreira Levy, and Sadi Sylvain Levy. Front row: Ruth Nina, Joaquim, and David Vieira Ferreira Levy, c. 1964

Sylvain Levy with children Ruth Nina, Joaquim, and David Vieira Ferreira Levy, c. 1966

Like his mother, Leon died unexpectedly, after being hit by a car in February 1978.[5] Shortly after the accident, Confortés wrote Leon's son, Sadi Sylvain, to offer condolences, to invite him to Salonica, and to respond to a number of Sadi Sylvain's legal questions concerning Leon's financial investments in Greece. Confortés outlined Leon's ongoing, implausible attempts to secure indemnities for the family's confiscated property in the Yeni Djami neighborhood of Salonica. He assured Sadi Sylvain that he was not obliged to see his father's claim through, but insisted that it was essential that Sadi Sylvain take Leon's place as family patriarch. To make the point, Confortés used formal French and the Hebrew word for family: *"Il faut prendre la succession de chef de 'Michpaha'* [sic] *laissé vide par Papa."* Intended as a reflection on the legal ramifications of Leon's death, Sam's remark had other implications as well. If Julie had come to serve as mother to the extended Levy family, Leon had become its patriarch. Mercurial, at times cantankerous, steadfast in his commitment to the familiy, Leon was *chef* of the Levy *"Michpaha"* (to use Confortés's formulation), and it was unlikely that anyone would, or could, ever take his place.

SADI SYLVAIN

Leon's son, Sadi Sylvain (1920–2001), honored and inherited his father's archival instinct. He, too, was a writer and saver of family papers. Sadi Sylvain also stewarded his father's legacy. After Leon's death, Sadi Sylvain donated his father's copy of the handwritten memoir of Sa'adi Besalel Ashkenazi a-Levi (which was also the sole extant copy) to the Jewish National and University Library of Jerusalem (today the National Library of Israel), catalyzing the chain of events that led to this book. Next, Sadi Sylvain donated Leon's professional papers and textile sample collection to the Museu de História e Artes do Estado do Rio de Janeiro in Niterói, while holding on to his father's personal papers. (Leon had himself differentiated his personal and professional papers before his death.) Sadi Sylvain would pass his father's personal papers on to the next generation after his own death.

An only child of unhappily married parents, himself a prominent surgeon, and the guardian of his unwell mother as of 1959, Sadi Sylvain inherited some of his father's testiness. Leon spent years worrying that his Brazilian-reared son would raise non-Jewish children. In fact, Sadi Sylvain turned out to have inherited his father's love of the past, too. When Sadi Sylvain became a father himself, he grew progressively more religious. His son Silvio remembers his father bringing him to Sinagoga Beth El, a Sephardic synagogue in Copacabana, on Friday nights and Saturday mornings—allowing Silvio to acquire a familiarity with the Talmud and biblical Hebrew unusual among his peers. Sadi Sylvain also amassed a sizable Judaica library during his lifetime.[1]

When Sadi Sylvain died in 2001, the portion of Leon's archive that remained with the family changed hands a second time, with stewardship passing to Sadi Sylvain's four children: Silvio, David, Joaquim, and Ruth Vieira Ferreira Levy.

Four generations, a century, and a distance of some seven thousand miles separated the Sa'adi with whom this book began and the Sadi with whom it ends. The first Sa'adi spent his entire life in Salonica, traveling no farther than Vienna, where he went only once, as a young man. The second Sadi, Sa'adi's great-grandson Sadi Sylvain, spent a fractured early childhood in transit across Europe and came of age in Brazil. Remarkably, these Levys were connected: not only by blood and name, but also by their Judaism and their Sephardic culture, and by their commitment to tradition. They were also connected by that most fragile of materials—paper. Sa'adi poured his memories into a small, inexpensive notebook that would outlive an empire, wars, genocide, and the dispersal of his descendants.

Sadi Sylvain was more a man of science than of letters. Still, he had the wisdom to preserve the papers of his father, Leon, who used the simple act of letter writing to bind the branches of the extended Levy family, grafting connections that would not otherwise have been made. The two men shared two names, each one altered by time, migration, and the dissolution of a concentrated, Sephardic cultural solution. As Sa'adi a-Levi became Sadi Sylvain Levy, a Jewish family undertook a century-long journey from an Ottoman to a nationalized world, across political borders, languages, and generations, and athwart a global diaspora. Through it all, the past continued to matter. The women and men in the extended Levy family were fiercely independent creatures of their eras, but they were also descendants.

DESCENDANTS

The far-flung descendants of Sa'adi Besalel Ashkenazi a-Levi are amiable, generous souls living culturally vibrant lives full of family, and integrated into the national and cultural contexts they call home. Most but not all identify as Jewish, though Jewishness means different things to different people. Today's Levy family has many constellations, each mapped according to its own sign. With the death of Leon and his generation, what was lost wasn't so much culture or loyalty or even memory: it was a personal link to an Ottoman Jewish past, and a sense of how various familial orbits exist in a larger sphere. These Levy descendants are not (in most cases) aware of their family's complex past, and apparently are not eager to broker relations with one another. And perhaps this is in the nature of things. The folly may lie in the historian, hungry to chart a unique system of coordinates in the ether.

I have met descendants of Sa'adi Besalel Ashkenazi a-Levi in an outdoor café in Lisbon overlooking the city's undulating hills, and in a wet, leafy suburb of Manchester. I have learned about the Levy family while trapped in an epic Rio de Janeiro traffic jam (five hours on the short road to Niterói, with Leon's immensely patient granddaughter Ruth Nina Vieira Ferreira Levy), and while listening to a trio jam the Grateful Dead on Berkeley's Solano Avenue. One particularly challenging conversation was interrupted at my gracious interlocutor's urging by a meander through a posh suburban mall, ostensibly to show off the site and maybe also to diffuse intensity. Some exchanges I carried out remotely, via e-mail or phone, fiber-optic cables bridging the distance between my office and South Africa, Brazil, or Greece in the blink of an eye. Many of these conversations have been carried out over the course of years. At times, I am included on family e-mails. This tickles me and delights me.

It is jolting for the historian, so buried in her sources and in the past, to realize that the historical figures she has come to know intimately have a relationship to the living. Rather foolishly, I was shocked to encounter Adolphe Nolté's magnificent, turn-of-the-century, hand-tinted portraits of Fortunée and Ascher Salem hanging in the stairwell of Alan and Hilary Salem's home in Alderley Edge, England; and unsettled to find Sa'adi's nineteenth-century studio portrait, reproduced by his grandson Leon, hanging in the Canadian bedroom of Liliane Hasson; and moved to hear an intimate depiction of Leon and Estherina from the couple's niece Giselle Alaluf Moskovitch (of blessed memory), shared just two years before her death.[1] I am grateful that in the course of my research almost no doors were closed to me, even if some family members I contacted proved more engaged than others. Those who availed themselves tended to remember ever more with time, to unearth further documents, photographs, and memories than they realized they possessed. Some leads, inevitably, ran cold, such as my attempts to locate the sons of Jacques Lévy.

These conversations and encounters have left me thinking about the ways in which the past does and does not matter to a family. The answer, I think, is that history emerges at unexpected moments, long after we assume it to be over, or even without our being aware of it. I can't help but see circularity in the Levy family history. One of Sa'adi's great-great-great-grandchildren is an accomplished musician, as was he. One of Daout Effendi's great-great-grandchildren now serves as a government official, as did he. Rachel and Elie Carmona, globe-trotting representatives of the Alliance Israélite Universelle, can count a French ambassador and a consul general among their descendants, including the first woman to represent France in San Francisco. Across the family, the high cheekbones endure; the height; the propensity for eye trouble; select, idiosyncratic personality traits. The will to preserve certain treasured objects, in the face of deportation or over a lifetime. The descendants of Vida a-Levi no longer gift *kemeás*, Sephardic amulets, but they do take the waters. Nevertheless, who could have anticipated that a descendant of Sa'adi's, Pamela Salem O'Hagan, would play Miss Moneypenny to Sean Connery's James Bond?[2] Jewish history, like history of all varieties, has continuities as well as bombshells.

It can happen, too, that the past unearths itself. In 2013, even as I was researching this book, representatives of the Jewish Community of Thessaloniki—working alongside Dr. Magda Parcharidou, Head of the Department of Byzantine and Postbyzantine Antiquities and Museums, Ephorate of Antiquities of Kilkis Prefecture—identified a number of Jewish tombstones in a pathway in the suburban neighborhood of Panorama, some five kilometers uphill from the city center. Among them was Sa'adi's pyramidal headstone, broken but nevertheless recognizable due to its text and distinctive shape. Moved to the Jewish Museum of Thessaloniki, it is visited, if not by family, then by a new generation (mostly foreign and Jewish) unaccustomed to thinking of Greece as a center of the modern Jewish world.[3]

No history of Vital Hasson has ever been written and he has

Fragment of the tombstone of Sa'adi Besalel a-Levi, found in a walkway in Panorama, Thessaloniki, in 2013

been excised from the Levy family trees that I have encountered.[4] He, too, has reemerged, as a villain, in a recent play that dramatizes the story of the Algava family, Salonican Jews saved from the Nazis by Christian protectors. Vital, described as swarthy and suspicious, hunts down a Jewish family in hiding and murders them. The play concludes triumphantly, with Jews and Christians dancing together in their new home, the United States.[5]

What is the Levy family to those descendants and friends I have located across the world, the youngest scarcely a teenager, the oldest in her late eighties—the great-grandchildren, great-great-grandchildren, and great-great-great-grandchildren of a nineteenth-century patriarch? What, if anything, ties them together? They are scattered across the globe, citizens of many countries, speakers of a multitude of languages, in almost every instance unaware of one another. Should Leon's death, and the gradual transformation of his letters into an archive, be understood to reflect the definitive fraying of this extended family—or the end of Sephardic culture? Or, more optimistically, did Leon's epistolary legacy create an opportunity for a household, in conjunction with a historian, to stir life from a dusty mountain of family papers?

Beyond what it tells us about Jews, Sephardic culture, or an Ottoman family in diaspora, to those of us who no longer write letters, by hand, on paper—to those of us who no longer receive letters or save them—the history of the Levys is a wistful tale. Other forms of communication may be speedier, more immediately gratifying. But letters are an inheritance. Their value, and the meanings we derive from them, are limitless. The longer we save them, the richer they become. The longer we save them, the better we understand one another, and ourselves.

NOTE ON NAMES, TRANSLITERATIONS, TRANSLATIONS, AND CITATIONS

The extended Levy family came from a multilingual Ottoman environment in which many languages were spoken and written, and in which people and places were known by various names. The Levy family surname itself morphed with time, from Ashkenazi a-Levi to a-Levi, and from a-Levi to Levy and Lévy, depending on the family branch in question. Family members also bore multiple first names—given names, biblical names, non-Jewish names, pet names, married names, adopted names, honorifics, as well as versions in French, Ladino, Hebrew, Ottoman Turkish, Greek, Italian, Portuguese, Spanish, or English.

In this book, I name people as did the family themselves, avoiding pet names that feel too intimate. If a person's name changed in the course of his or her life, which happened frequently to men as well as women in the extended family, I attempt to explain the shift and, if it was permanent, to honor that change in my writing.

Like the Levy family, the contemporary Greek city of Thessaloniki was known historically by many names (even after its formal renaming as Thessaloniki in 1937), including Saloniki in vernacular Greek, Hebrew, and German; Selânik in Ottoman and modern Turkish; Salonicco in Italian; Salonique in French; Solun in South Slavic languages; Sãrunã in Aromanian (Vlach); and variously as Saloniki, Salonika, Saloniko, Salonik, Selanik, Tesaloniki, and Thesaloniki in Ladino. Unless I am referring to the contemporary moment, I name the city as did the family themselves, changing only their favored usage of Salonique to Salonica, which will be more familiar to English-language readers.

The family's use of language reflected the multilingual world they inhabited. Family letters were occasionally written in Ladino but tended to be in French. Whatever language a correspondent preferred, she tended to intermingle other languages within it, including Ottoman Turkish (especially when it came to financial matters), Ladino (for affairs of the heart and benedictions), Hebrew (for religious sentiments), as well as Greek, Spanish, Portuguese, and English, depending on the writer's location, age, mood, and purpose. I attempt to give voice to these linguistic interweavings—but while they came naturally to the Levys, they are difficult to translate for a contemporary audience.

In my transliterations of Ladino, I employ the Aki Yerushalayim system, which represents the language phonetically. Transliterations published by other scholars have been modified to conform with this system, and are so noted. Other languages are transliterated according to Library of Congress rules, with diacritics removed. Sources originally published in English are left unchanged, even if the author uses a transliteration that differs from my own.

All translations are my own unless otherwise cited.

To spare the reader excessive notes, I have chosen not to cite the voluminous, uncatalogued family archive of Leon Levy of Rio de Janeiro document by document. Insights gleaned from all other archives, repositories, and published and unpublished works are cited in full in endnotes.

NOTES

ARCHIVES AND LIBRARIES CONSULTED

American Jewish Joint Distribution Committee Archives [JDCA]

Archives de l'Alliance Israélite Universelle, Paris [AIU, Paris]

Archives du ministère des Affaires étrangères, Paris—La Courneuve [AMAE, Paris]

Archivio Centrale dello Stato, Rome [ACS, Rome]

Avraham Harman Institute of Contemporary Jewry, Oral History Division, Jerusalem [AHICJ, Jerusalem]

Beit Hatfutsot, the Museum of the Jewish People, Tel Aviv [BH, Tel Aviv]

Brotherton Library, Special Collections Research Centre, University of Leeds, Leeds [BL, Leeds]

Central Archive for the History of the Jewish People, Jerusalem [CAHJP, Jerusalem]

Central Zionist Archive, Jerusalem [CZA, Jerusalem]

Centre de documentation juive contemporaine [CDJC, Paris]

Fortunoff Video Archive for Holocaust Testimonies, Yale University Library, New Haven [FVA, New Haven]

Franklin D. Roosevelt Presidential Library, Hyde Park [FDRPL, Hyde Park]

The German Federal Archives/Bundesarchiv, Koblenz

Imperial War Museums, London

Instituto Diplomático, Ministério dos Negócios Estrangeiros, Arquivo-histórico diplomático, Lisboa [AHD, Lisbon]

Jewish Museum of London

Jewish Museum of Thessaloniki [JMTh, Thessaloniki]
Joint Distribution Committee, New York City [JDC, New York City]
Library of Congress Prints and Photographs Division, Washington, DC
Manchester Jewish Museum Archives, Manchester [MJMA, Manchester]
Ministerio da Justiça Arquivo Nacional, Rio de Janeiro [MJAN, Rio de Janeiro]
Museu de História e Artes do Estado do Rio de Janeiro [MHAER, Niterói]
The National Archives of Hungary, Budapest
The National Archives of the United Kingdom, Kew [TNA, Kew]
Special Collections and University Archive, Stanford University
United States Holocaust Memorial Museum National Institute for Holocaust Documentation, Washington, DC [USHMM, Washington, DC]
Visual History Archive, University of Southern California Shoah Foundation, the Institute for Visual History and Education, Los Angeles [VHA, Los Angeles]
Yad Ben Zvi, Jerusalem [YBZ, Jerusalem]
Yad Vashem Archives, Jerusalem [YVA, Jerusalem]
YIVO Institute for Jewish Research, New York City [YIVO, New York City]

PRIVATE MANUSCRIPTS AND COLLECTIONS CONSULTED

Alaluf Moskovitch, Giselle Collection. Courtesy Giselle Alaluf Moskovitch.
Benmayor, Jacky Collection. Courtesy Jacky Benmayor.
Carmona, Yves, *"Une recherche familiale à l'Alliance Israélite Universelle."* Courtesy Yves Carmona.
Confortés (née Hasson, first married name Sarfatti), Julie Collection. Courtesy Liliane Hasson.
Hasson, Liliane Collection. Courtesy Lilane Hasson.
Levy, Leon David Family Collection. Courtesy Silvio, David, Joaquim, and Ruth Nina Vieira Ferreira Levy.
Levy, Mauricio, "A Espuma Dos Dias, Fotografias." Courtesy Claudia Wermelinger and Sara and Rita Levy.
Salem, Adolphe Albert, "Autobiographical Notes for Adolphe Albert Salem, 2005." Courtesy Tony (Anthony Ascher) Salem.
Salem, Adolphe Ascher, "Family Tree, c. March 1969," subsequently maintained by Rob Salem. Courtesy Rob Salem.

Salem, Alan Collection. Courtesy Alan Salem.

Salem, Karsa Collection. Courtesy Pamela Salem O'Hagan and Gillian Salem.

Sarfatty, Bouena Garfinkle, "The Memoirs of Bouena Garfinkle [Sarfatty], written in Ladino by Bouena Garfinkle, translated verbatim to English by Bouena Garfinkle, transcribed by Vera Kisfalvi, 1975." Courtesy Renee Levine Melammed.

Solomons, Esme Collection. Courtesy Esme Solomons.

Youchah, Isaac (Michael) Collection. Courtesy Elayna Youchah, also available as the Elayna J. Youchah Collection at the University of Washington Sephardic Studies Digital Library & Archive.

WRITERS

1. *A Jewish Voice from Ottoman Salonica: The memoir of Sa'adi Besalel a-Levi*, coedited and introduced by Aron Rodrigue and Sarah Abrevaya Stein, with translation, transliteration, and glossary by Isaac Jerusalemi (Stanford, 2012).
2. I am guided, here, by the extraordinary work of Deborah Cohen, *Family Secrets: Shame and Privacy in Modern Britain* (Oxford/New York, 2013).

OTTOMANS

1. *The Memoirs of Doctor Meir Yoel: An Autobiographical Source on Social Change in Salonika at the Turn of the 20th Century*, Introduction, Judeo-Spanish Text, Translation and Commentary by Rena Molho (Istanbul, 2011), 32.

SA'ADI

1. Devin E. Naar, *Jewish Salonica: Between the Ottoman Empire and Modern Greece* (Stanford, 2016), especially 53–58; Basil C. Gounaris, "Salonica," *Review (Fernand Braudel Center)* 16/4 (Fall 1993): 499–518.
2. Esther Benbassa and Aron Rodrigue, *Sephardic Jewry: A History of the Judeo-Spanish Community, 14th–20th centuries* (Berkeley, 2000). On the Jewish diversity of Salonica: Devin E. Naar, "The 'Mother of Israel' or the 'Sephardic Metropolis'? Sephardim, Ashkenazim and Romaniotes in Salonica," *Jewish Social Studies* 22/1 (Fall 2016): 81–129; Paris Papamichos Chronakis, "'Our Unfortunate Fatherland, Macedonia.' Regional Spatialities and the Greek Orthodox Middle Class of Salonica, 1870–1912," unpublished paper presented at "Bourgeois Seas: Revisiting the History of the Middle Classes in the Eastern Mediterranean Port Cities," European University Institute,

Department of History and Civilization RSCAS, Max Weber Programme, September 2008.

3. Mark Mazower, "Travelers and the Oriental City," *Transactions of the Royal Historical Society* 12 (2002): 65. On the shaping of the notion of "the Jerusalem of the Balkans," see Naar, *Jewish Salonica*.
4. At least, so bemoaned a critical contributor to *La Epoka*, the Ladino-language newspaper Sa'adi edited with his sons. "Orasion en la kaye," *La Epoka*, August 13, 1897, 1–2, cited and discussed in Cohen, *Becoming Ottomans*, 91.
5. On the working-class Jews of Salonica: Gilda Hadar, "Jewish Tobacco Workers in Salonica: Gender and Family in the Context of Social and Ethnic Strife," *Women in the Ottoman Balkans: Gender, Culture, and History*, eds. Amila Buturovic and Irin Cemil Schick (London/New York, 1997), 127–152; Donald Quataert, "The Workers of Salonica, 1850–1912," in *Workers and the Working Class in the Ottoman Empire and the Turkish Republic, 1839–1950*, eds. Donald Quataert and Erik J. Zürcher (London and New York, 1995), 61–69; Donald Quataert, "Industrial Working Class of Salonica," in Avigdor Levy, ed., *Jews, Turks, Ottomans: A Shared History, Fifteenth Through the Twentieth Century* (New York, 2002).
6. The first book published in the Ottoman Empire was Jacob ven Ascher's 1493 *Arba'ah Turim* [Four Orders of the Code of Law], which bore the imprint of the Sephardic brothers David and Shemuel Nahmias.
7. For an elaboration of this position: Rodrigue and Stein, *A Jewish Voice from Ottoman Salonica*, xxii–xxv.
8. Gounaris, "Salonica," 500.
9. Maureen Jackson, *Mixing Musics: Turkish Jewry and the Urban Landscape of a Sacred Song* (Stanford, 2013).
10. Sam Lévy, *Salonique à la fin du XIXe siècle* (Istanbul, 2000), 18.
11. Rodrigue and Stein, *A Jewish Voice from Ottoman Salonica*, 25.
12. For example, Haim Benveniste, *Sheyarei keneset ha-gedolah* (Salonica, 1757, and second edition, 1807); Haim Isaac Algazi, *Sefer derekh 'ets ha-hayim* (Salonica, 1804); Haim Palachi, *Semichah le-hayyim* (Salonica, 1826).
13. Rodrigue and Stein, *A Jewish Voice from Ottoman Salonica*, 9.
14. For an internal view, Michael Molho, *Traditions and Customs of the Sephardic Jews of Salonika*, ed. Robert Bedford (New York, 2006), esp. 145–148. For a scholarly discussion of these themes, Julia Rebollo Lieberman, "Introduction: What Is Family?," *Sephardic Family Life in the Early Modern Diaspora*,

ed. Julia Rebollo Lieberman (Lebanon, NH, 2011); Alan Duben and Cem Behar, *Istanbul Households: Marriage, Family, and Fertility, 1880–1940* (Cambridge, 1991).

15. This process ran roughly parallel to Mustafa Kemal Atatürk's Turkish-language reforms—though, in the Ladino case, some newspapers continued to utilize Rashi script even after the move to Romanization.
16. Alexander Benghiat, *Souvenires del meldar: Estudio verdadero de lo ke se pasava en un tiempo* (Izmir, 1920), translated by Olga Borovaya and republished as "Memoirs of the *Meldar*: An Ottoman Jew's Early Education," Julia Phillips Cohen and Sarah Abrevaya Stein, eds., *Sephardi Lives: A Documentary History 1700–1950* (Stanford, 2014), 94–96.
17. Rodrigue and Stein, *A Jewish Voice from Ottoman Salonica*, 13.
18. Aron Rodrigue, *French Jews, Turkish Jews: The Alliance Israélite Universelle and the Politics of Schooling in Turkey, 1860–1925* (Bloomington, 1990).

RACHEL

1. Iris Parush, *Reading Jewish Women: Marginality and Modernization in Nineteenth-Century Eastern European Society* (Waltham, 2004).
2. Frances Malino, "'Adieu à ma maison': Sephardic Adolescent Identities, 1932–36," *Jewish Social Studies* 15/1 (Fall 2008), 131–145.
3. Cited in Malino, "'Adieu à ma maison,'" 134.
4. Vassilios [Basil] Gounaris, *Steam over Macedonia: Socio-Economic Change and the Railway Factor, 1870–1912* (East European Monographs, 1993).
5. "Rachel-Elie Carmona," *Les Cahiers Séfardis* 2, 1 October 1948, 321–323.
6. Here I echo the conclusions of Aron Rodrigue, who argues the AIU maintained an extraordinarily invasive role in the lives of its teachers, serving for them as a paternalistic force. Rodrigue, *French Jews, Turkish Jews*, 76–77.
7. Esther Benbassa and Aron Rodrigue, eds., *A Sephardic Life in Southeastern Europe: The Autobiography and Journals of Gabriel Arié, 1863–1939* (Seattle, 1998), 75–76.
8. On inherited customs of Sephardic marriage (and other life-cycle events), Hannah Davidson, "Communal Pride and Feminine Virtue: 'Suspecting *Sivlonot*' in the Jewish Communities of the Ottoman Empire in the Early Sixteenth Century," *Sephardic Family Life in the Early Modern Diaspora*, 23–69.
9. Olga Borovaya, *Modern Ladino Culture: Press, Belles Lettres, and Theater in the Late Ottoman Empire* (Bloomington, 2012); Stein, *Making Jews Modern*;

Robyn K. Loewenthal, "Elia Carmona's Autobiography: Judeo-Spanish Popular Press and Novel Publishing Milieu in Istanbul, Ottoman Empire, circa 1860–1932," PhD diss., University of Nebraska, 1984.

10. Elias Canetti, "Ruschuk, 1905–1911," *The Tongue Set Free*, translated by Joachim Neugroschel (New York, 1979).
11. AIU, Paris, Bulgaire XVII E, Rachel Carmona to AIU, 6 April 1884 and 23 April 1885. The financial predicament the Carmonas found themselves in was not uncommon for AIU teachers. Lia Brozgal and Sarah Abrevaya Stein, eds., *Ninette of Sin Street, a novella by Vitalis Danon* (Stanford, 2017), 9, 13.
12. AIU, Paris, Bulgarie XVII E, Rachel Carmona to AIU, 12 February 1885.
13. AIU, Paris, Bulgarie XXVIII E, Rachel Carmona to AIU, 21 July 1890.
14. AIU, Paris, Bulgarie VI E 27, Rachel Carmona to AIU, 29 October 1895.
15. AIU, Paris, Maroc IC 1–2, Elie Carmona to AIU, 11, 12, 13, 25 May 1903, reprinted and translated in Aron Rodrigue, *Jews and Muslims: Images of Sephardic and Eastern Jewries in Modern Times* (Seattle, 2003), 209–211.
16. AIU, Paris, Morocco, Tetuan VI B 25–27, bobine MA-11, Jacques Berliawsky to AIU, 28 October 1903.
17. AIU, Paris, Liban III E 030, Rachel Carmona to the AIU, 10 and 15 April 1910.
18. For Elie's perspective on these events: AIU, Paris, Syrie XIV E 124, and Grece XXI E 272. For Rachel's: Syrie XIV E 125.
19. Yves Carmona, "Une recherche familiale à l'Alliance Israélite Universelle."
20. AIU, Paris, Grece III E 39, Secretary of the AIU to Rachel Carmona, 27 August 1906.
21. AIU, Paris, Grece III E 39, Rachel Carmona to the AIU, 13 September 1906. For a comparative perspective: Joy A. Land, "Corresponding Women: Female Educators of the Alliance Israélite Universelle in Tunisia, 1882–1914, *Jewish Culture and Society in North Africa*, eds., Emily Benichou Gottreich and Daniel Schroeter (Bloomington, 2011), 239–256. Aron Rodrigue has noted that women AIU teachers tended to retire at a younger age than their male colleagues. Rodrigue, *Jewish and Muslims*, 51.
22. "Une recherche familiale à l'Alliance Israélite Universelle."

SHEMUEL SA'ADI / SAM

1. Naar, *Jewish Salonica*, 149 and footnote 40.
2. Sam Lévy, "Mes memoires: Salonique à la fin du XIXe siècle," in Isaac Rafael Molho, ed., *Tesoro de los judíos sefardíes: Estudios sobre la historia de*

los judíos sefardíes y su cultura, vol. 6 (Jerusalem, 1959), lviii-lxii. Translated selection published as "Ambivalent Recollections of a Jewish Boarder in an Ottoman Imperial High School {1890}," in Cohen and Stein, *Sephardi Lives*, 72–75.

3. Olga Borovaya, *Modern Ladino Culture*, 91–92. The friend I invoke is Meir Yoel: Molho, *The Memoir of Meir Yoel*, 32.
4. Molho, *The Memoirs of Doctor Meir Yoel*, selection republished as "Salonican Jewish Students in Paris Respond to the Dreyfus Affair {1890s}," Cohen and Stein, *Sephardi Lives*, 200–206.
5. Hélène Guillon, *Le Journal de Salonique: Un périodique juif dans l'Empire ottoman (1895–1911)* (Paris, 2013), 106.
6. I draw my description from Leon Sciaky, *Farewell to Salonica: City at the Crossroads* (New York, 1946).
7. Sarah Abrevaya Stein, *Making Jews Modern: The Yiddish and Ladino Press in the Russian and Ottoman Empires* (Bloomington, 2004); Borovaya, *Modern Ladino Culture*.
8. *Le Journal de Salonique*, 8 August 1927, 1. On the Federation: Paul Dumont, "A Jewish, Socialist and Ottoman Organization: The Worker's Federation of Salonica," in *Socialism and Nationalism in the Ottoman Empire 1876–1923*, eds. Mete Tunçay and Erik Jan Zürcher (London, 1994), 49–75; Abraham Benaroya, "A Note on 'The Socialist Federation of Saloniki,'" *Jewish Social Studies* 11 (1949): 69–72; H. Sükrü Ilicak, "Jewish Socialism in Ottoman Salonika," *Southeast European and Black Sea Studies* 2/3, 2002:115–146.
9. Tony Michels, *A Fire in the Hearts: Yiddish Socialists in New York* (Cambridge, 2009).
10. Sam Lévy, "Mes mémoires," translated as "Ambivalent Recollections of a Jewish Boarder in an Ottoman Imperial High School {1890}," in Cohen and Stein, *Sephardi Lives*, 74.
11. Borovaya, *Modern Ladino Culture*.
12. AIU, Paris, Maroc, Mazagan-Maroc XXX E 493, Suzanne Sultana Claire Levy to AIU, 5 April 1929. Suzanne's letter refers only to "her grandmother," not specifying if it was her maternal or paternal ancestor—but Sam's own mother, Esther, did not accompany her husband even on his one trip to Vienna, and could not read French.
13. "Vive la liberté," *Le Journal de Salonique*, 27 July 1908, 2; Paris Papamichos Chronakis, "From Pillars of Stability to Symbols of Conflict: Class and

Ethnicity among the Jewish and Greek Orthodox Entrepreneurs of Young Turk Salonica, 1908–1912," unpublished paper presented at UCLA, 22 May 2012.

14. On Jews' patriotism to empire, Julia Phillips Cohen, *Becoming Ottomans: Sephardic Jews and Imperial Citizenship in the Modern Era* (Oxford/New York, 2014), and Michelle Campos, *Ottoman Brothers: Muslims, Christians and Jews in Early Twentieth-Century Palestine* (Stanford, 2011).
15. *Le Journal de Salonique*, 17 September 1908, 2. Cited in Borovaya, *Modern Ladino Culture*, 126. As Borovaya notes, Sam's stance did not prevent him from accepting a subsidy for his journals from the Zionist movement in return for putting the periodicals at the service of Zionism—"so long as he was not compelled to challenge the territorial integrity of the Ottoman Empire nor campaign against Ladino," 126.
16. The *Grand Cercle* was founded in 1890. Yosef Uziel, "Moadonim (kuluvim) ve-agadot," *Saloniki: ir va-em be-Yisrael* (Tel Aviv, 1967).
17. For a vivid description and analysis of the sultan's visit, see Cohen, *Becoming Ottomans*, 108–119. Sam Lévy, *Souvenir du voyage* (Salonica, 1911). My thanks to Julia Phillips Cohen for sharing her copy of Sam's album with me. Select photographs from Sam's album, along with translations of his captions, appear in: Yannis Megas, *Souvenir: Images of the Jewish Community, Salonika 1897–1917* (Athens, 1993), 170–174.
18. Rodrigue and Stein, *A Jewish Voice from Ottoman Salonica*, xxxiii–xxxiv, 202–208.
19. *El Liberal*'s first issue appeared on 12 December 1911. In addition to acknowledging the joint editing of Sa'adi's sons, the paper identified Matarasso as director and Nefussy as administrator. Its lead editorial indicated that the journal was meant to replace both *La Epoka* and another family product, *El Imparsial*.

DAVID / DAOUT EFFENDI

1. Sarah Abrevaya Stein, *Extraterritorial Dreams: European Citizenship, Sephardic Jews, and the Ottoman Twentieth Century* (Chicago, 2014).
2. Molho, *Memoirs of Doctor Meir Yoel*, 33. Names, as well as the spelling of the word *tezkere*, have been transliterated to accord with those used in the present book.
3. Daout Effendi's pen frequents the various collections that emanated from

Salonica, including those held by the CAHJP, Jerusalem; the JMTh, Thessaloniki; and the YIVO Collection.

4. "Societé mutuelle de Salonique," *Le Journal de Salonique,* 4 October 1908, 2; Chronakis, "From Pillars of Stability to Symbols of Conflict."
5. Much has been written about the creation of the millet system and the *Tanzimat* [Reorganizing, the Ottoman centralizing, administrative reforms that began in 1839 and continued until 1876] of which this system was a part. For a recent review of the literature as pertains to Salonica, Naar, *Jewish Salonica,* especially 17–24.
6. "Echos," *Le Journal de Salonique,* 3 April 1910, 3.
7. AIU, Grece, IC 51, letter by Joseph Nehama to the AIU, 12 November 1912.
8. Eyal Ginio, *The Ottoman Culture of Defeat: The Balkan Wars and Their Aftermath* (Oxford, 2016); Mark Mazower, *Salonica, City of Ghosts: Christians, Muslims, and Jews, 1430–1950* (New York, 2006), 275–286.
9. Paris Papamichos Chronakis, "De-Judaizing a Class, Hellenizing a City: Jewish Merchants and the Future of Salonica in Greek Public Discourse, 1913–1914," *Jewish History* 28, 3–4 (December 2014): 373–403; Orly Meron, *Jewish Entrepreneurship in Salonica, 1912–1940: An Ethnic Economy in Transition* (Brighton, 2011).
10. I borrow the language from the Zionist intellectual and journalist David Florentin, who penned from Salonica an anguished letter to the Zionist Organization during the course of the Balkan Wars. CZA, Jerusalem, Z 3/2, Letters from David Florentin to the Zionist Committee, Berlin, 15 December 1912, and 3 January 1913. Translated and published in Cohen and Stein, *Sephardi Lives,* as "A Zionist's Proposal to Make Salonica an International City." Similar sentiments surface in AIU, Grece, I C 51, letter by Joseph Nehama to the AIU, 27 November 1912.
11. As Devin Naar has shown, other Jews sought to emulate and deploy the language and ideals of Venizelism, seeing Jews as a natural component of the Second Hellenic Republic. Naar, *Jewish Salonica,* especially 121–123. On the Sunday-rest law, 29–30.
12. Besalel and Vida's children Jacques, Maurice, and Ino worked as agents for Maison Walker & Charhon, a firm of "buying agents and exporters" created by the brother of Maurice's second wife, Flor Charhon (also a Salonican Jew), in 1924. Maurice and his first wife, Juliette (née Weill), divorced in 1930 through the Salonica *Beit Din* [Jewish court], citing

marital incompatibility. USHMM, Washington, DC, RG-11.001M, "Osobyi Archive (Moscow) records," Divorce of Maurice Besalel Lévy and Juliette Weill, 30 June 1930.

13. Rachel harbored fantasies of opening a bookstore in the city with a relative, following in the footsteps of her uncle Hayyim. But soon she and Elie, too, left for Paris, whether because the envisioned commercial endeavor could not be realized, because of the encroaching war, or because Jewish Salonica was diminished under the current political circumstances. AIU, Paris, Grece, X E 143, Rachel Carmona to the AIU, 28 January 1914.
14. To the Portuguese, Spanish, and Austro-Hungarian consuls who extended this legal opportunity, the benefit was also clear. These states hoped to recruit as citizens a large, Jewish, mercantile population at the moment that their own political future was uncertain. Stein, *Extraterritorial Dreams*. Documentation pertaining to Leon and Estherina's papers is contained within the Leon David Levy Family Collection: documentation pertaining to Ino's papers within AHD, Lisbon, MISC 2PA50M40, "Repatriacão de judeus portugueses residentes no Reich e territorios ocupados, incluindo a França 1913–1942."
15. AIU, Paris, Grece ID3, Joseph Nehama to the AIU, 28 May 1913.

FORTUNÉE

1. The children pictured are Jacques, Esther, and Karsa. MJMA, Manchester, 2005. 120/12.12; Adolphe Albert Salem, "Autobiographical Notes for Adolphe Albert Salem," 2005.
2. Basil Judah's interview with Esther Michael references Ascher's frequent business trips to Manchester: MJMA, Manchester, 200S.123.22, Interview with Esther Michael conducted by Basel Judah, 18 February 1994. The quotation is drawn from "Elégance-Solidité," *Le Journal de Salonique,* 1 November 1906. Ascher's partnership with his brother Elie ended in 1924. Alan Salem Collection.
3. Among the firms and merchants with which Ascher partnered were Karsa Frères, Hassid Benrubi & Cie, Youssouf Moustafa, Alfred Calderon, and Emmanuel Navarro. Ascher also partnered with his brothers David and Elie, the latter of whom was working out of Manchester by 1907. Alan Salem Collection.
4. Evidence of the business partnership between the firms is contained in

the Alan Salem Collection. Mustafa Karsa was hosted by the Salems in 1907: "Arrivées et départs," *Le Journal de Salonique* 30 May 1907, 1.

5. Marc Mazower, *Salonica, City of Ghosts*, 234. On the shifting urban fabric of the city: Méropi Anastassiadou, *Salonique, 1830–1912: Une ville ottoman à l'âge des Réformes* (Leiden, 1997); Alexandra Yerolympos and Vassilis Colonas, "Un urbanisme cosmopolite," in *Salonique, 1850–1918: La "ville des Juifs" et le réveil des Balkans*, ed. Gilles Veinstein (Paris, 1992), 158–176.
6. "Autobiographical Notes for Adolphe Albert Salem," 2005.
7. "Autobiographical Notes for Adolphe Albert Salem," 2005, 1; MJMA, Manchester, Interview with Esther Michael.
8. TNA, Kew, HO 144/3420, "Nationality and Naturalisation: Jacob Ascher Salem"; Unpublished manuscript, "Autobiographical Notes for Adolphe Albert Salem," 2005.
9. In later years, after the textile industry hit a slump, Jacques would abandon business in favor of work as a translator. Author conversation with Alan Salem, 27 July 2017, Alderley Edge.
10. Paris Papamichos Chronakis, "Global Conflict, Local Politics: The Jews of Salonica and World War I," *World War I and the Jews: Conflict and Transformation in Europe, the Middle East, and America*, Marsha L. Rozenblit and Jonathan Karp, eds. (New York: 2017); Mazower, *City of Ghosts*, 286–297.
11. "Autobiographical Notes for Adolphe Albert Salem," 2005.
12. TNA, Kew FO 383/88. The number of Ottoman-born residents of Great Britain was small at this time, numbering in the hundreds rather than the thousands. This population, Christian as well as Jewish, was dwarfed by the far larger population of German and Austrian "enemy aliens," some 32,000 of whom were arrested and interned in the course of the war. Stein, *Extraterritorial Dreams*, chapter 3.
13. MJMA, Manchester, Interview with Esther Michael.
14. TNA, Kew, HO 144/3420, "Nationality and Naturalisation: Jacob Ascher Salem." I am also thankful to Esme Michael for her reflections on the history of her maternal uncle Jacques Ascher Salem, shared in a series of e-mails including, most recently, of 28 March 2015.
15. "British Treatment of alien prisoners. Journalist's visit to Manx camps," *Manx Quarterly* 17, October 1916.
16. Jacques was released on the penultimate day of 1918, several weeks after

the armistice that ended the Great War. Upon his discharge, he was granted a rail ticket home to the Manchester suburb of Urmston, and instructions to obtain from the police, immediately upon his arrival, a certificate marking him as a friendly alien.

ESTHER

1. MJM, Manchester, 1988.5/1a-b, Letters written by Esther Michael (née Salem) to Jacques Salem, 23 and 28 August and 6 September 1917. Also translated by Alma Heckman as "Eyewitness to the Fire in Salonica [1917]," in Cohen and Stein, *Sephardi Lives*, 87–93.
2. Other family members who sought refuge with the Salems included Esther's aunt Djentil (Fortunée's sister) and her cousins Moise "Kirbatch" (son of Fortunée's brother Hayyim), and Juliette and Esther (daughters of Fortunée's sister Fakima).
3. Minna Rozen, "Money, Power, Politics, and the Great Salonika Fire of 1917," *Jewish Social Studies* 22/2 (Winter 2017): 78.
4. AIU, Paris, Grèce II C 53/10 (bobine 13), "Reponse au questionnaire de la Mission Hoover."
5. Letter from Yomtov Samuel Saltiel to the Superior Commission of the Communal Schools, YIVO, New York City, RG 207, file 135. Translated from Ladino and introduced by Devin E. Naar in Cohen and Stein, *Sephardi Lives*, 168–169.
6. "Autobiographical Notes for Adolphe Albert Salem," 2005.
7. The saying appears in Judeo-Spanish *musar* discussing charity: Matthias B. Lehmann, *Ladino Rabbinic Literature and Ottoman Sephardic Culture* (Bloomington, 2005), 95.
8. Jacob Ascher Salem.
9. Alan Salem Collection.
10. Translated in Naar, *Jewish Salonica*, 253–254; full transcription of Hebrew original into Judeo-Spanish in Michael Molho, *Kontribusion ala Istoria de Saloniko* (Salonica, 1932), 28–29, 76–78.
11. "Autobiographical Notes for Adolphe Albert Salem."

SAM

1. FO 265/589, "To Foreign Office: Political, Treaty, Parliamentary," Letter by Sir Francis Elliot to the Foreign Office, 5 September 1916; Paul Du-

mont, "Le français d'abord," *Salonique, 1850–1918: La ville des Juifs et le réveil des Balkans*, ed. Gilles Weinstein (Paris, 1992): 7. Also discussed in Borovaya, *Modern Ladino Culture*, 96.

2. Hélène Guillon, "Sam Lévy, un intellectual salonicien," *Itinéraires sépharades: Complexité et diversité des identités*, ed. Esther Benbassa (Paris, 2010), 278; Borovaya, *Modern Ladino Culture*, 89–97; Olga Borovaya, "Shmuel Saadi Halevy/Sam Lévy Between Ladino and French; Reconstructing a Writer's Social Identity," *Modern Jewish Literatures: Intersections and Boundaries*, Sheila E. Jelen, Michael P. Kramer, L. Scott Lerner, eds. (Philadelphia, 2011), 83–103.
3. *Le Guide Sam, annuaire de l'Orient: France, Italie, Turquie, Egypte, Syrie, Grece, Bulgarie, Palestine* also published as *Le Guide Sam: Pour l'expansion économique française dans le Levant* (Paris, S. Lévy: 1922–1930).
4. *L'Opinion*, 1 June 1916; 4 June 1916; 5 June 1916. Among the topics Sam covered in his lecture was the lamentable state of Salonica's Jewish cemetery, which he contrasted with the orderly cemeteries of Europe.
5. Curiously, the photograph seems to be a crude montage, as if Sam's face was sutured to another's body—or as if he replaced his own face with a more favorable portrait. *Les Cahiers Séfardis*, 5 November 1946, 58.
6. AIU, Paris, Grece II C 53/12, b. 13, Sam Lévy, "Le Salut des Balcans."
7. Naar, *Jewish Salonica*, 3.
8. Borovaya, *Modern Ladino Culture*, 96–97.
9. Suzanne's time in Morocco, like Rachel's, did not end well. Both women's experiences were clouded by accusations that they were rough with their pupils. These episodes were traumatic for the two Levy women, whose letters to their shared employer suggest that they engaged in similar soul-searching a generation apart. AIU, Paris, Maroc XXX E 493 [Suzanne Sultana Claire Levy]. The charge against Suzanne may have been exaggerated by a supervisor with whom she did not get along: Mazagan-Maroc XXX E 492, Messody Lévy to the AIU, 12 July 1935.
10. Fragments of Sa'adi's memoir appeared in the family newspaper *La Epoka* in 1907, with Sam Lévy's name in the byline, and again in the 1930s in the Ladino journal *L'Aksyon*, which acknowledged Sam's work in their preparation. At roughly the same time Sam published a second version of Sa'adi's reminiscences in the Paris-based, French-language *Le Judaïsme Sépharadi*. Rodrigue and Stein, *A Jewish Voice*, lv–lvi.

LEON

1. "Canteen," *The Encyclopedia Britannica, The New Volumes,* Volume XXX (London, 1922), 562–563.
2. Elie Florentin.
3. AMAE, Paris, Correspondance politique et commerciale, dite "Nouvelle série" (1896–1918), vol. 970, "Ottomans en France," "Dossier général, 1917, mars–juil," letter by the Minister of Foreign Affairs to the Minister of the Interior, 22 May 1917; Sarah Abrevaya Stein, "Citizens of a Fictional Nation: Ottoman-born Jews in France during the First World War," *Past & Present* 226/1, February 2015: 227–254.
4. Mirjam Zadoff, *Next Year in Marienbad: The Lost Worlds of Jewish Spa Culture* (Philadelphia, 2012).
5. Molho, *Traditions and Customs,* 75, 272–273.
6. Mary Dewhurst Lewis, *The boundaries of the Republic: Migrant Rights and the Limits of Universalism in France, 1918–1940* (Stanford, 2007); Stein, "Citizens of a Fictional Nation."
7. Elie's wife, Léa (née Sion), had emigrated from Izmir. MJAN, Rio de Janeiro, "Elie Alaluf," A9.0.PNE.3351/1927, and "Léa Alaluf," A9.0.PNE.6733/1927.
8. On Brazil's Jewish community: Jeffrey Lesser, *Welcoming the Undesirables: Brazil and the Jewish Question* (Berkeley, 1999).

DAOUT EFFENDI

1. Devin Naar, "Who Will Save Sephardic Judaism? The Chief Rabbi," *Jewish Salonica,* 89–138.
2. JMTh, Thessaloniki, "Declaracion responsavle, Daout Levy," file 26. Thanks to Devin Naar for drawing my attention to this source. Relative wages of the Community's employees are explored in Naar, *Jewish Salonica,* 157, note 185.
3. USHMM, Washington, DC, RG-11.001M, "Osobyi Archive (Moscow) records," Divorce of Maurice Besalel Lévy and Juliette Weill, 30 June 1930.
4. Mazower, *Salonica, City of Ghosts,* 311–347; K. E. Fleming, *Greece: A Jewish History* (Princeton, 2008), 80–84.
5. Meron, *Jewish Entrepreneurship in Salonica.*
6. "Tribune Publique: Un Scandale," *Pro Israel,* 10 October 1923, 5; "À l'Attention de Mes. J. Kohn & Daoud Levy," *Pro Israel,* 2 November 1923, 7.
7. London Metropolitan Archives, Board of Deputies of British Jews, File ACC

3121.E3.158.2, Letter by Joseph Nehama to the Alliance Israélite Universelle, 12 February 1931. On the Jewish cemetery: Naar, *Jewish Salonica*, chapter 3.

8. Naar, *Jewish Salonica*, 246, 248, 251, 265.
9. Aristotle Kallis, "The Jewish Community of Salonica Under Siege: The Antisemitic Violence of the Summer of 1931," *Holocaust and Genocide Studies* 20/1 (Spring 2006): 34–56. For a firsthand account of the riots, see November 2015 interview with Mico Alvo by Paris Papamichos Chronakis for "Centropa, Preserving Jewish memory—Bringing history to life," www.centropa.org/biography/mico-alvo.
10. Sa'adi's memoirs were selectively published in installments as "Mis Memorias," in the Ladino *La Aksion* and the French *Le Judaisme Sepharadi*, over 1931–1932 and 1933–1937, respectively. Rodrigue and Stein, *A Jewish Voice from Ottoman Salonica*, liv; Naar, *Jewish Salonica*, 237.
11. A photograph documenting the naming of the street showing Daout Effendi and a cluster of other unidentified people appears in *Zikhron Saloniki: Grandeza i Destruyicion de Yeruchalayim del Balkan*, ed. David A. Recanati, volume II (Tel Aviv, 1972–1985), 475.
12. Naar, *Jewish Salonica*, 128.
13. Daout Effendi strayed from the truth. Moise Allatini had also been decorated, some years earlier. Henri Nahum, "Charisme et pouvoir d'un médecin juif. Moise Allatini (1809–1882), 'le père de Salonique,'" in Anastassiadou Meropi, ed., *Médecins et ingénieurs ottomans à l'âge des nationalismes* (Paris, 2003), 59.
14. Rodrigue and Stein, *A Jewish Voice from Ottoman Salonica*, xxiii–xxiv, 142–148. Julia Phillips Cohen has described the celebrations of sultan and empire that Ottoman Jews crafted and performed in the late imperial era. Cohen, *Becoming Ottomans*.
15. *El Mesajero*, 26 January 1936, 1.
16. As early as December 1935, Salonica's Ladino periodical *El Mesajero* reported that Daout Effendi might be included among the list of parliamentary candidates, but ensuing coverage of the election elided mention of his candidacy until January 15, 1936, when his intention to run was at last declared. "Kandidatos djidios en las listas Metaksas i Republikana: Sres. Daout Levi, Saby Saltiel i Moiz Saltiel," *El Mesajero*, 15 January 1936, 4.
17. Daniel Alaluf and Shabetai Saltiel.
18. *Efimeris ton Valkanion*, 3 February 1936, 2. Thanks to Paris Papamichos Chronakis for drawing my attention to this source.

ELEANOR

1. Sarie Shabetai, Michael's wife, was the daughter of Jewish immigrants from Ottoman Aleppo: her father, like Michael's father (and, for that matter, like Michael himself), was a successful textile merchant. Lydia Collins, *The Sephardim of Manchester, Pedigrees and Pioneers* (Manchester, 2006), 281. Today, the glass plates taken by Michael are in the hands of Michael and Sarie's son, Alan, who diligently scanned each one for me. Alan Salem Collection.
2. Renée Levine Melammed, *An Ode to Salonika: The Ladino Verses of Bouena Sarfatty* (Bloomington, 2013), 153. I have modified Melammed's transliterations and translations so that they are consistent with the style employed in this book.
3. The fiancé was Joseph Mordokay Menasse.
4. Melammed, ed., *An Ode to Salonika*, 60–61. I have modified Melammed's translation and transliteration.

EMMANUEL

1. Roger Saby Lévy.
2. Emmanuel's house was rented, for a time, to the Egyptian consulate in Salonica.
3. Daout Effendi also took out a loan from the House of Amar, a Jewish-owned, international banking operation based in Salonica.
4. Maria Vassilikou, "Post-Cosmopolitan Salonika—Jewish Politics in the Interwar Period," *Jahrbuch des Simon-Dubnow-Instituts* 2 (2003); Meron, *Jewish Entrepreneurship in Salonica*.

ESTHER

1. E-mail by Esme Solomons to author, 24 November 2016. Silhouette from Esme Solomons Collection.
2. Alan Salem Collection.
3. TNA, Kew, HO 144/3420, "Jacques Salem."
4. TNA, Kew, HO 144/40/83999, and HO 334/9/2911, "Nationality and Naturalisation: Michael, Moise, from Turkey. Resident in Manchester. Certificate A2911 issued 26 May 1879."
5. MJMA, Manchester, Interview with Esther Michael. The second household was of the family Kalderon.

6. Conversation with Tony (Anthony Ascher) and Gill Salem, 26 July 2017, London.
7. Isaac Carasso. The company was named after Carasso's son, Daniel, whose nickname was Danone. Later, the corporate name would be modified to Dannon for the American market.
8. Alan Salem Collection.
9. The family friend is Victor Roditi.

LEON

1. I visited the collection with Leon's granddaughter Ruth Vieira Ferreira Levy, who holds a prominent staff position at another of Rio's cultural institutions, the Eva Klabin Museum. For decades—since the Levy family donated the material in the early 1980s—the collection has sat in the museum's basement, uncatalogued and unexplored. Recently, in hopeful anticipation of the opening of a Museum of Fashion in Rio, the Leon Levy collection has captured the interest of a small team of textile curators and conservationists, who view it as the basis of a compelling exhibit. The holdings warrant the attention. Nevertheless, Ruth wondered, on our way back to Rio, if the dream of the Museu de História e Artes do Estado do Rio de Janeiro's team might never come to fruition. Though a great deal of money was poured into sports venues for the 2016 Rio Olympics, none of that money would reach the museum.
2. MJAN, Rio de Janeiro A9.0.PNE.3351/1927, "Pedido de naturalização de Elie Alaluf," and A9.0.PNE.6733/1927, "Pedido de naturalização de Léa Alaluf."
3. Elie Alaluf's stationery and business papers occasionally made reference to his work with farming products, which was possibly a means of dodging import taxes upon European luxury goods. His previous place of business was at Rua 7 de Setembro.
4. Jeffrey D. Needell, *A Tropical Belle Epoque: Elite Culture and Society in Turn-of-the-Century Rio de Janeiro* (Cambridge, 1987), 161. My thanks to Cassia Paigen Roth for her help with these insights.
5. Teresa A. Meade, *"Civilizing" Rio: Reform and Resistance in a Brazilian City, 1889–1930* (University Park, 1997), 84–88.
6. Susan K. Besse, *Restructuring Patriarchy: The Modernization of Gender Inequality in Brazil, 1914–1940* (Chapel Hill, 1996), 29–30.

7. The precise valuation of the brothers-in-law's business in Brazilian milréis was 262:574$301. The Brazilian milréis was written as 1$000 by the early nineteenth century. One thousand milréis equaled 1:000$000. William R. Summerhill, *Inglorious Revolution: Institutions, Sovereign Debt, and Financial Underdevelopment in Imperial Brazil* (New Haven, 2015), xiii. My thanks to Summerhill for his help in understanding the relative value of Elie's and Leon's shares of the business.
8. Robert Levine, *Father of the Poor? Vargas and His Era* (Cambridge, 1998); Daryle Williams and Barbara Weinstein, "Vargas Morto: The Death and Life of a Brazilian Statesman," in *Death, Dismemberment, and Memory: Politics of the Body in Latin America*, Lyman Johnson, ed. (Albuquerque, 2004); Daryle Williams, *Culture Wars in Brazil: The First Vargas Regime, 1930–1945* (Durham, 2001).
9. Francisco Vidal Luna and Herbert S. Klein, *The Economic and Social History of Brazil Since 1889* (Cambridge, 2014), 64–65.
10. AHD, Lisbon, 3PA12 M312, "Inspeções em Levante, Inspector Roza de Oliveira"; Stein, *Extraterritorial Dreams*, chapter 2.

ESTHERINA

1. MJAN, Rio de Janeiro, "Levy, Estherina," 6200/54.
2. I am grateful to Silvio Levy and Giselle Alaluf Moskovitch for helping me flesh out a vivid and well-rounded picture of Estherina.
3. "Austria-Hungary," *The Advocate, America's Jewish Journal* 42, 16 September 1911, 157; Julius Hirschberg, *A History of Ophthalmology*, 11 volumes, volume 10, "The Second Half of the Nineteenth Century" (Bonn, 1991), 556.
4. MJAN, Rio de Janeiro, "Levy, Estherina," 6200/54.

KARSA

1. This story, and much of the information that follows, was kindly provided to me by Karsa's daughter Pamela Salem O'Hagen in a conversation of 12 January 2017. Some of the information Pamela provided is at odds with other sources: I have done my best to square the story with existing information. On the 1936 Olympics, David Clay Large, *Nazi Games: The Olympics of 1936* (New York, 2007).
2. TNA, Kew HO 334/251/1229, "Naturalisation Certificate: Karsa Salem."
3. Karsa Salem Collection.

4. The head of AEG, Hermann Bücher, was later condemned by the Nazi leadership as being a "defeatist," for having held the position that Germany should participate in an international settlement that would limit arms development. Peter Hayes, *Industry and Ideology: I. G. Farben in the Nazi Era* (Cambridge, 1987), 130–131, 323.
5. "Firmengeschichte der AEG," www.gerdflaig.de/AEG_Geschichte/AEGalles.htm. Last accessed 24 April 2019.
6. Pamela Salem O'Hagen, 12 January 2017.

VIDA

1. For consistency, I have transliterated the Ladino sentence according to Aki Yerushalayim norms. Daout Effendi's original "Gallicized" the Ladino, as he had formal training in French but none in Ladino. This was typical of Levy family correspondence, and of much written Ladino of the time.
2. Melammed, ed., *An Ode to Salonika*, 94–97. I have modified Melammed's translation and transliteration.

CAPTIVES

1. Melammed, ed., *An Ode to Salonika,* 224–225. I have modified Melammed's translation and transliteration.

ESTHER

1. E-mail by Esme Solomons to author, 14 November 2012.
2. Sari Salem.
3. "Adolphe Salem," www.youtube.com/watch?v=VrY7H3Ll91I. Last accessed 24 April 2019.
4. E-mail by Esme Solomons to author, 14 November 2012. Esme's brother was also changed by the war. Eric served in the Royal Air Force as soon as he came of age, eventually rising to the rank of squadron leader.
5. Esme Solomons Collection.

EMMANUEL

1. Jacques B. Lévy, "Recit de Captivité," *Les Cahiers Séfardis,* 15 March 1947, 178. Jacques's testimony continues, in that journal, on 20 June 1947, 227–231, and 30 September 1947, 339–345.

2. Ralph Carmona was also Carola's paternal uncle. "Une recherche familiale à l'Alliance Israélite Universelle."
3. Mauricio Levy, "A Espuma Dos Dias, Fotografias."
4. JDC, New York City, "Jewish Displaced Persons and Refugee Cards, 1943–1959," Item 115345, [Jean] Daniel Lévy.
5. Michael Ebner, *Ordinary Violence in Mussolini's Italy* (Cambridge, 2011), 206–207.
6. Renée Poznanski, *Jews in France During World War II* (Hanover, NH, 2001); Susan Zuccotti, *The Holocaust, the French, and the Jews* (New York, 1993).
7. Susan Zuccotti, "Surviving the Holocaust in France," in Michael Berenbaum and Abraham J. Peck, eds., *The Holocaust and History: The Known, the Unknown, the Disputed, and the Reexamined* (Bloomington, 1998); Corry Guttstadt, *Turkey, the Jews, and the Holocaust* (Cambridge, 2013), especially "France," 180–247.
8. Jean-Marc Dreyfus, *L'impossible réparation. Déportés, biens spoliés, or nazi, comptes bloqués, criminels de guerre* (Paris, 2015); Jean-Marc Dreyfus and Sarah Gensberger, *Nazi Labor Camps in Paris: Austerlitz, Lévitan, Bassano, July 1943–August 1944* (New York, 2011).
9. Zuccotti, *The Holocaust, the French, and the Jews*, 207.
10. The July roundup, begun at dawn on July 16, targeted the 28,000 (mostly foreign or stateless) Jews of the city and resulted in some 13,000 individuals, including approximately 4,000 children, being held for days in the Vélodrome d'hiver sports stadium before their internment in Drancy and deportation to the east. Michael Robert Marrus and Robert O. Paxton, *Vichy France and the Jews* (Stanford, 1981), 250–255.
11. Sam Lévy and Leon Rousseau to the German Embassy in Paris, 13 January 1942, Document T12 in Irith Dublon-Knebel, *German Foreign Office Documents on the Holocaust in Greece (1937–1944)* (Tel Aviv, 2007), 84–87; CDJC, Paris, Sam Lévy to Marshal Pétain, 9 September 1941.
12. Serge Klarsfeld, *Memorial to the Jews Deported from France 1942–1944: Documentation of the Deportation of the Victims of the Final Solution in France* (New York, 1983), 344.
13. Sam Lévy, "La Nuit Tragique," *Les Cahiers Séfardis*, 7 January 1947, 81–82.
14. Avraham Milgram, *Portugal, Salazar, and the Jews* (Jerusalem, 2011), 236.
15. Stein, *Extraterritorial Dreams*, 118–125.
16. Milgram, *Portugal, Salazar, and the Jews*, 236–244.

17. Such was the case of Yaco Soulam, a Turkish-born Jew who managed to communicate encoded, Ladino-language letters to his wife, Rebecca, in the course of his internment. "A Turkish Jew Interned at Drancy Writes Home," Cohen and Stein, *Sephardi Lives*, 265–266.
18. Zuccotti, *The Holocaust, the French, and the Jews*, 158; Poznanski, *Jews in France During World War II*, 304–305.
19. Klarsfeld, *Memorial to the Jews Deported from France*, 344–345. Klarsfeld contains a translation of a portion of Jacques's account in his volume, 346–347.

DAOUT EFFENDI

1. *The Trial of Adolf Eichmann: Record of Proceedings in the District Court of Jerusalem* (Jerusalem, 1992), 850.
2. Fleming, *Greece*, 106.
3. Joseph Néhama, "Les bibliothèques juives de Salonique détruites par les Nazis," *Les Cahiers Séfardis*, 15 March 1947, 134–136.
4. *The Trial of Adolf Eichmann*, 850. I have modified the translation for clarity.
5. Mazower, *Inside Hitler's Greece*, chapter 3; see also Fleming, *Greece*, 115.
6. TNA, Kew FO 371/33175, "Conditions in Greece," British Consulate General, Zurich to Foreign Office, 4 August 1942; British Legation, Berne to Foreign Office, 21 March 1942; Berry to Wadsworth, 5 March 1942.
7. TNA, Kew FO 371/33175, "Conditions in Greece," Berry to Wadsworth, 5 March 1942.
8. TNA, Kew FO 371/33175, "Conditions in Greece," British Consulate General, Zurich to Foreign Office, 4 August 1942; British Legation, Berne to Foreign Office.
9. TNA, Kew FO 371/33175, "Conditions in Greece," British Consulate General, Zurich to Foreign Office, 4 August 1942.
10. Daout Effendi's report opens with the explanation that Saltiel requested he produce the document in a letter of 23 December 1941. For the original: JMTh, Daout Effendi Levy, *"Rapporto sovre la Communidad Djudia de Thessaloniki a partir del anio 1870 asta el 1940 sea por ouna perioda de circa 60/70 anios,"* June 1942, folder 20. On this subject, see also: Minna Rozen, "Jews and Greeks Remember Their Past: the political career of Tzevi Koretz (1933–1943)," *Jewish Social Studies* 12/1 (Fall 2005), 112, 145–146 n.5.
11. On the pillaged and dispersed archive of Salonica's Jewish Community:

Naar, *Jewish Salonica*, 13–16. On the rediscovery of documentation in Thessaloniki: *"The Day after the Holocaust,"* exhibition catalogue, Jewish Community of Thessaloniki/Historical Archive (Thessaloniki, 2017), 60.

12. Minna Rozen, "Jews and Greeks Remember Their Past," 850–851; Yomtov Yacoel, "The Memoir of Yomtov Yacoel," in *The Holocaust in Salonika: Eyewitness Account*, Steven B. Bowman, ed. (New York, 2002), 88.
13. Mazower, *City of Ghosts*; Steven B. Bowman, *The Agony of Greek Jews* (Stanford, 2009).
14. Rozen, "Jews and Greeks Remember Their Past," 111–166.
15. Devin Naar, "Memory and Desecration in Salonica," *Jewish Review of Books* (Winter 2017). https://jewishreviewofbooks.com/articles/2417/memory-and-desecration-in-salonica. Last accessed 24 April 2019.
16. George Ioannou, "In Those Days," *Chronika*, September 1984, 73, cited in Michael Matsas, *The Illusion of Safety*, 163.
17. Erika Kounio-Amarilio, *From Thessaloniki to Auschwitz and Back, Memories of a Survivor from Thessaloniki*, transl. by Theresa Sundt (née Amarigilio [sic]) (London/Portland, Or., 2000), 46.
18. Minna Rozen, "Jewish Working-Class Neighborhoods Established in Salonica Following the 1890 and 1917 Fires," in Minna Rozen, ed., *The Last Ottoman Century and Beyond: The Jews in Turkey and the Balkans, 1808–1945*, vol. II (Tel Aviv, 2002): 173–194.
19. Yomtov Yacoel, "The Memoir of Yomtov Yacoel," 100.

VITAL

1. On Hasson's migration to Palestine, Rozen, "Jews and Greeks Remember Their Past," 150, n33.
2. Accounts differ on the size of the police force. One source places the group at 100, another at 250. For the figure cited: Daniel Carpi, *Italian Diplomatic Documents on the History of the Holocaust in Greece, 1941–1943* (Tel Aviv, 1999), Doc. 1943.12; Yomtov Yacoel, "The Memoirs of Yomtov Yacoel," 111.
3. Daniel Carpi, "Salonika During the Holocaust, a New Approach," in Minna Rozen, ed., *The Last Ottoman Century and Beyond: The Jews in Turkey and the Balkans 1808–1945* (Tel Aviv, 2002–2005), 269–275.
4. Steven B. Bowman, *Jewish Resistance in Wartime Greece* (London/Portland, OR, 2006); Michael Matsas, *The Illusion of Safety* (New York, 1997), Parts IV and V.

5. Carpi, *Italian Diplomatic Documents*, 46–47; Doc 1943.38; Doc 1943.58; Doc 1943.64; Doc 1943.68.
6. For a map of the ghetto, YVA, Jerusalem, O.33, "Testimonies, Diaries, and Memoirs Collection," File 1147, "12 short testimonies regarding the conditions in the Baron Hirsch Ghetto in Salonika, the deportations to Auschwitz, Rabbi Chaim Habib in the ghetto, the fate of the Greek Jews in Birkenau, labor in the Canada Kommando and in the kommando assigned to clear away the rubble from the [former] Warsaw Ghetto," "Plan du faubourg 'Baron Hirsch,' de Thessalonique, Transformé en camp de concentration et antichambre des camps de Pologne," 3–11. I also lean on a description of the ghetto offered by Bouena Sarfatty, a Jewish native of Salonica who escaped internment because she was an Italian citizen. "The Memoirs of Bouena Garfinkle [Sarfatty], written in Ladino by Bouena Garfinkle, translated verbatim to English by Bouena Garfinkle, transcribed by Vera Kisfalvi." Unpublished transcript, 1975. A selection of this memoir was generously shared with me by Renée Melammed. See also: Melammed, ed., *An Ode to Salonika*, xi, 191–192, 233, 239; Renée Levine Melammed, "Les *Mémoires* d'une résistante de Salonique," *Itinéraires Sépharades: Complexité et diversité des identités* (Paris, 2010), 205–222.
7. Danuta Czech, "Hashmadat yehudey yavan be-Oshvits," *Dapim: le-heqer ha-sho'ah ve-ha-mered*, second series, Tel Aviv, 1973: Danuta Czech, *Auschwitz Chronicle, 1939–1945* (New York, 1990); Bowman, *The Agony of Greek Jews*, chapter 5.
8. The formulation offered by Asher Moissis, president of the Jewish Community, was that Vital served as an "active director" of the Baron Hirsch ghetto. YVA, Jerusalem, O.33, "Testimonies, Diaries, and Memoirs Collection," File 1147, "12 short testimonies"; "Salonika. Report of Asher Moissis—President of the Jewish Community," 28–35.
9. VHA, Los Angeles, interview with Dan Saporta [40729], 15 February 1998 (Greek).
10. VHA, Los Angeles, interview with Izi Revach [40024], 18 January 1998 (Greek); USHMM, Washington, DC, 2003.4, "The Hasson Trial," testimony of Joseph Gategno, 31–33.
11. VHA, Los Angeles, interviews with Ely Cohen [30425], 14 April 1997 (Hebrew), and Henry Levy [26580], 10 February 1997 (English).

12. VHA, Los Angeles, interview with Lya Cohen [450] 22 December 1994 (English).
13. Isaac Aron Matarraso, "And Yet Not All of Them Died," in *The Holocaust in Salonica, Eyewitness Accounts*, ed. Steven B. Bowman and Isaac Benmayor (New York, 2002), 158; VHA, Los Angeles, interview with Dan Saporta [40729].
14. YVA, Jerusalem, O.33, "Testimonies, Diaries, and Memoirs Collection," File 1147, "12 short testimonies"; "Miss Bela Bivas (Mrs. Kattan now)," 16.
15. "The Memoirs of Bouena Garfinkle [Sarfatty]," Unpublished transcript, 1975, 179.
16. USHMM, Washington, DC, 2003.4, "The Hasson Trial," testimony of David Bitran (39–40), Raphael Cohen (46–47), Joseph Karasso (12–14); Anasasios Maretis (33–34); VHA, Los Angeles, interview with Lily-Nina Benroubi [37989], 12 February 1988 (Greek); Molho, *In Memoriam: Hommage aux Victimes Juives des Nazis en Grèce* (Salonica, 1948), 91–92.
17. VHA, Los Angeles, interview with Lily-Nina Benroubi [37989], 12 February 1988 (Greek).
18. USHMM, Washington, DC, 2003.4, "The Hasson Trial," 23.
19. Fleming, *Greece*, 167.
20. Some 367 Salonican Jews who held Spanish passports were also included in this transport. Haim Avni, *Spain, the Jews, and Franco* (Philadelphia, 1982), 158; Stein, *Extraterritorial Dreams*, 120.
21. Carpi, *Italian Diplomatic Documents*, 1943.119, Consul General Castruccio to the Ministry for Foreign Affairs and the Italian Mission to Athens, 11 August 1943.
22. Carpi, *Italian Diplomatic Documents*, 11 August 1943, and Michael Molho, *In Memoriam: Homage aux victims juives des Nazis en Grèce* (Salonique, 1948), 143–144; Testimony of Emilio Neri, *Zikhron saloniki*, vol. 2, 571; Interestingly, Neri's testimony, reproduced in *Zikhron saloniki*, does not appear in the English- or Greek-language transcripts of the trial held by the USHMM or the JMTh, Thessaloniki. From which transcript Recanati drew Neri's testimony is uncertain. In his study of the case, Daniel Carpi refers to a "photograph of the complete minutes" held by the Wiener Library in London. The Wiener Library is today unable to locate the source. Carpi, "Salonika during the Holocaust," 275–279.
23. At Vital's trial, Emilio Neri, a member of the Italian consular staff, testified to this arrangement. His testimony is not contained in the partial

minutes of the trial held by the USHMM or the Archives of the Jewish Community of Thessaloniki, which I have consulted—it is, however, cited by Daniel Carpi.

24. *Italian Diplomatic Documents*, 119, Consul General Castruccio to the Ministry for Foreign Affairs and the Italian Mission to Athens, 11 August 1943. Other accounts of the episode highlight the same details: Joseph Nehama, *In Memoriam* (Salonica, 1949), 143–144; Bouena Sarfatty Garfinkle, "The Memoirs of Bouena Garfinkle [Sarfatty]," unpublished typescript, courtesy Renée Levine Melammed, 179; Matsas, *The Illusion of Safety*, 407–408.
25. Carpi, *Italian Diplomatic Documents*, 119, Consul General Castruccio to the Ministry for Foreign Affairs and the Italian Mission to Athens, 11 August 1943.
26. According to the online digital database "Ebrei stanieri internati in Italia durante il periodo bellico" curated by Anna Pizzuti, Ida and Enrico were in Dubrovnik before they reached Bari, www.annapizzuti.it/index.php. Last accessed 24 April 2019.
27. Someone in Liliane's family requested a copy of the Italian baptism certificate in September 1947, possibly around the time the child returned to Salonica. Subsequently a Greek translation of the document was procured, in March 1949. Liliane Hasson Collection.
28. The mother and son were registered in Italy as foreign refugees: ACS, Rome, Ministero dell'Interno 1814–1986, Direzione Generale Pubblica Sicurezza (1861–1981), A16, "stranieri ed ebrei stranieri (comprende i Centri di raccolta profughi stranieri, campi IRO) 1930–1956," b.52, f.10/1, "BARI."
29. JDC, New York City, "Jewish Refugees in Italy Receiving Aid, 1946," 1 January 1946. The list itself carries a date of 1945, though the document is so filed in the Archives of the JDC.
30. FDRPL, Hyde Park, Records of the War Refugee Relief Board, 1944–1945, Box 31, "Union of Jews from Greece in Palestine," Letter from J. Beja and A. Alcheh, representatives of the Central Committee of the Union of Jews from Greece in Palestine, to the World Jewish Congress, 4 August 1944.
31. A number of sources repeat the story of Hasson's escapes and arrests, with the foundational source being Molho, *In Memoriam* (1949), 144. See also

Michael Molho and Yosef Nehama, *The Destruction of Greek Jewry, 1941–1944*, 91; Michael Matsas, *The Illusion of Safety*, 407–409; FVA, New Haven, Sara B. Holocaust testimony (HVT-2773) [videorecording] interviewed by Jaša Almuli (English), June 3, 1993.

DINO

1. USHMM, Washington, DC, 2003.4, "The Hasson Trial," 10.
2. USHMM, Washington, DC, 2003.4, "The Hasson Trial," testimony of Joseph Gategno, 31–33.
3. Yad Vashem, the Central Database of Shoah Victims' Names, "Sara Hasson, née Gatenio [sic]," Item ID 9163814.
4. Yad Vashem, the Central Database of Shoah Victims' Names, "Dino, Hason," Item ID 9163453.
5. USHMM, Washington, DC, 2003.4, "The Hasson Trial," testimony of Alberto Safan, 5–12; Solomon Saltiel (31); Dr. Ovadia Beja (16–18, see also 32); Joseph Gategno, 31–33.
6. USHMM, Washington, DC, 2003.4, "The Hasson Trial," testimony of Alberto Safan, 38–39. Haim Meir may also be referring to Dino when he describes the murder, in Auschwitz, of one of two collaborators from Salonica—just before launching into a description of the second collaborator, Vital Hasson. AHIJC, Jerusalem, Interview with Haim Meir, Interview No. (146)9A3.
7. Author conversation with Rosy Saltiel, 4 July 2016, Thessaloniki, with Paris Papamichos Chronakis participating.

ELEANOR

1. Yad Vashem records Daout Effendi's death as having taken place slightly earlier, on April 28, 1943. This would roughly place his deportation in the middle of the eighteen transports from Salonica to Auschwitz, ten of which had left by April 13. Yad Vashem, the Central Database of Shoah Victims' Names, "Daut David Levi," Item ID 9169587. In reparation requests filed by Leon, Daout Effendi's date of death is noted as June 10, 1943: this date was provided to him by Thessaloniki Protodikon, through his lawyer, Sam Nahmias.
2. Bowman, *The Agony of Greek Jews*, 96.

JACQUES

1. Jacques Lévy, "Récit de Captivité," *Les Cahiers Séfardis*, 20 June 1947, 227.
2. Wolf Gruner, *Jewish Forced Labor Under the Nazis, Economic Needs and Racial Aims* (New York, 2006), 228.
3. Jacques Lévy, "Récit de Captivité," 227; "Blechhammer," Yad Vashem, Holocaust Research Center, www.yadvashem.org/odot_pdf/Microsoft%20Word%20-%206094.pdf. Last accessed 24 April 2019.

INO

1. The firm Maison Walker & Charhon was created by the brother of Maurice's second wife, Flor Charhon, in 1924. The Sephardic and Salonican surname Charhon also appears as Sharhon.
2. For documentation pertaining to Ino's petitions for papers and repatriation: AHD, Lisbon, MISC 2PA50M40, "Repatricão de judeus portugueses residentes no Reich e territorios ocupados, incluindo a Franca 1913–1942."
3. More than 2,800 other Jews in France were granted Portuguese papers illegally by the Portuguese consul in Bordeaux, Aristides de Sousa Mendes. For these humanitarian efforts, Sousa Mendes was found guilty of "disobeying orders" and shamed by the Portuguese government. Only decades later, when Yad Vashem named him Righteous Among the Nations, was he celebrated for his actions. In 1988, the Portuguese Republic rehabilitated de Sousa Mendes, granting him a posthumous Order of Liberty medal. Milgram, *Portugal, Salazar, and the Jews*, 80–83, 241.
4. Stein, *Extraterritorial Dreams*, 118–129.
5. "Turkish Community of Vienna, Austria, 1845–1935: Births Register," An index compiled by Mathilde Tagger, www.Sephardigen.com/databases/viennaBirthsSrchFrm.html. Last accessed 24 April 2019. Beatrice's mother was Elise Eliakim, from Ruschuk.
6. I am indebted for this information to Sara Levy, Ino and Beatrice's granddaughter, who remembers her grandmother's romantic stories of her and Ino's courtship in Paris. Personal e-mail by Sara Levy to author, 12 October 2016.
7. I do not know whether this postcard has been preserved: I have encountered references to it in Ino's correspondence with his cousin Leon.
8. The precise date or circumstances of Maurice's death are not known. In 2004, Maurice's daughter Claude registered his name with Yad Vashem's

database of Holocaust victims, erroneously fixing the year of death as 1942. "Maurice Besalel Lévy," Yad Vashem, the Central Database of Shoah Victims' Names, Item 5578307.

9. For this insight, I thank Claudia Wermelinger, a dear friend of Mauricio's with whom I have corresponded since 2012. Mauricio Levy, "A Espuma dos Dias, Fotografias." According to his daughters, Mauricio's parents enrolled him in Lisbon's Lycée Français Charles Lepierre.
10. Author conversation with Gillie Salem and Pamela Salem O'Hagan, 23 July 2017, London.

JACQUES

1. The sons are Henri Daniel and Jean Lévy: the relative is unidentified.
2. Brief histories of the Dannon label and Carasso's personal history may be found here: "Danone nació en El Raval," *El Mundo*, 28 June 2015; and www.dannon.com/our-history. Last accessed 24 April 2019.
3. Besalel's ashes were interred in Paris, in the Père Lachaise Cemetery.

VITAL

1. SCUL, Leeds, Cecil Roth Collection, MS Roth, 8/3/1, Ann Molho, "Relief and Rehabilitation Work for Greek Jewry, 4th June 1946," 10. Molho was herself of a Salonican Jewish family.
2. The other accused parties were Aliki Amora, Amster Avraam, Agop Boudarian, Hagouel, Edgar Kounio, Sam Max, and Leon "Tipouz" Sion. The number of accused had been whittled down from an initial list of fifty-five drawn up by the Jewish Community of Salonica in September 1945.
3. To be clear, there are parallels with the trials that took place in Greece, notably the June 1947 trial of the Recanati brothers, accused of abetting the deportation and annihilation of the Jews of Rhodes. This trial resulted in a death sentence for Ino (Costa) Recanati that was not carried out, for he was deemed insane and transferred from prison to an asylum before his sentence could be completed. Interestingly, the Jewish press of Salonica reported that Vital's execution was the last straw in driving Recanati to insanity (or at least to the claim of mental illness, which the paper viewed with suspicion). A few days before the trial, *Evraiki Estia* reported, Recanati tried to commit suicide by swallowing oil from his cell's

lamp, whereupon he was transferred to a mental institution. "Hasson's execution," *Evraiki Estia*, 23 April 1948.

4. Mark Mazower, "Three Forms of Political Justice: Greece, 1944–1945"; Eleni Haidia, "The Punishment of Collaborators in Northern Greece, 1945–1946"; and Polymeris Voglis, "Between Negation and Self-Negation: Political Prisoners in Greece, 1945–1950," in *After the War Was Over: Reconstructing the Family, Nation, and State in Greece, 1943–1960* (Princeton, 2000).
5. During the war, Greece, in no way recovered from famine or occupation, entered a violent civil war (1943–1949) and state-sponsored crackdown on the left. During these years, recriminations, political purges, and executions continued to be horribly familiar to Greeks. Within this climate, Jewish vitriol against perceived collaborators (Vital and others, including especially Rabbi Koretz, whom one historian has called the scapegoat of Salonican survivors) was stoked. Rozen, "Jews and Greeks Remember Their Past," 119; see also Bowman, *The Agony of Greek Jews*, 65; *After the War Was Over: Reconstructing the Family, Nation, and State in Greece, 1943–1960*, ed. Mark Mazower (Princeton, 2000); André Gerolymatos, *An International Civil War: Greece, 1943–1949* (New Haven, 2016), 236.
6. Such were the findings of two British consuls general who toured the city's prisons in November 1945: TNA, Kew FO 996/2, "Visit to Salonica Prisons, 28th/29th November, 1945."
7. Bouena Sarfatty attended the Hasson trial with the intention of testifying, until the proceedings triggered traumatic memories. She became dizzy and tried to push her way through the crowd but fainted, reviving only when cold water was splashed on her face. Garfinkle, "The Memoirs of Bouena Garfinkle [Sarfatty]," 178. See also: Renée Levine Melammed, "The Memoirs of a Partisan from Salonika," *Nashim* 7 (2004): 151–173, 171, footnote 47. Some testimony failed to make it into the available transcripts. In Yale University's Fortunoff Video Archive of Holocaust Testimonies, an interview exists with a native of Salonica referred to as Sara B., who describes testifying at Hasson's trial, but whose words do not appear in existing transcripts. FVA, New Haven, Sara B. Holocaust testimony (HVT-2773) [videorecording] interviewed by Jaša Almuli, 3 June 1993 (English).
8. VHA, Los Angeles, interview with Edgar Kounio [42145].

9. The presiding judge sentenced two others on trial to death: Agop Boudourian and Avraam Aster. Boudourian was sentenced in absentia, having escaped the country after the war's end. Aster's sentence was eventually reduced to prison time. Leon "Tipouz" Sion was sentenced to life imprisonment, Jacques Albala to fifteen years, and Edgar Kounio to eight years. None of the sentences but Vital's were carried out in full.
10. VHA, Los Angeles, interview with Edgar Kounio [42145]. Kounio is incorrect about the length of time Vital spent in the prison in the wake of his trial—he mentions a span of three years, but other sources point to Vital being on Corfu as early as the spring of 1947.
11. "Our brothers' traitors," *Evraiki Estia*, 11 April 1947, and 6 June 1947.
12. On Vital's July 1946 request for clemency: *Evraiki Estia*, 15 August 1947; on the Minister of Justice Christos Ladas's February 1948 reply, *Evraiki Estia*, "The Minister of Justice on the traitors Recanati and Hasson," 10 October 1947, and "The requests for clemency of Hasson and Recanati have been rejected," *Evraiki Estia*, 30 January 1948.
13. "Hasson's execution," *Evraiki Estia*, 23 April 1948.
14. "Hasson's execution," *Evraiki Estia*, 23 April 1948. The presence of a Jewish witness (if not an executioner) at the execution is confirmed in one oral testimony: AHICJ, Jerusalem, Interview with Haim Meir, Interview No. (146)9A3.

JULIE

1. Author conversation with Rosy Saltiel, 4 July 2016, Thessaloniki, with Paris Papamichos Chronakis participating.
2. Author conversation with Liliane Hasson, 17 October 2016.
3. Julie (née Hasson, first married name Sarfatti) Confortés Collection.
4. Cecil Roth, "The Last Days of Jewish Salonica: What Happened to a 450-Year-Old Civilization," *Commentary* 10 (1 January 1950), 49.
5. For this and the previous details, K. Fleming, *Greece*, chapter 9.
6. Yad Vashem Holocaust Research Center, "Salonica Jews Sponsor Trial of Collaborators," 11 September 1945, available at the Jewish Virtual Library—American-Israeli Cooperative Enterprise, www.jewishvirtuallibrary.org/jsource/Holocaust/Collaboration.html. Last accessed 24 April 2019. For a discussion of the particular forms of guilt that Bergen-Belsen deportees suffered after the war: Rika Benveniste, *Autoi pou epezēsan: antistasē,*

ektopisē, epistrophē: Thessalonikeis Evraioi stē dekaetia tou 1940 [*Those Who Survived, Resistance, Deportation, Return: Thessaloniki Jews in the 1940s*] (Athens, 2014), especially chapter 3.

7. Julie (née Hasson, first married name Sarfatti) Confortés Collection, Communauté Israélite de Salonique certificate documenting service of Julie Sarfatty [*sic*] to the Community, 12 May 1943; see also JMTh, "Declarasion Responsavle, J. Hasson," 28 June 1934, File 26. Thanks to Devin Naar for drawing my attention to this source.
8. USHMM, Washington, DC, 2003.4, "The Hasson Trial," testimony of Joseph Gategno (31–33).
9. Bea Lewkowicz, *The Jewish Community of Salonica: History, Memory, Identity* (Portland, OR, 2006), 201; Bowman, *The Agony of Greek Jewry*, 228; see also VHA, Los Angeles, conversation with Rosy Sarfatty [44581], 18 May 1998.
10. Beginning in February 1934, Sarfatti served the communal offices as a translator. JMTh, "Declarasion Responsavle, Michel Sarfatti," 15 February 1934, File 26. Thanks to Devin Naar for drawing my attention to this source.
11. Sources conflict on Michel Sarfatti's death date, as they do for a good number of those lost in the Holocaust. Julie's own records include the German identity papers of her first husband, issued in July 1941. Handwritten in pencil on the cover of this small booklet, in Julie's hand, is a death date of 17 May 1945/5 Sivan 5705. Julie (née Hasson, first married name Sarfatti) Confortés Collection. Official databases record his death as having taken place in Tröbitz twelve days earlier. "The Lost Train: Bergen-Belsen to Tröbitz," www.jewishgen.org/databases/Holocaust/0170_lost_train.html. Last accessed 24 April 2019.
12. According to Liliane Hasson, the property's address is Leoforos Nikis 47, now home to the Swiss consulate. Author conversation with Liliane Hasson, 17 October 2016.
13. Author conversation with Pamela Salem O'Hagan, 12 January 2017; Author conversation with Gillie Salem and Pamela Salem O'Hagan, 23 July 2017, London; Gillie Robic (née Salem), *Swimming Through Marble* (Live Canon, 2016), 24.
14. Author conversation with Rosy Saltiel, 4 July 2016, Thessaloniki, with Paris Papamichos Chronakis participating. For more on Rosy's marriage and life: Interview with Nico Saltiel by Paris Papamichos Chronakis, October 2006, Centropa.org.

SAM

1. The cousin in California was Ovadia Haim, who was among the first Sephardic Jews to settle in Los Angeles (he arrived in 1905).
2. Klarsfeld speculates that four original carbon copies of each deportation list originally existed. Two were destroyed by the Nazis in Auschwitz; a third remained with the secretariat of the camp in Drancy. The fourth was likely given to the Union Générale des Israélites de France (UGIF)—the office created by the Vichy government to oversee all Jewish affairs during the war. The UGIF received its copy of the Drancy deportation lists with the authorization of the police prefecture; their copy was in time donated to the Contemporary Jewish Documentation Center, where it remains today. In a letter to Leon, Sam wrote that he had been granted personal access to the documents by the *Ministre des prisonniers, déportés et réfugiés*. The work required him to read through each of the onion-skin documents in order to identify the Sephardic names.
3. Naar, *Jewish Salonica*, 209–219.
4. The windfall turned once Sam's relationship with the organization soured, and its representatives demanded the machine back. JDCA, 1945–1954 Geneva Collection, World Sephardic Congress, *Les Cahiers Séfardis*, 1947–1951, Items 2142804 and 2142801, Letters from Charles Malamuth to Monsieur Sam Lévy, 2 March 1950, and 7 March 1950.
5. In December 1945, the Union des Israélites Séfardis de France celebrated Sam's seventy-fifth birthday, acknowledging the impact of his life's labors. It was a grand affair, Sam reported, and he was given a handsome Bible two hundred years old. On the historic unprofitability of the Ladino press, Borovaya, *Modern Ladino Culture*, 59.
6. JDCA, 1945–1954 Geneva Collection, World Sephardic Congress, *Les Cahiers Séfardis*, 1947–1951, Item 2142816, Letter from Solomon Tarshansky to Sam Lévy, 3 November 1948.
7. Earlier, in the 1920s, Sam saw New York City as a potential bastion for Sephardism. At other moments, he trumpeted Salonica and Paris as its "citadel." For example: Sam Lévy, "La cité martyre," *Les Cahiers Séfardis*, 5 November 1946.
8. JDCA, 1945–1954 Geneva Collection, World Sephardic Congress, *Les Cahiers Séfardis*, 1947–1951, Item 2142815, Letter from Sam Lévy to Dr. Joseph Schwartz, 28 November 1948.

LEON

1. In 1946, a new Jewish cemetery was established in the suburb of Stavroupolis. Julie's letter was either written prior to its construction, without knowledge of its impending construction, or made reference to the historic, desecrated Jewish cemetery with which Leon would have been familiar.
2. The friend was Israel M. Rousso. Rousso told Leon that he had been informed of the details by the president of the postwar Salonican Jewish Community, Haim Saltiel. MI, Rio de Janeiro, uncatalogued papers and textile samples of Leon Levy, letter to Levy from Israel M. Rousso, 25 April 1946.
3. The cemetery, Cemitério Comunal Israelita do Cajú, opened in 1956 and bears a plaque acknowledging Leon's leadership in unifying ten Jewish organizations dedicated to the cause.
4. Confirmation of Elie Florentin's death may be found in: Klarsfeld, *Memorial to the Jews Deported from France*, "List of Jews Executed in France," 645. Klarsfeld notes that Florentin was shot in neighboring Bron on 12 August 1944.
5. Stein, *Extraterritorial Dreams*, 34–35.
6. Kateřina Králová, *Das Vermächtnis der Besatzung Deutsch-griechische Beziehungen seit 1940* (Cologne, 2015), especially 1.6.1; Kateřina Králová, "In the Shadow of the Nazi Past: Post-war Reconstruction and the Claims of the Jewish Community in Salonika," *European History Quarterly* 46/2, 2016: 262–290.

LILIANE

1. Bea Lewokowicz, "'After the War We Were All Together,' Jewish Memories of Postwar Thessaloniki," *After the War Was Over*, Mazower, ed., 264.
2. CZA, Jerusalem, ISA1\15501\1, Passenger list of immigrants arriving in Palestine on board the *Jerusalem*, 26 July 1959.
3. Author conversation with Liliane Hasson, 17 October 2016.
4. Author conversation with Liliane Hasson, 17 October 2016.

JULIE

1. Mazower, *Salonica, City of Ghosts*, 18.
2. Author conversation with Gillie Salem and Pamela Salem O'Hagan, 23 July 2017, London.

3. Email by Alan Salem to author, 25 March 2019.
4. Photographs from Julie (née Hasson, first married name Sarfatti) Confortés Collection.
5. Králová, *Das Vermächtnis der Besatzung*, especially 1.6.1; Katerina Králová, "The 'Holocausts' in Greece: victim competition in the context of postwar compensation," *Holocaust Studies, a Journal of Culture and History* 23/1–2 (2017).

LEON

1. Tax filings from 1951 suggest that in that year, Leon imported nearly 45 percent of all wool to Rio de Janeiro. The city was tropical, to be sure, but the importer had found his niche and was thriving as a result. This bit of sleuthing is thanks to Cassia Paigen Roth and Comissão Executiva Textil (CETEX), *Indústria têxtil algodoeira* (Rio de Janeiro, 1946), 30.
2. It appears that a portion of the family land in the Yeni Djami neighborhood (located roughly at the present-day intersection of Delfon and Archeologikou Mousiou Streets) was claimed by the Greek government in the course of an expansion of the Archaeological Museum of Thessaloniki. Thanks to Silvio Levy for this insight. On the history of the erstwhile mosque, see also the work of the research collective Sonor Cities, http://sonor-cities.edu.gr. Last accessed 24 April 2019.
3. Molho, *Traditions & Customs of the Sephardic Jews*, 365.
4. Though Leon never knew it, his cousin Adolphe Ascher Salem in Manchester used Leon's fragmentary translation of Sa'adi's memoir to produce an English-language version of his own, never published, yet preserved today by his family. My thanks to Tony (Anthony Ascher) Salem for sharing Adolphe's papers with me.
5. Announcements of Leon's death appear in *O Dia*, 19 January 1978, 14, and *Jornal do Brasil*, 2 October 1978, 22.

SADI SYLVAIN

1. Personal e-mail by Silvio Levy to author, 21 March 2017.

DESCENDANTS

1. Author conversation with Giselle Alaluf Moskovitch, with Ruth Levy and Diana Moskovitch participating, 7 October 2015, Rio de Janeiro.

2. *Never Say Never Again*, directed by Irvin Kershner, produced by Jack Schwartzman, performed by Pamela Salem (O'Hagan) (1983; London: Warner Bros.), film.
3. On the extent to which the modern city of Thessaloniki is paved with Jewish tombs, Naar, "Memory and Desecration in Salonica," *Jewish Review of Books*, Winter 2017.
4. One of the family trees I have viewed is held by the JMTh, Thessaloniki. Its creator is unidentified. A second, different tree was compiled by Adolphe Ascher Salem in 1969, a copy of which his nephew Tony (Anthony Ascher) Salem shared with me. Tony's son Rob continues to update his grandfather's family tree.
5. Joan Coch, "Safe Harbor, based on the true story as related by Andrew Algava," 2000.

ACKNOWLEDGMENTS

My first and deepest debt of gratitude is due to the various branches of the Levy family who opened their collections, homes, and hearts. Joaquim Ferreira Levy, David Ferreira Levy, Silvio Ferreira Levy, and Ruth Nina Vieira Ferreira Levy—the grandchildren of Leon and Estherina Levy and the children of Sadi Sylvain and Ruth Vieira Ferreira Levy, and the stewards of Leon's extensive personal archive—have provided this book with its archival backbone. Silvio, who has read much of his grandfather's collection, has been particularly unstinting in his generosity. Ruth served as a most companionable host in Rio de Janeiro, joining me in visiting the Museu do Ingá to peruse her grandfather's professional archive. Ruth also facilitated and participated in a wonderful conversation in Rio with Leon and Estherina's remarkable niece Giselle Alaluf Moskovitch (*zikhronah livrakha*, may her memory be for a blessing) and her daughter Diane.

Alan Salem, the son of Michael and Sari Salem, has proven himself a prodigious student of family history and, with his wife, Hilary, a delightful conversation partner. In e-mail after e-mail, Alan shared scans of precious documents and images, pairing them with detailed insights. I carry the fondest memory of a three-generational five-hour summer lunch at their home, from which I (and my infinitely patient son Julius) left feeling fully a part of the family.

For years, I have carried on a shimmering e-mail conversation with Esme Solomons, the daughter of Esther Michael (née Salem). A writer of great talent and a most sensitive soul, Esme helped me gain a feeling for her mother's world that no archive could yield. From the senior center at which she lives on the outskirts of Johannesburg, Esme also sent scans of precious photographs I delighted in dissecting with her.

Thanks to Gillie Salem Robic and Pamela Salem O'Hagan, the daughters of Karsa and Pearl Salem, for a magical afternoon spent in the dreamy poet's jewel-box of a home belonging to Gillie and her husband, Michel. Gillie and Pamela allowed me to peruse their father's photographs and papers, complementing them with their own memories and stories.

I was, additionally, pleased to meet Tony Salem, the son of Adolphe Albert Salem, as well as Tony's wife, Gill. They, with their son, Rob Salem—a teacher of history and diligent pupil of his family's story—kindly shared Adolphe's unpublished memoir, as well as an interview he conducted in his advanced age. Alas, I was not able to meet Jacqueline Appleton, the daughter of Fortunée Salem's son Jacques; however, she has been most giving via e-mail. Elayna Youchah, whose father, Isaac (Michael) Youchah, is the grandson of Samuel and Esther [née a-Levi] Covo and the great-grandson of Sa'adi's eldest child, Hayyim, kindly discussed family history, and (with the help of Devin Naar and Ty Alhadeff of the University of Washington's Sephardic Studies Program) shared her father's remarkable collection of photographs and historical documents. Yves Carmona is a keen student of family history, and his writing granted me insight into the lives of Rachel (née a-Levi) and Eli Carmona and their descendants.

Liliane, the daughter of Regina and Vital Hasson, welcomed me repeatedly into her home, sharing memories of her childhood, her mother, her aunt Julie Hasson Sarfatti Confortés, and her grandfather Aron, all whom I know only through print and whom she loved deeply. Liliane also graciously shared Julie's papers and photographs, which she has treasured since her aunt's death.

Claudia Wermelinger, a close friend of Mauricio Levy, shared her insights into the history of Mauricio and his father, Ino, and introduced me to Mauricio's children, Sarah, Rita, and Miguel. I am grateful to these Levy siblings for allowing me to read their father's unpublished memoir and view family photographs.

Others outside the Levy family provided other forms of nourishment. Rosy Saltiel, whom I met thanks to the assistance of her daughter, Solita Saltiel, and her friend Paris Papamichos Chronakis, divulged memories of her friend Julie Hasson Sarfatti Confortés. Renée Levine Melammed shared her copy of the unpublished memoir of Bouena Garfinkle Sarfatty, and Frances Malino her ever-insightful impressions of Rachel Carmona, gleaned in the course of her own scholarly investigations.

Research carried me to thirty archives and libraries in Brazil, England, France, Germany, Greece, Portugal, Israel, Italy, Spain, and the United States. I am grateful to these institutions (which I list in the bibliography) and their staff. I am, additionally, indebted to Samuel Josafat, Director of the Jewish Community of Thessaloniki, and Jacky Benmayor for granting me permission to publish a photograph taken in 2013, in the course of unearthing Jewish tombstones desecrated during and after World War II; to David Recanati of the Salonika and Greece Jewry Heritage Center; and to Beit Avot Leon Recanati of Petah Tikvah, Israel, for granting me permission to reproduce images from his landmark *Zikhron Saloniki: Gedulata ve-hurbana shel Yerushalayim de-Balkan* (Tel Aviv, 1972–1985). Last but not least, Minna Rozen and Shmuel Refael deserve praise for facilitating my exchange with Mr. Recanati and, in Minna's case, for sharing her erudition.

I presented portions of this book at various institutions, and appreciation is due to my hosts and conversation partners at Princeton University; Rutgers University; the University of Pennsylvania; the University of Chicago; Columbia University; Vanderbilt University; Institut für Jüdische Studien und Religionswissenschaft, Berlin; New York University; Washington University; the University of North Carolina; the University of Colorado Boulder; the University of Minnesota, Twin Cities; the University of Wisconsin–Madison; Fordham University; and the University of Salento, Italy (in collaboration with Lehigh University). Special thanks for their company and conversation at these venues go to Anne Albert, Leora Auslander, Orit Bashkin, Zvi Ben Dor Benite, Clemence Boulouque, Ra'anan Boustan, Julia Phillips Cohen, Carolyn Dean, Hasia Diner, Katy Fleming, Liora Halperin, Marion Kaplan, Seth Koven, Cecile Kuznitz, Hartley Lachter, Fabrizio Lelli, Lital Levy, Tony Michels, Sina Rauschenbach, Nancy Reynolds, Mary Louise Roberts, Marina Rustow, Lise Schreier, Sasha Senderovitch, David Shneer, Bonnie Smith, Julia Stephens, Judith Surkis, Francesca Trivellato, and Steven Weitzman.

Alma Heckman, Pauline Lewis, and Chris Silver—an all-star cast of doctoral students (now all-star scholars in their own right)—offered help in the course of my research. I thank them for their virtuosity. For years I have sung Rachel Deblinger's praises for the intricately searchable digital note-taking system she created for this project. Cassia Paigen Roth assisted with Portuguese sources, and by lending her own knowledge of Brazilian history.

Farther from home, Molly FitzMorris shared expertise with Ladino transliterations and translations, Tamir Karkason assisted me in combing through Salonica's Ladino press, and Guilherme Babo Sedlacek plumbed archival material in Rio de Janeiro that I had missed in the course of my visit. Marina Aivaliotou gamely reviewed Greek-language Holocaust testimonies and other, related sources for me, yielding extraordinary findings with modesty and efficiency.

Colleagues and friends have given conversation, companionship, support, and levity. My warmest thanks to Amir Alexander, Andrew Apter, Steve Aron, David Biale, Olga Borovaya, Aomar Boum, Lia Brozgal, Chris Chism, Greg Cohen, Norma Mendoza Denton, Robyn Derby, Nathaniel Deutsch, Barbara Fuchs, Andrea Goldman, Kelly Lytle Hernandez, Carolyn Starman Hessel, Lynn Hunt, Ali Iğmen, Robin Kelly, Chris Kelty, Hannah Landecker, Caroline Libresco, Jessica Marglin, Valerie Matsumoto, Tony Michels, Ken Moss, David Myers, Minayo Nasiali, Carla Pestana, Eddy Portnoy, Todd Presner, Michael Rothberg, Teo Ruiz, Joshua Schreier, Todd Shepard, Susan Slyomovics, Brenda Stevenson, William Summerhill, Lynn Thomas, Tommaso Treu, and Stefania Tutino. The stellar cast of staff in the History Department and Alan D. Leve Center for Jewish Studies deserve heaps of praise, especially Reina Chung, Vivian Holenbeck, Jay Jang, Caroline Luce, Ann Major, Chelsea White, and David Wu. Last but not least, a shout-out to Will Bentley and the Santa Monica Swim Center gang, who have kept me going lap after lap, year after year.

Instrumental financial support for this project came from the Maurice Amado Chair in Sephardic Studies at UCLA, which I am honored to hold. My warmest wishes are owed to the extended family of Maurice Amado, the Board of the Maurice Amado Foundation, and Executive Director Pam Kaizer for nurturing my scholarship. I am also immensely grateful to the John Simon Guggenheim Foundation, which named me a Fellow in 2015–2016, allowing me the time to focus on this book. Additional support came from UCLA's Council on Research.

What a joy to have Andrea Ventura's gorgeous, historically astute art grace a second book of mine—thanks, Andrea, for "packing the VW camper" ever fuller. Again, Bill Nelson has mapped my dreams to perfection.

Jordanna Bailkin, Paris Papamichos Chronakis, Julia Phillips Cohen, Devin Naar, Aron Rodrigue, Sarah Friedman Solomon, Richard Stein, Fred

Zimmerman, and Steven Zipperstein read and commented on this manuscript, offering exceptional insights and sparing me from errors and infelicities. With Marina Aivaliotou, Paris Papamichos Chronakis hosted me in Salonica and environs, quite literally leaving no stone unturned in his determination to share the city and history he knows so deeply. Alongside Paris, Aron, Devin, and Julia have been unstinting in sharing their extraordinary historical know-how. For decades, Steve has offered mentorship and friendship, for which I am most grateful. This book is in certain respects a sequel to another, the translated memoir of Sa'adi Besalel a-Levi, which I edited with Aron Rodrigue. It is an honor to take our shared project and conversations a step farther.

To my great delight, this book was represented by Charlotte Sheedy and the Charlotte Sheedy Literary Agency. I share with Charlotte a passion for vintage Marimekko (as well as books), and am most appreciative of her panache and vision. Working with Farrar, Straus and Giroux has been a dream. To Susan Goldfarb, Jackson Howard, Abby Kagan, Veronica Ingal, and Lottchen Shivers, profound thanks for your ingenuity and efficiency.

It is an honor to collaborate with so brilliant an editor as Ileene Smith for the second time. Like a master arborist, Ileene pruned the straggly branches of this book until a bird could fly through without scratching its wings. Whatever airiness it possesses, I owe to her.

As I conclude a book about another family's history, I save the greatest thanks for my own. Joan, Lorrie, and Alvin (z"l), aunts and uncle extraordinaire. Frederick Michael and Joanell, gracious in-laws. My mother, Carole, for showing me that everyone has a story worth telling. My father, Richard, for his sage editorial hand, love of words, and characteristic empathy. My sister, Rebecca; brother-in-law, Andrew; and nephews Isaac and Saul for their appreciation of a good yarn and all-around fabulousness. This book is for Fred, Ira, and Julius—for tolerating my obsessions, for traveling with me to so many sites of Levy history, and for being, above all, the most magnificent family.

Illustration Credits

pages x and xi: Courtesy of the author.

page 5: Map © Bill Nelson.

page 15: National Archives of Hungary, Festetics Family Keszthely Archives, Festetics Family, Photographs, MNL OL P240-1-r/9-No.31.

page 21: Studio portrait of Sa'adi Besalel Ashkenazi and his unidentified second wife, c. 1890s. Courtesy of the family of Leon Levy.

page 24: © Beit Hatfutsot, Oster Visual Documentation Center, Tel Aviv. Courtesy of Salonika Collection, Photo Unit Number 1527.

page 26: Mémorial de la Shoah/Musée, Centre de documentation, MLVII_0336.

page 31: *Les Cahiers Séfardis,* 1 October 1948, 323. With the assistance of the YIVO Institute for Jewish Research.

page 40: Courtesy of Vagelis Kostoglou.

page 43: *El djiro del mundo kon sinko metalikes* (Salonica, 1905). Courtesy of Yad Ben Zvi Library, Jerusalem.

page 48: David Recanati, *Zikhron Saloniki: Gedulata ve-hurbana shel Yerushalayim de-Balkan* (Tel Aviv, 1972–1985), 472. Courtesy David Recanati.

page 56: Courtesy of the family of Leon Levy.

page 58: Courtesy of Manchester Jewish Museum [2005.120.12.12] and Alan Salem.

page 60: Courtesy of Alan Salem.

page 61: Courtesy of Paris Papamichos Chronakis.

page 63: Courtesy of Jewish Museum of London, 735.

page 65: Courtesy of Jewish Museum of London, 735.8.

page 70: Mémorial de la Shoah/Musée, Centre de documentation, MLVII_1482.

page 72: Imperial War Museums, London, 90487.

pages 74 and 75: Courtesy of Alan Salem.

page 79: Courtesy of Special Collections and University Archive, Stanford University.

page 89: Courtesy of Liliane Hasson.

page 93: David Recanati, *Zikhron Saloniki: Gedulata ve-hurbana shel Yerushalayim de-Balkan* (Tel Aviv, 1972–1985), 475. Courtesy David Recanati.

page 94: David Recanati, *Zikhron Saloniki: Gedulata ve-hurbana shel Yerushalayim de-Balkan* (Tel Aviv, 1972–1985), 127. Courtesy David Recanati.

page 99: Courtesy of Alan Salem.

page 112: Courtesy of Gillie Salem Robic and Pamela Salem O'Hagan.

page 114: Courtesy Alan Salem.

page 115: Courtesy Alan Salem.

page 117: Museu de História e Artes do Estado do Rio de Janeiro in Niterói, Brazil. Photograph by author.

page 118: Library of Congress Prints and Photographs Division, Washington, D.C. LC-F81-1338.

page 120: Courtesy of the family of Leon Levy.

page 129: Courtesy of Gillie Salem Robic and Pamela Salem O'Hagan.

page 130: Courtesy of Gillie Salem Robic and Pamela Salem O'Hagan.

page 131: Courtesy of Gillie Salem Robic and Pamela Salem O'Hagan.

page 135: Courtesy of the family of Leon Levy.

page 146: Courtesy of Esme Solomons.

page 149: The Image Works, Inc.

page 152: Bundesarchiv: Illus. 183, General German Intelligence Service—Zentralbild Fig. 183-B10917.

page 161: United States Holocaust Memorial Museum, Photograph Number 49493.

page 166: Bundesarchiv Illus. 101I-168-0895-11A. Courtesy the German Federal Archives/Bundesarchiv.

page 168: Photograph Number 64140A. Courtesy United States Holocaust Memorial Museum.

page 173: Courtesy of Centropa/Vienna.

page 186: Courtesy of Yad Vashem Archives.

page 194: Courtesy of Sara and Rita Levy.

page 195: Courtesy of Sara and Rita Levy.

page 196: Courtesy of Sara and Rita Levy.

page 201: Courtesy of Sara and Rita Levy.

page 208: Courtesy of Liliane Hasson.

page 211: Courtesy of Liliane Hasson.

page 212: Courtesy of Liliane Hasson.

page 238: Courtesy of Liliane Hasson.

page 239: Courtesy of Liliane Hasson.

page 248: Courtesy of Sara and Rita Levy.

page 249: Courtesy of Liliane Hasson.

page 250: Courtesy of Liliane Hasson.

page 255: Courtesy of the family of Leon Levy.

page 257, top and bottom: Courtesy of the family of Leon Levy.

page 268: Courtesy of Jacky Benmayor and the Jewish Community of Thessaloniki.

A Note About the Author

Sarah Abrevaya Stein is the Sady and Ludwig Kahn Director of the Alan D. Leve Center for Jewish Studies as well as a professor of history and the Maurice Amado Endowed Chair in Sephardic Studies at UCLA. She is the author or editor of many books, including *Extraterritorial Dreams: European Citizenship, Sephardi Jews, and the Ottoman Twentieth Century* and *Plumes: Ostrich Feathers, Jews, and a Lost World of Global Commerce*. The recipient of the Sami Rohr Prize for Jewish Literature, two National Endowment for the Humanities Fellowships, a Guggenheim Fellowship, and two National Jewish Book Awards, Stein lives with her family in Santa Monica, California.